SACRED BRITAIN

A Guide to Places that Stir the Soul

MARTIN SYMINGTON

Edition 1

Bradt Travel Guides Ltd, UK
The Globe Pequot Press Inc, USA

Bradt

Sacred site/place.
Numbers refer to the
page the site or place is
described in the text.

ATLANTIC OCEAN

Fair Isle

Shetland Islands

ORKNEY ISLANDS

Kirkwall

171

John o'Groats

Thurso

St Kilda

OUTER HEBRIDES

Stornoway

177

North Uist

South Uist

North Minch

Coll

Tiree

Rum

Mallaig

Oban

Mull

181

NORTH CHANNEL

NORTHERN IRELAND

Arran

Ayr

Stranraer

189

Carlisle

Glasgow

185

Clyde

192

SCOTLAND

EDINBURGH

200

Perth

Dundee

96

Montrose

Aberdeen

Peterhead

Fraserburgh

Spey

Inverness

Moray Firth

NORTH SEA

Newcastle upon Tyne

105

110

115

Durham

195

Shakespeare is honoured with a statue at Westminster Abbey's Poets' Corner. (P)

Soul mates commune with Karl Marx at his tomb in Highgate Cemetery. (AA)

London

'This vast, ancient and constantly renewed city is painted from an amazing palette.'

A rectangle of poppies frames the Grave of the Unknown Warrior in Westminster Abbey, a focal point for Remembrance Sunday. (SS)

Diana Memorial markers guide walkers along a seven-mile route through central London. (TC/D)

The gilded dome of Central London Mosque at the edge of Regents Park. (P)

Established at a time when Jews were not permitted to build on a public thoroughfare, Bevis Marks Synagogue is tucked away out of sight. (P)

Neasden's gleaming Shri Swaminarayan Mandir is the largest Hindu temple outside India. (P)

Darshan ceremonies to Hindu gods take place within Hertfordshire's half-timbered Bhaktivedanta Manor, a Hare Krishna Temple.

(below: MS & left: JH/A)

The mysteries of Stonehenge endure despite the brutal intrusion of new roads. (P)

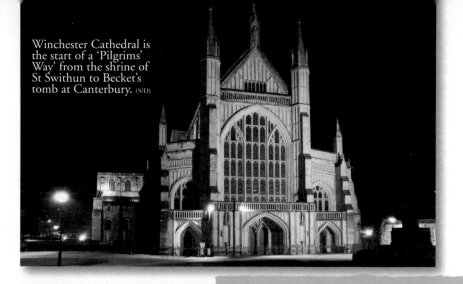

Winchester Cathedral is the start of a 'Pilgrims' Way' from the shrine of St Swithun to Becket's tomb at Canterbury. (S/D)

Southeastern England

'Pilgrims have been hiking across the plains and chalk downs of the southeast for more than 3,000 years and pilgrimage sites, ancient and modern, are still strewn across this region.'

The Chiltern Hills are alive with the sound of Thai spiritual music at the Amaravati Buddhist Monastery. (DB/A)

The Great Cloister of Canterbury Cathedral, near the spot where Becket was butchered. (RM/D)

Manchester United fans make pilgrimages from across the globe to 'The Theatre of Dreams'. (GC/D)

Hallowed be thy game?

'The great thing about football is that it can attract the sort of emotion and passion that becomes a sort of religion in people's minds.' (Sir Alex Ferguson)

Welsh rugby fans at Twickenham Stadium. Here even the brawniest of men can sob with raw emotion. (P)

Turf does not come more hallowed than at Lord's cricket ground. (SS)

SACRED BRITAIN

A Guide to Places that Stir the Soul

MARTIN SYMINGTON

Bradt

The Bradt story

The first Bradt travel guide was written in 1974 by George and Hilary Bradt on a river barge floating down a tributary of the Amazon. In the 1980s and 1990s the focus shifted away from hiking to broader-based guides covering new destinations - usually the first to be published about these places. In the 21st century Bradt continues to publish such ground-breaking guides, as well as others to established holiday destinations, incorporating in-depth information on culture and natural history with the nuts and bolts of where to stay and what to see.

Bradt authors support responsible travel, and provide advice not only on minimum impact but also on how to give something back through local charities. In this way a true synergy is achieved between the traveller and local communities.

First published October 2011
Bradt Travel Guides Ltd
IDC House, The Vale, Chalfont St Peter, Bucks SL9 9RZ, England
www.bradtguides.com
Published in the USA by The Globe Pequot Press Inc,
PO Box 480, Guilford, Connecticut 06437-0480

Text copyright © 2011 Martin Symington
Maps copyright © 2011 Bradt Travel Guides Ltd
Photographs & illustrations copyright © 2011 Individual photographers & illustrators (see below)
Managing Editor: Anna Moores

ISBN: 978 1 84162 363 4

British Library Cataloguing in Publication Data
A catalogue record for this book is available from the British Library

Cover design James Nunn (*www.jamesnunn.co.uk*)

Photographs
Athar Abidi (AA); Alamy (A): Doug Blane/Doug Blane Photography (DB), Robert Estall Photo
Agency (RE), Nic Hamilton Photographic (NH), Jane Hobson (JH), BL Images Ltd (BL), Mike
Kipling Photography (MK), Eddie Linssen (EL), S and J Photography (S&J); Karen Beal (KB);
Dreamstime (D): Giovanni De Caro (GC), Tiziano Casalta (TC), Creativehearts (C), Gail Johnson
(GD), Daniela Lenzinger (DL), Richard Majlinder (RM), Snapper99 (S), Whiskybottle (W); Flickr
(F): karlonsea (K); Holly Hayes/www.sacred-destinations.com (HH); www.photolibrary.com (P);
SuperStock (SS); Martin Symington (MS); Wikipedia Commons (WC)

Maps Chris Lane/Artinfusion (Contains Royal Mail data © Crown copyright and database 2011)
Illustrations Peter Gates (*www.petergates.co.uk*)

Typeset from the author's disc by Artinfusion (*www.artinfusion.co.uk*)
Production managed by Jellyfish Print Solutions; printed in India

Foreword

There is something about the sacred sites of Britain – how they have settled into the landscape, how they have taken hold quietly and convincingly. An American poet once wrote '*Into this house we are born, into this world we are thrown*'; it is the same for every generation – we arrive on this planet halfway through the film not knowing the ending. Sacred sites provide us with the story of what went before – from the enigmatic chalk images slung across the hills in southern England, to standing stones, the intimacies of hidden wells and churches rising up from the middle of fields. Each provides us with a fragment of the story of the human quest for meaning and purpose, and the fact that so many of these sacred sites remain highlights the extent to which this essential human quest is honoured by subsequent generations.

I rather like the way that we cannot quite understand all of the sacred sites, that we cannot hear them completely – that they invite us to imagine their meaning, and ours. But there is little doubt that they speak a common human language that celebrates existence, love, the cycle of the seasons, acts of courage and the human experience of the numinous, the sacred, which in many instances they reflect.

This guide recognises the quest for the sacred as something that *has* happened but also as something that *is* happening all the time. Within these pages you will find long-established holy islands alongside pagodas and shrines to princesses and rock stars. This excellent guide acknowledges that each generation leaves behind its own expression of what is sacred: its contribution – our contribution – to this unfolding story.

Rev Peter Owen-Jones
BBC television presenter of
Around The World In 80 Faiths,
Extreme Pilgrim and
How To Live A Simple Life

Author's story

© Neill Menneer

I was born and grew up in Portugal, from which sunny idyll I paid yearly visits to Leicester to spend summer holidays with grandparents. To return to this industrial city at the heart of Middle England years later, and find it pulsing with Hindu, Sikh and Jain temples was one inspiration for *Sacred Britain*.

Other seeds were sown when I followed in the footsteps of millions of medieval pilgrims across the salty sea cliffs of north Wales to drink from a holy rock pool below the high tide mark which, miraculously, was bubbling with clear, sweet water; and when I first observed the remarkable similarities between the faith displayed at religious shrines, and the ardent devotion shown by his followers at the tomb of Karl Marx.

A sense of the sacred in 21st-century Britain, I realised, takes manifold forms and is to be found in unlikely places. Accordingly I set off on a quest for the sacred which took me from Orkney, north of mainland Scotland, to the southwest tip of Cornwall; and from the wilds of west Wales to the expanses of East Anglia. Time and again, I was astonished by what I discovered.

Dedication

Sacred Britain is for Hennie.

Acknowledgements

Countless people went out of their way to help me as I scoured the length and breadth of Britain in search of the sacred. My special thanks go to the following: Father Anil Akkara, Ajahn Amaro, Denise Allen, Maurice Bitton, John Cattini, Penta Clark, Reverend John Crutchley, Radha Mohan Das, Paul Dickson, Hilary Dominey, Lisa Donohue, Christine Evans, Paul Fletcher, Paul Gogarty, Katherine Gorbing, Simon Gribbon, Jimmy Guy, Kay Hyde, Brother Damian Kirkpatrick, Andrew Lawson, Lama Yeshi Losal Rimpoche, Ani Lhamo, Ged Lynn, Diana Massey, Robert Maxwell, Tim McDonald, Matthew Moore, Nimisha Mehta, Dr Ranesh Mehta, Marion Milne, Mary Murtagh, Jim Procter, Ian Robinson, Anne Semler, James St Aubyn, Dave Steel, Kate Sussams, Barry Taylor, Robert Tremain, Orange Trevillion, Bob Trimmer, Bishop Lindsay Urwin, Carole Vivian, Ellen Watson and Damon Willcox.

A big thank you also to everybody in the Bradt team, especially Hilary Bradt and Adrian Phillips for taking up the idea with such alacrity; and to Anna Moores for being eager, patient, thorough and fun to work with. Finally thanks to Iona, Toby and Sebastian for all sorts of things.

CONTENTS

INTRODUCTION

The idea that a place is 'sacred' means myriad things to different people. For some, the word simply implies a place of devotion to a deity or creed. For many more, it is a multi-purpose term, suggesting that a particular location, monument, structure or journey evokes responses of emotion, soul or spirit.

Such sentiments cannot be pinpointed, much less rationalised, but my starting point in this guidebook is that sacred Britain is a reality. That there are places in England, Scotland and Wales that are sacred in the sense that they hold the power to move people to feelings of wonder, awe or transcendence.

Many of the places I travel to are prehistoric in origin – ancient monoliths, stone circles, burial mounds or chalk hill carvings. The faiths of the people who created them are lost to us, and as religious sites they have changed entirely. Why are such places 'sacred'? My answer is that from world-famous monuments such as Stonehenge, to forlorn chunks of rock attended only by half-forgotten legend, these ancient signatures on the British landscape have powerful moods attached to them and so hold a grip on the imagination. They can transport the visitor into a realm beyond the weariness of mere historical or archaeological information.

Similar senses of the mystical are waiting to be discovered at destinations of pilgrimage, which are another cornerstone of *Sacred Britain*. Travel to sacred places is, after all, the world's oldest form of tourism. In Britain, the heyday of pilgrimage was the Middle Ages when millions made journeys to the sacred, trying to score credit against the whims of fate and hoping for reward in this life or the next.

Tombs of saints and martyrs, scenes of visions and miraculous cures, or simply places associated with revered people, were the targets. Vast edifices, such as the cathedral that rose around the relics of St Cuthbert at Durham, safeguard some; others are obscure shrines or holy wells whose existence will, I suspect, frequently surprise. And many more places of pilgrimage are at remote and far-flung extremities of Britain, such as the islands of Iona, Lindisfarne or Bardsey where holy people have found refuge from worldly temptations.

Such sites are, in the words of George MacLeod, '*thin places, where only a tissue separates the material from the spiritual*'. It is no coincidence that these are often also places of raw beauty and elemental high drama. Then, as now, the dividing line between pilgrims and tourists is blurred; the *Canterbury Tales*, for example, paint pictures of high jinks among the hair shirts. And it is in this spirit that, in an age when we can speed in a couple of hours along a route that took pilgrims weeks to walk, I have chosen as sacred places, some of the Christian pilgrimage trails of the pre-Reformation era.

In more recent times, the flowering in Britain of other religions, particularly from the East, has woven fresh threads into the weft of sacred Britain. 'Guests in Quest' meditate at a Tibetan Buddhist temple in the Scottish Borders; followers of Islam make pilgrimages to London's Regent's Park, there to pray facing Mecca under a huge gilded dome; and devotees, as well as tourists lured by tales of the exotic, flock to a dazzling temple in Neasden, Hinduism's largest outside India. All these, and numerous other places of worship, are part of sacred Britain.

And so to the places of 'secular pilgrimage' which also take their place in my choice of sacred sites. The term sounds oxymoronic, but it is apparent that in this rationalist age where scientists seek to strip the mystery from existence, the yearning to visit places that evoke responses of emotion, soul or spirit remains immutable. Karl Marx's irreligion contributes pointedly secular overtones to his tomb in Highgate Cemetery, but his philosophical soulmates nevertheless seek to commune with him at the site.

Marx himself famously described religion as *'opiate of the masses'*, but might he have concluded that sport was a new religion, had he witnessed the stadiums, stars and crowds which echo cathedrals, prophets and devotees? And what to make of the extraordinary, constantly changing shrine to Princess Diana at the railings of Kensington Palace? Despite lacking any specific spiritual focus, this has become the most resonant pilgrimage destinations in modern Britain.

In the end, the innate and acquired atmosphere of a place – which is what makes it 'sacred', or otherwise – is a matter of how visitors experience it and hence is individual to them. My feeling is that a sacred place is one that needs to be felt in the heart, as well as viewed with the eye. I hope this book helps people find such places.

How to use this book

The nature of the sites and journeys that I have chosen to include varies hugely. However, the subject matter means that they cannot be comprehensive – far from it. Rather, this book is a **personal selection** in which I have tried to cover as many different regions of Britain as is practical.

For each region a **sketch map** is included. To guide you round, each featured site or place is given a **circled number** both on the map and in the text. Each site is numbered consecutively as they occur in the text, making it easy to locate them on the map. Basic information on **public transport** and **roads** is included as a starting point for planning a visit, along with the nearest **tourist information centre**. A handful of **accommodation options and restaurants** are listed for their proximity to the sacred sites. No admission charges are included in this guide, but if access is free (or a donation is expected), this is mentioned at the start of each entry.

For a full **list of the sacred sites** included in this guide, see page 206.

Updates website and feedback request

If you have any comments, queries, grumbles, insights, news or other feedback please contact us on ☏ 01753 893444 or e info@bradtguides.com. Alternatively you can add a review of the book to 🖰 www.bradtguides.com or Amazon.

We'd also love to hear from you if there are places or sites you consider particularly sacred – write to us and let us know.

Periodically our authors post updates and reader feedback on the website. Check 🖰 www.bradtguides.com/guidebook-updates for any news.

1. London

Looking down from the grassy summit of Primrose Hill on the north side of Regent's Park, an extraordinary panorama of London unfurls. This vast, ancient and constantly renewed city is painted from an amazing palette. Framed by soaring office blocks in the distance, you can see the towers of Westminster Abbey where Saint Edward the Confessor lies buried, next to the Houses of Parliament. Not far away is the leafy expanse of Hyde Park and Kensington Gardens, the site where a more secular age seems to have conferred unofficial and unlikely sainthood on Diana, Princess of Wales.

Nevertheless, the glinting golden dome of the Central London Mosque in Regent's Park is a reminder of spiritual variety in multi-faith, multi-cultural Britain. The presence of other Eastern religions is also visible to eyes keen enough to pick out temple spires and minarets pricking the horizon.

It might be worth reflecting that in the record of humanity in Britain, virtually everything visible from this hill is recent.

Where to stay and eat

London has literally thousands of hotels, guesthouses, B&Bs and hostels to choose from. They encompass every style, cover all budgets and are easily located through an internet search. Moreover, all the sites covered in this chapter are easily reached from a single location. For these reasons, this chapter does not include *Where to stay* entries, except in a couple of instances. The website www.visitlondon.com is a useful starting point if you're looking for accommodation.

Similarly, there are no listings of London's eateries, although a few of the sites covered have restaurants attached which are included under the relevant entries.

Tourist information

Britain and London Visitor Centre (BLVC) 1 Lower Regent St, SW1 4XT
08701 566 366 www.visitlondon.com. London's main centre for tourist information. The nearest Tube station is Piccadilly Circus.

The following local tourist offices are also useful:

Euston Travel Information Centre Opposite platform 8, Euston Train Station NW1 2HS.

Greenwich Tourist Information Centre Pepys House, 2 Cutty Sark Gardens, SE10 9LW.

Heathrow Travel Information Centre Terminals 1,2,3 Underground Station Concourse TW6 1JH.

King's Cross St Pancras Travel Information Centre Western Ticket Hall (through brick arches at St Pancras to LUL), Euston Rd, N1 9AL.

Twickenham Tourist Information Centre The Atrium, Civic Centre, 44 York St, TW1 3BZ.

Victoria Station Travel Information Centre, Opposite Platform 8, Victoria Train Station SW1V 1JU.

① Westminster Abbey

20 Dean's Yard, SW1P 3PA ☎ 020 7222 5152 🖰 www.westminster-abbey.org.

Numberless historical associations bind Westminster Abbey to the spirit of Britain. Every monarch since William the Conqueror has been crowned here. Scores of the nation's most revered people are buried or honoured in tombs, effigies, statues and memorial stones: saints, kings, queens, statesmen, heroes and heroines, the cream of the establishment – and also of the anti-establishment, in political and literary figures who have challenged orthodoxy over the ages.

The foundations of the original abbey were built on a 7th-century Anglo-Saxon church on what was then the 'Isle of Thorns' in the Thames. By 960 it had become a Benedictine monastery and in 1065 King Edward the Confessor consecrated the major church he had built on the site, which he intended as his burial place. Little remains of this today (above ground, anyway), though at the time it was said to be greater in scale than any church in Normandy.

The building of the present abbey church was begun by King Henry III in 1245. He demolished most of Edward the Confessor's church and had a replacement designed in the new, soaring Gothic style. Over the centuries, numerous magnificent architectural features were added. The amazing vaulted nave was completed in the early 16th century, closely followed by the mesmerising Lady Chapel with its fan-vaulted ceiling and statues of 95 saints; it is dedicated to Henry VII, who lies behind the altar. The last phase of construction, the West Towers in all their imperious grandeur, was finished in 1745.

Westminster Abbey is both famous and familiar around the world, through the royal weddings and funerals beamed via satellite to billions. It is among the most popular of all Britain's tourist attractions, despite a hefty entrance fee, yet also remains a prayerful place, a working church with a daily rhythm of worship. On the hour, every hour, a short liturgy is conducted during which visitors, whatever their beliefs, are asked to pause for a moment in contemplation.

Amid its astounding wealth of historical, temporal and spiritual riches, I have chosen a trio of spots which self-evidently hold special powers to stir the soul.

The shrine of St Edward the Confessor

Edward, son of Ethelred the Unready, was the penultimate Anglo-Saxon king of England. He ruled from 1042 till 1066, just a few months before the Norman invasion, and was buried in a tomb behind the high altar in Westminster Abbey. This is where his remains still rest.

Long before he was formally canonised by Pope Alexander III in 1161, Edward the Confessor's tomb had become a shrine, and he was being venerated as a saint. Why was he styled 'the Confessor'? In old English to 'confess' meant to bear witness to saintliness by living the faith, rather than through martyrdom. Edward had done this by practising austerity and monk-like simplicity; it is sometimes said that, although married, his self-imposed chastity was the reason he died without issue. He was peaceful, performed countless acts of kindness and charity, and used his influence to endow churches and monasteries. He also testified to his faith by raising Westminster Abbey to the glory of God.

When Edward III began the rebuilding of the abbey in 1245, he installed his namesake the Confessor as its patron saint and had his remains moved to a magnificent new shrine encrusted with gold and jewels. During the Reformation the treasures were looted and the shrine desecrated. Edward's remains, however, were preserved and reburied in another part of the church. Then, during her brief restoration of the Catholic faith, Queen Mary had the shrine rebuilt and moved Edward's relics back. Edward the Confessor is possibly the only English saint other than Cuthbert at Durham (see page 119) who still lies in a medieval shrine.

For this is the shrine still there today, in a raised chapel behind the high altar. Eleven kings, queens and princesses lie in tombs around the shrine, which faces the Coronation Chair where every monarch has been crowned since Edward II in 1307 (apart from Edward VIII who was never crowned).

A cordon bars the staircase up to the shrine, which is not generally accessible to the public. All the same, it is not impossible to visit; it is worth asking one of the green- or red-robed abbey stewards to let you in. The alternative is that every weekday, at 11.00 and 15.00, after the hourly pause for prayer throughout the abbey, there is a short liturgy at the shrine. Anybody is welcome to take part, though very few do.

While crowds milled around the abbey, I was one of only four people to follow Reverend John Crutchley up the stairs to the chapel where Edward's tomb is raised high on a platform, surrounded by a processional ambulatory. At the foot of the shrine is a simple altar and six niches, three on each side, where the faithful would kneel and pray for cures from their ailments.

In recent years, some aspects of pilgrimage have been restored. Every so

3

often a parish pilgrim group from somewhere around the country comes here. There is also an annual national pilgrimage at 'Edwardtide' in October, sometimes officiated ecumenically by the Archbishop of Canterbury together with the Catholic Archbishop of Westminster. And it is here at Edward the Confessor's shrine that the former prayed with Pope Benedict XVI during the September 2010 papal visit.

Poets' Corner

It is estimated that around 375 million people speak English as their mother tongue, and more than a billion as a second language. Poets' Corner, in the South Transept and lit by a large rose window, is the sacred place that commemorates the English literary tradition. Its sacredness lies in the genius of those honoured here, with atheists and agnostics buried or remembered alongside the pious.

It all started with Geoffrey Chaucer, who would of course have merited his place by any measure of literary genius. Chaucer was, however, interred here in 1400 simply because he had been Clerk of the Works at the Palace of Westminster. When Edmund Spencer was laid to rest in the abbey 150 year later, it was seen fitting that he should be placed near Chaucer. And hey presto, a tradition was established!

The company that Chaucer and Spencer now keep is phenomenal: Tennyson, Browning, Dickens, Hardy, Kipling – you name them, they're all buried here. Others are marked by memorial statues or stones: Milton, Wordsworth, Keats, Shelley, Austen, the trio of Bronte sisters, Betjeman … and, of course, Shakespeare. I wouldn't expect anybody from the Holy Trinity Church in Stratford-upon-Avon to agree with me, but it does seem a shame that the greatest literary genius is remembered by a statue rather than a tomb.

My prize for the most intoxicating epitaph goes to T S Eliot's quotation, from his poem 'Little Gidding' (see page 90), on his own memorial:

> *The communication of the dead is tongued with fire beyond the language of the living.*

Wow.

Grave of the Unknown Warrior

On the morning 11 November 1920, the second anniversary of the armistice ending World War I, a casket borne on a gun carriage drawn by six black horses processed through London. Immense crowds lined the silent streets. The procession reached the Great West Door of Westminster Abbey, where 100 recipients of the Victoria Cross formed a guard of honour. In the presence of King George V, Prime Minister David Lloyd George, members of the government and military chiefs, the casket was interred in the abbey nave.

The inscription on the tombstone begins:

Beneath this stone rests the body
of a British warrior
unknown by name or rank
brought from France to lie among
the most illustrious of the land
and buried here on armistice day

The original idea is credited to the Rev David Railton, an army padre serving on the Western Front, after seeing a grave on which had been scrawled the epitaph, '*An unknown British soldier*'. After the war Railton wrote to the Dean of Westminster, suggesting that an unidentified serviceman should be '*buried among the kings*' in commemoration of all those who had given their lives in the war.

The suggestion took hold, and military search parties were dispatched to the battlefields of the Sommes, Ypres, Arras and the Aisne. Their grisly instructions were to dig up one corpse from each. They should be sure from uniform or badges that they were British, but should be without any further form of identification. The four bodies, draped in union flags, were brought together in a hut at the village of St Pol near Arras. A blindfolded officer then selected one of them at random which was placed in a waiting casket, while the other three were solemnly reburied. The casket was taken to London for the Armistice Day burial.

No place in Westminster Abbey is treated as more sacred than the Grave of the Unknown Warrior. Nowadays it is generally regarded as a memorial also for the unknown dead in World War II and subsequent conflicts. It requires no cordon, as the multitudes wander about the nave. A rectangle of poppies frames the tombstone, the final monument in the abbey before visitors proceed to the abbey shop and exit.

Getting there
Westminster Abbey is in central London and can be reached from Westminster **Underground** station, served by the District, Circle and Jubilee lines.

② Diana, Princess of Wales

You will forever be the Queen of My Heart. Michele, P.Ed. Island, Canada.

Diana you set the downtrodden free!!

These are just two of the written messages left at the railings of Kensington

Palace in west London, along with flowers, poems and tea-light candles flickering in front of photographs of the late Princess of Wales. People from all over the world – pilgrims, if you like – cling to the memory of a 36-year-old woman who died in 1997; in other words, they pray to the dead Diana.

Year-round, a trickle of such pilgrims make their way to the Kensington Palace railings. Then on 31 August, the anniversary of Diana's death in a road tunnel in Paris, it all steps up a few gears. The flowers, votive offering and prayers multiply as this, and other sites commemorating Diana, expose the extent of Britain's most resonant contemporary pilgrimage.

The anniversary gatherings are an echo of the astonishing upwelling of spontaneous public devotion caused by Diana's death. On the morning after the crash, bunches of flowers began to appear at the south gates of Kensington Palace. Over the coming days, more than a million bouquets were left there, creating a vast 'field of flowers', left by the sobbing multitudes. Kensington Palace stayed open 24 hours a day for the 136,000 mourners who came to leave messages in books of condolence. The outpouring of emotion seemed to reveal that Diana occupied a personal or symbolic place in the lives of millions of individuals and hence in the collective national psyche.

At the time, and more particularly in retrospect, some Britons felt embarrassed – ashamed even – of the way in which the country displayed so publicly its paroxysms of anguish. There was something disturbingly 'un-British' about incontinent displays of sentiment. Here was a nation long renowned for the stiffness of its upper lip, suddenly indulging itself in an orgy of recreational grieving.

Taking a more measured approach Dr Rowan Williams, now the Archbishop of Canterbury, wrote at the time that he regarded the public response as '*a potent lament for a lost sacredness, magical and highly personal, but equally a ritualised focus for public loyalty.*' By '*lost sacredness*', Dr Williams seemed to be referring to the incoming tide of secularism. In other words, an intangible God had been replaced by an all-too-mortal goddess.

There are various memorials to Diana, where modern pilgrims may pay their respects.

Kensington Palace and Gardens

Kensington W8 4PX ☎ 0870 751 5170 🖥 www.hrp.org.uk/kensingtonpalace. Free access to gardens.

This is the palace where monarchs held court in the 17th and 18th centuries before royalty moved on to Buckingham Palace. More recently, it has been divided into apartments as 'grace and favour' residences for members of the wider royal family. Diana lived in Apartment 8, Kensington Palace from the

Althorp Estate, Northamptonshire

Northampton NN7 4HQ ☎ 01604 770107 🖳 www.althorp.com.

Althorp Estate in the Northamptonshire countryside is the ancestral home of the Spencer family, and is open to the public in July and August. Lady Diana Spencer lived here for much of her childhood and, as Diana, Princess of Wales, was buried here on the day of her funeral, 6 September 1997. Accompanied only by immediate family and close friends, her body was rowed across Round Oval, an ornamental lake in the estate grounds, to the island where her grave is. She was buried wearing a black dress, and holding a rosary which had been given to her by Mother Teresa of Calcutta who herself died two days before Diana's funeral.

Persistent reports that Diana's grave can be visited by the public once a year, on the anniversary of her death, are untrue. The grave is strictly private and is hidden from view by a thicket of trees on the island. The only monument on the island visible to visitors is a memorial urn which can be seen from the lakeside. A path lined with 36 young oak trees, marking the years of her life, leads to the lake where a summerhouse, styled as a Classical temple, serves as a memorial to Diana.

There is also a permanent, six-room exhibition, **Diana: A Celebration**, devoted to the princess's memory, housed in a converted stable block. The rooms are filled with exhibits plucked from her life such as school reports, childhood letters and her wedding dress. Other displays explore her influence on the fashion world, and the impact of her charitable work.

Getting there

Althorp is 7 miles west of Northampton off the A428. Directions are signposted from exits 16 and 18 on the M1.

time of her marriage to the Prince of Wales in 1981 until her death. This is why the crowds gathered here, transforming the railings into the unofficial shrine which they remain today.

At the time of going to press, Kensington Palace was undergoing a wholesale refurbishment and the view from the railings was just of green sheeting and scaffolding. All the more extraordinary, then, that Diana's devotees should still be coming here to attach their offerings to the wrought iron.

However, next to the palace in Kensington Gardens, which are open to the public and are effectively an extension of Hyde Park, is the **Diana, Princess of Wales Memorial Playground**. Thus Diana's love of, and charitable work for, children is honoured. There are teepees and an enormous wooden pirate ship where nearly a million children a year are brought to clamber and race around.

The Diana, Princess of Wales Memorial Fountain expresses the spirit of informality and accessibility for which she is remembered. This rather unusual water feature, designed by American landscape architect Kathryn Gustafson, allows visitors to wade through the shallow, running stream cooling their feet in quiet contemplation if they so wish. Or instead, to gambol about and splash each other, if Diana's spirit moves them to do this. The fountain is at the southwest corner of Hyde Park near the bank of the Serpentine Lake, a few minutes' walk from Kensington Palace.

The Royal Parks have waymarked a seven-mile **Diana Princess of Wales Memorial Walk** (*www.royalparks.org.uk/tourists/dianamemorialwalk.cfm*). The route begins at the Black Lion Gate entrance to Kensington Gardens on Bayswater, opposite Queensway Underground Station on the Central Line; it then weaves through Kensington Gardens, Hyde Park, Green Park and St James Park. The walk is marked by 90 plaques featuring a five-petalled rose symbol and leads devotees past several places associated with Diana's life, such as Kensington Palace, Spencer House, St James Palace, Clarence House and Buckingham Palace.

Getting there
The palace is accessed via Orme Square Gate, off Bayswater Road. The nearest **Underground** stations are Queensway and High Street Kensington.

Where to stay
Kensington House Hotel 15/16 Prince of Wales Terrace, W8 5PQ ℃ 020 7937 2345 www.kenhouse.com. A beautiful boutique hotel in a townhouse within a blown kiss of the Kensington Palace railings and the Diana memorial.

Harrods
87–135 Brompton Rd, Knightsbridge SW1X 7XL ℃ 020 7730 1234 www.harrods.com. Free access.

If the memorials to Princess Diana in Kensington Gardens and Hyde Park are seen as restrained and tasteful in their informality, those in London's most famous department store are likely to evoke the opposite reaction. Garish and tacky they may be, but these memorials still have the power to move many of Diana's devotees – particularly those who identify with her as a victim of the establishment.

The memorials are in Harrods because the store was owned by Mohamed Al-Fayed, the Egyptian father of Dodi Al-Fayed who died with Diana in the 1997 Paris car crash. (Mr Al-Fayed sold Harrods to a Qatari company in 2010, but the memorials remain.)

The main shrine, dedicated simply to 'Diana and Dodi' is prominently positioned at the bottom of the imperious Egyptian escalator on the lower-ground floor. It consists of four large candles, intertwined portraits of the couple, and an acrylic pyramid containing a wine glass, a ring and a stick of lipstick (Diana's, apparently). An inscription claims:

The wine glass has been preserved in the exact condition it was left on the couple's last evening together at the Imperial Suite at the Hotel Ritz in Paris. Dodi bought this engagement ring for Diana on the day before the tragedy.

The second memorial, at Harrods' door 3, is a little more controversial. It is a bronze sculpture of the couple dancing, beneath the outstretched wings of a bird. It is titled *Innocent Victims* apparently in reference to Mohamed Al-Fayed's claim that the couple were murdered as a result of a conspiracy involving the British intelligences services and the Duke of Edinburgh.

Getting there
The nearest **Underground** station is Knightsbridge, on the Piccadilly line.

③ Marc Bolan's Rock Shrine
Queens Ride, Barnes SW15 5RG 🖐 www.marc-bolan.org. Free access.

On the night of 16 September 1977 the guitarist, singer, song-writer and poet Marc Bolan (born Mark Feld) of 'glam-rock' band T-Rex was killed. He died instantly when the purple Mini, in which he was a front-seat passenger, careered off the road and hit a sycamore tree on Queens Ride in Barnes, southwest London. Within hours of the wrecked vehicle's removal, the first fans began arriving at the tree to grieve, tie strips of cloth to the trunk, and leave photographs and jam jars of flowers. A rock shrine was born.

Meanwhile, spine-chilling tales began to circulate about the accident. Bolan had foreseen the manner of his own death years before. This was why the 29-year-old, who owned several cars, had always been too afraid to learn to drive himself. And how about those lines in his hit single 'Solid Gold Easy Action':

Woman from the east with her headlights shining,
Eased my pain and stopped my crying.

The driver of the car had been his girlfriend Gloria Jones from Ohio. Not convinced? Well, another couplet from the same song goes:

Life is the same and it always will be,
Easy as picking foxes from a tree, easy as picking foxes from a tree.

The registration number of the fated Mini which Jones wrapped around the sycamore was FOX 661L.

All of which was like oil poured on the flames of fervour surrounding the nascent Marc Bolan's Rock Shrine. The shrine grew. The faithful made pilgrimages and every year, on the anniversary of the accident, crowds gathered to pay tribute to Bolan and his music. On the 20th anniversary a memorial

stone and bronze bust was unveiled by Bolan and Gloria Jones's son, Rolan Bolan. A T-Rex Action Group (TAG) was formed to protect the shrine, and was granted a permanent lease on the site with responsibility for caring for the 'Bolan Tree'. There are now steps up the eroded embankment from Queens Ride to the tree.

While the Mark Bolan Rock Shrine is a unique phenomenon, in recent years a vogue has developed across Britain for establishing small shrines at the sites of fatal road accidents: the shrines typically consist of flowers (real or plastic), photographs, football strips and sometimes, in poignant commemoration of dead children, soft toys. Sometimes these objects are taped to road signs or tree trunks. While roadside shrines have long been common in other countries, their rather sudden prevalence in Britain does seem to suggest that the national stiff upper lip is relaxing somewhat as the decades go by.

Getting there

Barnes **railway** station is just a few minutes' walk from the shrine. Regular services run from Waterloo Station.

④ Twickenham Stadium

Rugby Rd, Twickenham TW11DZ ☎ 020 8892 8877 🖥 www.rfu.com.

'Dad, why is that man crying?' asked a boy of about six who was on the Twickenham Stadium Tour I had joined. 'Nathan, *shshsh*', answered his father admonishingly. But I knew the answer. While we waited for the tour, Fernando has told me he played tight-head prop for a team in Buenos Aires and that he had been 'loco' about rugby since he was about Nathan's age. Now he had arrived at 'the home of rugby, my spiritual home' as he put it, 'and the main reason for my first visit to London.'

Fernando's moment of truth came at the end of the tour – a run through the players' tunnels onto the hallowed turf (there is no avoiding the cliché here, it is just too apt). There he stood, 19 stone of barrel-chested Argentine beef, his glazed eyes gazing up between the upright posts and tears coursing down his stubbly cheeks.

'Because he can't quite believe he's here, Nath', I heard the Dad try to explain, *sotto voce*.

True, most of our ten-strong group had come to Twickenham for reasons a little shorter on raw, spiritual emotion. On the other hand, our guide Phil Taylor, a retired businessman, club player and lifelong rugby devotee did greet us with the words, 'I am delighted to welcome you all here on your pilgrimage to Headquarters'.

Mr Taylor whisked us, by lift, high up to the top of the north stand from where we looked out across a rippling sea of 82,000 empty seats. 'Just listen to the silence for a while, then hear the roar as England takes the field against the All Blacks', he said, deftly evoking the stirring sense of fervour and belonging that has Twickenham crowds bawling 'God Save the Queen' and swaying to 'Swing Low, Sweet Chariot'.

Our tour took us round the stadium, calling at the television commentary box; the Royal Box where we were invited to park our posteriors on the very leather where Her Majesty does the same on her occasional visits; the President's Suite; and the Medical Suite and Doping Centre. For the anorak tendency, our guide was able to call on a vast array of facts and statistics, both about the stadium and the history of the game. Then it was down to the ultimate inner sanctum, the tradition and superstition-soaked England players' dressing room.

'The front row always use these three pegs', said Mr Taylor, his voice dropping in hushed reverence. Somehow, we were all duly awestruck when shown the giant, 75-year-old iron baths. 'Twenty minutes before kick-off, everybody leaves the room except the players. The captain then addresses them.'

The build-up to our fantasy run through the players' tunnel was now complete. Out we went into the roaring, capacity-crowd stadium for the uplifting national anthems and the blood and thunder of international confrontation. Poor old Fernando. It was all just too much for him.

The tour includes entry to the **World Rugby Museum**, which is under the east stand. It is a sophisticated, ultra-modern museum that keeps people enthralled for a couple of hours or more. High-tech visuals and acoustics skillfully recreate the atmosphere of Twickenham on match days: you enter through a mock-up turnstile into a cauldron of life-size model players in action, surrounded by singing, shouting crowds projected on to the walls.

The 'medical suite' and 'dressing room' are even more authentic, with gory bits of blood-stained bandage, mud, boots and dirty kit on the floor, while the whiff of liniment hangs in the air. On the interactive computers, you can also call up any team or era you like and watch choice pieces of action, complete with original commentary.

Getting there

There is ample free parking, except on match days, in the car park by entrance Gate 11. Twickenham **train** station is about 10 minutes' walk from the stadium.

Where to stay and eat

London Marriot Hotel Twickenham 198 Whitton Rd, TW2 7BA ✆ 020 8891 8200 🌐 www.marriott.co.uk. A comfortable hotel built into the stadium's south stand with roofs overlooking the pitch. Also a good place to eat before or after a stadium tour.

Hallowed be thy game

Karl Marx famously referred to religion as 'the opiate of the masses'. Had he been around in today's infinitely more secular world (well, Western world anyway), the philosopher might have had observations to make about the way sport has come to mirror the sacred themes, ritual and practice of religion. Are stadiums the new cathedrals? Are the spectating fans the equivalents of congregations? Can sporting stars and celebrity managers be seen as priests and prophets?

A while ago Manchester United Manager Sir Alex Ferguson commented in a television interview that, 'The great thing about football is that it can attract the sort of emotion and passion that becomes a sort of religion in people's minds'. So has football become a religion? My Argentine friend Fernando who I met at Twickenham (see page 10) was unquestionably on a pilgrimage to a place sacred to him. He said as much himself. 'My spiritual home.' Admittedly, he belonged to a different denomination ... round balls, oval balls ...

Thinking about it, the parallel between religion and modern sport goes on and on: the powerful rhythm of noise and chanting, stirring people to a sense of identity and communion; sublime moments of transcendent 'magic'. As for the vocabulary in common: prayer, faith, worship, sacrifice, devotion, dedication, commitment, spirit, suffering, celebration ... and pilgrimage.

Along with Twickenham, the following complete a holy trinity – the most prominent among innumerable sporting shrines and sacred places in Britain.

Old Trafford

Sir Matt Busby Way, Manchester M16 0RA ☎ 0161 868 8000
🖰 www.manutd.com.
Manchester United's stadium is nicknamed 'The theatre of dreams'. A tour of Old Trafford and a visit to the Manchester United Museum are billed as 'the greatest football story ever told'. As a visitor, you are summoned to 'immerse yourself in a legend still being made'. About 350,000 people a year accept the invitation, more than half of them from overseas. Typically, they spend a little over an hour

⑤ Bevis Marks Synagogue

4 Heneage Lane, City of London EC3A 5DQ ☎ 020 7626 1274
🖰 www.bevismarks.org.uk.

I got a bit lost trying to find Britain's oldest continually used synagogue. Wandering around the City of London in the shadow of temples to mammon such as Norman Foster's 'Gherkin', I eventually found my way to the unnamed alley off Bevis Marks Street. The fact that it was hard to find, however, is sort of the point. In 1699 when permission was given to establish the first synagogue in the country, Jews were still not permitted to build on a public thoroughfare so the synagogue was deliberately tucked away out of sight.

paying homage to their heroes at the world's most famous sports stadium; many linger for longer in the extensive museum.

Old Trafford is licensed for civil weddings which take place regularly at a special Marriage Suite in the south stand, overlooking the 'hallowed turf' (that phrase again!). The scattering of ashes, post-cremation, on the grass round the edge of the playing surface is another 'service' offered.

Lords Cricket Ground

St John's Wood Rd, London NW8 8QN ☎ 020 7616 8595 🖰 www.lords.org.
'Cricket is not a game, it is a religion', claims a very old joke about adherents of the game. The adage is more likely to conjure an image of tea with the vicar, than an outpouring of spiritual fervour. However, to the faithful, Marylebone Cricket Club's historic grounds at St John's Wood in north London is, as the Lords website puts it, cricket's global 'spiritual headquarters'. In this context, the name 'Lords' sounds all too apt, although in truth it takes its name not from the Almighty, but from professional player Thomas Lord who founded the MCC in 1787.

Upwards of 60,000 visitors a year tour the ground and Cricket Museum. A majority are from the Indian sub-continent followed by Australians, with British pilgrims only a distant third.

The standard tour takes about 100 minutes. It starts at the MMC museum, home of the famous Ashes Urn (which never leaves Lords, even if the Ashes have been 'lost' to Australia by England). After that, there are years of history to revel in, from the days of W G Grace, who is honoured at the Grace Gates, to the 'Old Father Time' weather vane and futuristic Lords Media Centre. In recent years there have been requests for private visits by gentlemen who wish to propose marriage at Lords (granted), and for the deceased to have their ashes scattered there (denied).

The façade is meaningfully discreet, rather like a nonconformist meeting house. The master builder was, in fact, a Quaker called Joseph Avis who, after completing the building in 1701 decided to return his fee on the grounds that it was wrong to profit from building a house of God. Inside, I was immediately struck by the beautiful, serene simplicity of the architecture which Maurice Bitton, the building's curator, told me was patterned on the Spanish and Portuguese Great Synagogue in Amsterdam.

With seating for about 500, Bevis Marks felt much larger than the exterior had led me to expect. Light floods in from a big bay window and there is a magnificent ark or 'Ehal' at the east end crafted from dark oak and containing the sacred Hebrew parchment scrolls of the Pentateuch, the five books of

Moses. Seven dramatic candelabra hang from the ceiling symbolising the days of the week with the largest, central one signifying the Sabbath. As an Orthodox synagogue, the sexes are seated separately – a women's gallery is supported by 12 columns representing the tribes of Israel.

Maurice has been a lifelong worshipper at the synagogue. He attending Schul here from the age of five and had his Bar Mitzvah eight years later. To

call him a mere walking encyclopedia of Bevis Marks would be to miss the passion he displays for the detail and significance of this place in the history of Judaism in Britain.

There had been Jews in England since the 11th century, Maurice reminded me, but they suffered perennial persecution and were expelled in 1290 under King Edward I. Jews have only been permitted to live and worship openly since 1656, following Rabbi Menasseh Ben Israel's petition to Oliver Cromwell. Bevis Marks, affiliated to the Sephardic rite established by expelled Spanish and Portuguese Jews in Amsterdam, became the centre of the Anglo-Jewish world.

The Register of Births records that the infant Benjamin Disraeli was circumcised at Bevis Marks by his uncle Rabbi David Ararbanel Lindo in 1804. The future Prime Minister's father Isaac Disraeli, however, subsequently left the synagogue under a cloud after being chosen to be Warden of the Congregation in 1813. Not only did he decline the honour, but Disraeli Senior refused to pay the fine of £40 which rejection mandated, and left the congregation. He then had his children baptised as Christians. Jews were still not allowed to be Members of Parliament so, as it turned out, this event made a penetrating impact on English history.

A more pious worshipper at Bevis Marks seems to have been the celebrated pugilist Daniel Mendoza, who is credited with turning boxing from a contest of brute force into an art form. In 1798 Mendoza even published a book entitled *The Art of Boxing* and is said to have been the first Jew King George III conversed with. However, according to Maurice Bitton, it was Mendoza's transformation of the stereotype of an English Jew from weakling into person able to defend himself and deserving of respect, which really packed a punch.

Bevis Marks is the only synagogue in Europe to have had continuous services for over 300 years. Today it remains the flagship of the Anglo-Jewish community and holds regular daily Saturday morning and Friday evening Kabbalat Shabbat worship.

Getting there
The nearest **Underground** stations are Liverpool Street and Aldgate.

Where to eat
Bevis Marks Restaurant EC3A 5DQ ☎ 020 7283 2220

🍴 www.bevismarkstherestaurant.com. Classy décor and mouth-watering food served with contemporary flourishes. Probably the finest, and most expensive, kosher restaurant in London. Reached through the synagogue's main entrance.

⑥ Highgate Cemetery

Swain's Lane, Highgate N6 6PJ 📞 020 8340 1834 🍴 www.highgate-cemetery.org.
This is one of the world's most famous and beautiful cemeteries. A densely wooden area, the cemetery is also a nature reserve, rich in birdlife and a haven for foxes. It is divided into two parts, the West and East. **Highgate Cemetery West** opened in 1839 as part of a plan to provide seven (later to be known as 'The Magnificent Seven') new cemeteries around what was then the periphery of London. It soon became one of the most fashionable places to be buried. Today, the West with its magnificent Victorian funerary architecture is only accessible to the public on pre-booked group tours. Highlights are the Lebanon Circle, Terrace Catacombes and Egyptian Avenue.

The first interment at **Highgate Cemetery East** was in 1861, since then numerous famous people have been laid to rest here. The most famous of all is Karl Marx, an object of secular pilgrimage and hence the reason for the cemetery's inclusion in this book. Highgate remains a working Church of England burial ground, although there are both consecrated and unconsecrated areas. It is run by the Friends of Highgate Cemetery Trust charity, and maintained using the charge paid by some 70,000 visitors a year.

Karl Marx's Tomb

Since Karl Marx's death in 1883, his soulmates have been making pilgrimages to commune with him at this resting place in Highgate. His tomb is inscribed with the epitaph:

Workers of all lands unite

and below these words, the less familiar:

*Philosophers have only interpreted
the world in various ways.
The point however is to change it.*

Marx's lack of, hostility to, and disregard for religion, categorises any reverential journey to his tomb as a secular pilgrimage par excellence. Nevertheless, on my own visit to the most famous occupant of Highgate Cemetery I was struck by how many of the characteristics of religious observance are on display. Marx's thick-bearded face gazes out from the portrait bust atop his imperious tombstone like an Old Testament prophet. Irrelevant this may be, but it sets a tone. Flowers lie at the foot of the tomb – quite a few posies in glass vases, and other bunches unwatered but touchingly fresh. '*Keep the Faith*' somebody had stencilled on a piece of red cardboard propped up against the back of the tomb.

While Marx is the patriarch of the tomb, an inscriptions tablet lists other members of his family who share it. His wife Jenny von Westphalen; his daughter Eleanor Marx, the political activist who tragically committed suicide in 1895; Marx's grandson Harry Longuit; and Mrs Marx's companion Helena Demuth, later housekeeper to Friedrich Engels.

I did not speak to any of the other visitors who paused at the tomb. It would not have been right, amid the reverential aura of the place. Were they 'Marxists' here to demonstrate solidarity with the ideology? Or just curious onlookers? I have no idea.

According to Bob Trimmer, a trustee of Friends of Highgate Cemetery, who met me at the entrance, I was entirely typical of visitors in making a beeline for Karl Marx's tomb. True, numbers have fallen significantly since the collapse of Communism in 1989, but the tomb is still a powerful magnet.

Bob explained to me that Marx was not originally buried where his monument now stands. When he died in 1883 only a dozen or so people attended his simple funeral and he was interred in a grave with a modest headstone about 200yds from his present tomb, now hidden in dense undergrowth. It was not until well into the 20th century that his growing influence began to be reflected in significant numbers of pilgrimages to his grave at Highgate.

In 1956, the present plot on a prominent pathway bend was purchased by the Marx Memorial Library. Marx's remains, along with those of the other family members, where exhumed and reburied there. The new memorial was commissioned by the Communist Party of Great Britain and sculpted by Lawrence Bradshaw, who incorporated the inscription tablet taken from the original grave.

Around the tomb are the graves of other famous people, apparently buried here in a spirit of solidarity with Marx and his philosophy. Some of Marx's neighbours are from the north London left-wing elite, such as Paul Foot ('*Writer and Revolutionary 1937–2004*') and Ralph Miliband (the Marxist sociologist and father of British Labour Party politicians David and Ed). And, since Communism is by its nature international, also buried here are the likes of Saad Saadi Ali ('*Iraqi Communist Leader and Campaigner for Democracy and Freedom*') and Dr Yusuf Mohamed Dadoo ('*1909–1903, Chairman of the South African Communist Party*').

How, I asked Bob Trimmer, does somebody get to be buried within spitting distance of Marx?

'Marx has a strong and ardent following, and Marxists tend to be deeply sensitive people. Wreaths are laid for Marx. People are willing to die for Marxism, just as others are for the deities they believe in. But the desire to be buried near Marx is actually quite a recent thing. Before, the idea never seemed to have occurred to people,' said Bob. 'But I think a notion of wanting to be part of a political community has come about. There are no hard and fast rules about who gets to be buried where. People are buried here because of their wishes during their lifetimes, and those of their families, and after that it is a matter of private negotiation.'

Devotion and pilgrimage motivated by ideology, I could only conclude, are strikingly similar to a religious quest.

Getting there
The West and East cemeteries are on either side of Swain's Lane in Highgate, north London, next to Waterlow Park. The nearest **Underground** station is Archway on the Northern line.

⑦ Central London Mosque and Islamic Cultural Centre

146 Park Rd, NW8 7RG ☎ 020 7725 3363 🌐 www.iccuk.org. Free access.
A resplendent gilded dome glints between the trees which fringe the western edge of Regent's Park while a 140ft minaret rockets above. The Central London Mosque (often called the Regent's Park Mosque) is an unmistakable landmark in a fabulous location just a stone's throw from the boating lake and not much further than the range of a fulsome six hit from Lord's cricket ground.

I had tried without success to find, in advance, somebody to show me around and answer questions. Approaching the mosque I found I was similarly ignored – neither welcomed, nor made to feel the slightest bit out of place either. I entered through a wide though rather unattractive concrete courtyard typical of 1960s functional architecture. The complex includes offices, a halal restaurant, a bookshop and the largest Islamic library in Britain.

I took off my shoes to walk through the lobby into the main prayer hall, orientated towards Mecca. Its scale and sheer grandeur took my breath away; a huge, glittering chandelier hung beneath a vast dome sparkling with mosaics and shimmering with colours from stained-glass windows. Underneath, I luxuriated on an expanse of plush, red-and-white carpet. It was a weekday afternoon and a few men were praying round the edges while one or two others seemed to be asleep on the floor; nevertheless, the overall impression was one of majesty and opulence beyond anything I had expected.

I finally found an attendant, and asked him how many people come here for Friday prayers. 'Upwards of 1,500 worshippers', Salim Khan told me, adding that, 'for Muslim festivals such as Eid we can fit in 5,000 men.' In addition, women pray in a balcony overlooking the main hall.

History

The Central London Mosque can trace its roots to 1940, when Winston Churchill's War Cabinet authorised the allocation of £100,000 to acquire a site for a mosque in London, in recognition of the fact that soldiers from across the Islamic world were fighting for the British Empire. The 2.3-acre plot adjacent to Hanover Gate was purchased and the Islamic Cultural Centre (though not yet the mosque) was officially opened in 1944 by King George VI.

Over the next few decades development of the mosque stalled, with various proposals being rejected. Only in 1969 was a design finally approved, after an international competition was won by English architect Frederick Gibbert (who had already won global renown for Liverpool's Catholic cathedral). A sizeable donation by King Faisal of Saudi Arabia allowed the extravagant project to proceed and the mosque was finally completed in 1977.

Getting there

The nearest **Underground** stations are St John's Wood on the Jubilee line and Baker Street on the Bakerloo line.

Where to eat

Zaitoon Restaurant 146 Park Rd, NW8 7RG ☏ 020 7723 2228 ⊕ www.zaitoonrestaurant.co.uk. A good-value restaurant and cafeteria within the cultural centre, serving halal meat and vegetable curries, and other Asian dishes.

⑧ Shri Swaminarayan Mandir

105–119 Brentfield Rd, Neasden, Brent NW10 8LD ☏ 0208 965 2651 ⊕ www.mandir.org. Free access.

It has been called Neasden's Taj Mahal. The very idea of juxtaposing this backwater London suburb on the droning North Circular with the world's most romantic and beautiful building is, of course, absurd. Until, that is, you face the Shri Swaminarayan Mandir for the first time. My epiphany came as I emerged from behind a truck trying to reverse into an office furniture depot: suddenly, there before me was the world's largest Hindu temple outside India. Blinding white sikhara pinnacles', golden spires, domes, pillars and staircases rose up in wedding cake layers. For me, it really was a moment of Taj Mahal-esque wonder. In Neasden.

The Swaminarayan sect is a branch of Hinduism with its roots in Gujarat, from where about 60% of British-Indian families originate. The Neasden temple was built and funded entirely by the Hindu community. They bought 2,800 tonnes of quarried limestone from Bulgaria and 2,000 tonnes of Carrara marble from Tuscany, all of which was shipped to India to be carved by a team of more than 1,500 master craftsmen (and women) using traditional skills.

Back in Neasden, members of the community gave up their time to work, unpaid, on the complex which consists of the Mandir (temple) and the adjoining Haveli (a Hindu cultural centre with a huge assembly hall, offices and a bookshop). Construction began in 1992 with what was, according to *The Guinness Book of Records*, the biggest ever concrete-pour in the UK to lay the foundations. Over the next two years more than 26,000 individual pieces of carved stone were shipped back from India to be assembled at the temple, which opened in 1995.

My only disappointment on reaching Shri Swaminarayan was that airport-style security is apparently necessary, with bag searches and scanners. However, this was compensated for by the openheartedly hospitable volunteer staff. I was welcomed at the gates by Karan Patel, a young man with a broad smile and a leather jacket, who suggested to me in his north London accent that I, 'completely forget about the outside world, while you are in the Mandir. This is a sacred place, where God is present.'

Karan's advice was unexpectedly easy to follow. Within moments I was transported into a resplendent world of intricate carvings and milky marble; flickering lights amid forests of pillars; sacred statues to deities being ritually fed, bathed and clothed in gold and crimson silk by sadhu holy men; and the scents of incense and camphor.

There were hundreds of people at the Mandir on the morning I was there – Hindu devotees, tourists, pensioners on outings and numerous school parties. People wandered between the seven separate shrine rooms housing Murtis (statues of the deities), each one a centre of worship at which Darshan rituals are held five times a day, the first at 09.00, the last at 16.30. Lamps are lit and offered to the deities along with garlands of marigolds and water, to the nasal chanting of songs of praise.

I found the quietest place to be the Understanding Hinduism exhibition (the only part of the Mandir for which there is a charge). The effect of this series of paintings, life-sized tableaux, 3D dioramas and other visual effects was to glorify the ancient wisdoms of Hinduism and India. The exhibition also includes a video film of the Mandir's construction, from the digging of the foundations to the arrival of the Murtis.

Getting there
The nearest **Underground** stations are Neasden (Jubilee) and Stonebridge Park (Bakerloo).

Where to eat
Shayona 54–62 Meadow Garth, off Brentfield Rd, NW10 8HD ☎ 020 8965 3365
🖥 www.shayonarestaurants.com. Delicious, contemporary-style Indian vegetarian restaurant right opposite the Mandir entrance. Numerous regional dishes and thalis. Very different from your average curry house.

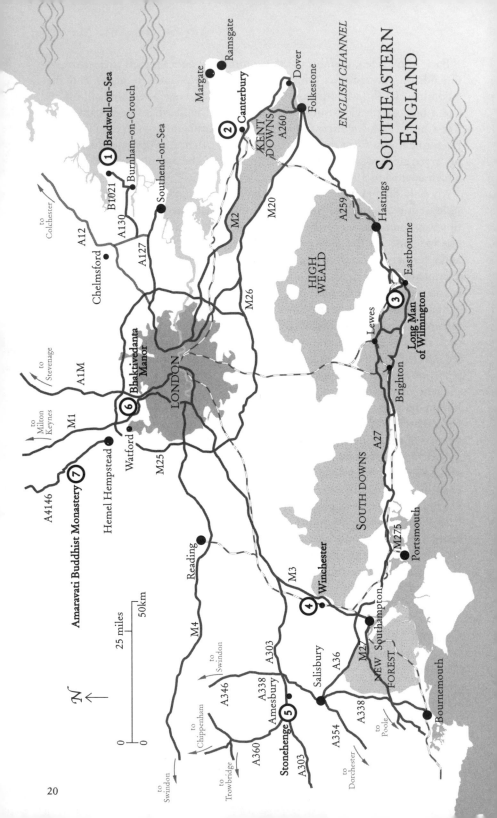

SOUTHEASTERN ENGLAND

ENGLISH CHANNEL

1 Bradwell-on-Sea

2 Canterbury

3 Long Man of Wilmington

4 Winchester

5 Stonehenge

6 Bhaktivedanta Manor

7 Amaravati Buddhist Monastery

Ramsgate

Margate

Dover

Folkestone

KENT DOWNS

A260

Hastings

Eastbourne

HIGH WEALD

Lewes

Brighton

SOUTH DOWNS

A27

Portsmouth

M275

NEW FOREST

Bournemouth

Southampton

M27

M3

A36

A338

to Poole

Salisbury

A354

to Dorchester

A303

Amesbury

A338

A346

A360

to Trowbridge

to Swindon

to Chippenham

M4

Reading

M25

Watford

Hemel Hempstead

M1

A4146

to Milton Keynes

A1M

to Stevenage

LONDON

M26

M20

M2

Chelmsford

A127

A12

A130

B1021

Burnham-on-Crouch

Southend-on-Sea

to Colchester

A259

M2

N

0

0

25 miles

50km

2. SOUTHEASTERN ENGLAND

Pilgrims have been hiking across the plains and chalk downs of the southeast for more than 3,000 years, if we include the young men from beyond the Alps who made the journey to the great monuments on the isle at the western fringe of the known world. Centuries later these worshippers were followed by streams of medieval penitents on a trail from the tomb of St Swithun, mentor to King Alfred the Great, to the shrine of Thomas Becket, the politician and saint murdered in the cathedral. Pilgrimage sites, ancient and modern, are still strewn across this region. In more recent times, modern multi-faith pilgrims are making their way through the suburbs north of London towards Hertfordshire (of all places), there to find some of Britain's foremost temples and retreat centres founded on beliefs from the East.

① Bradwell-on-Sea

Chapel of St Peter-on-the-Wall: Bradwell-on-Sea CM0 7PX ✆ 01621 776203
🌐 www.bradwellchapel.org.

On the first Saturday of every July, about 2,000 pilgrims process from the Essex village of Bradwell, though fields and along a sea-fringed promontory, to the isolated, ancient and beautifully simple chapel of St Peter (or St Peter-on-the-Wall). The pilgrimage is ecumenical, and evangelical in flavour; participants – including many youth groups and families with children – sing, dance and share picnics before worshipping together at this place of history and extraordinary aura.

As I hiked to St Peter's in solitude on a cool, late-autumn morning, I tried to imagine the summer scene of holy revelry. I had only seabirds for company and their sharp screeches for music as I followed the six-mile, waymarked 'Wildside Walk' round the promontory towards the stark and curiously barn-like, red-roofed stone chapel. It was a moment to remember **St Cedd**, but for whom there would be no chapel, pilgrimage or magnetic atmosphere.

Cedd was a monk of Lindisfarne (see page 105), probably born in Northumbria around 620, who was brought up and tutored by St Aidan. We know from the Venerable Bede's *Ecclesiastical History of the English People* (see page 114) that he was the oldest of four brothers who were all Lindisfarne monks. He became a priest and later a bishop, and was present at the 664 Synod of Whitby (see page 135) where he played a central role.

Before this, Cedd was one of several monks sent out from Lindisfarne to carry the gospel all over Saxon England and beyond. One of Cedd's allotted patches was East Anglia where he travelled in 653, perhaps sailing down the North Sea coast with a retinue of junior monks and assistants. It is not hard to see why they settled on this remote promontory. Isolation from the world and the call of the sea were at the heart of Celtic monastic life; just as Lindisfarne mirrored these features of Iona (see page 181), so Cedd must have imagined Bradwell replicating the sublime elements that he had grown up with at Lindisfarne.

Cedd founded the new Celtic monastery on the deserted foundations of Othona, a ruined Roman fort at the mouth of the River Blackwater. His church, St Peter-on-the-Wall (dedicated to Peter the Fisherman, and referring to the Roman foundations) was consecrated in 664. The new community consisted of living quarters for both men and women, and a guesthouse, library, hospital, school and farm. It also served as a base for evangelical missions into the region. So successful were these missions that Cedd was made Bishop of the East Saxons and, by the time of his death from the plague in 664, he had converted much of East Anglia to Christianity.

The monastery survived after Cedd's time and, following the Norman invasion, was taken over in 1068 by Benedictines from St Valery in France. Little is known of its fortunes after that, except that it was sold to William of Wykeham in 1391, and that it was a small monastery which went the way of others at the Reformation. There is evidence that in 1750 the church was being used as a barn for storing grain and sheltering livestock.

All the same, tall, gaunt St Peter's has a fair claim to being the oldest church in England still in regular use. The church that perches on the sea-fringe is the nave of St Cedd's original 7th-century building. Among the surrounding windswept grass are the remains of the chancel and side chambers, while ruins of the further-distant Othona are today an archaeological site.

In 1920 the chapel was restored and re-consecrated. It is used daily by the nearby Othona community, a Christian-based retreat centre open to people of all faiths or none. The church continues to attract spiritual tourists year round, as well as the annual July pilgrimage.

Getting there
Bradwell-on-Sea is 8 miles north of Burnham-on-Crouch. St Peter-on-the-Wall is about half-a-mile further on, down a track reached on foot.

Where to stay and eat
Ye Olde White Harte Hotel The Quay, Burnham-on-Crouch CM0 8AS ☎ 01621

786376. A 17th-century inn with 11 rooms, some of them overlooking the fishing harbour. Good local seafood.

Tourist information
Burnham-on-Crouch Information Centre The Old Customs House, The Quay, CM0 8AS ✆ 01621 786376 ✆ www.aboutbritain.com/towns/burnham-on-crouch.asp.

② Canterbury

Penitents no longer arrive at Canterbury on their knees seeking the intercession of the unlikely knight, scholar, politician, sometime intimate of King Henry II and finally churchman, who became the most venerated saint in the history of Britain. Large numbers of tourists do, however, still visit the small city of beguiling alleys thronging with university students (in term time, at least). Canterbury Cathedral, a UNESCO World Heritage Site, is the city's heart. St Thomas Becket is its soul.

History
St Augustine, the Benedictine monk from Rome who became the first Archbishop of Canterbury, landed with 40 followers at the Isle of Thanet off the Kentish coast in 597. According to some accounts it was 9 June, the very day that St Columba died on Iona (see page 181).

This curious coincidence highlights the fact that Augustine did not, as is sometimes suggested, bring Christianity to Britain. Far from it. There had, of course, been Christians in Britain since Roman times. For example, the Christian St Patrick, patron saint of Ireland, was born in Britain in the late 4th century before being taken across the Irish Sea and sold as a slave. And before Augustine's arrival saints Ninian (see page 189) and Columba had crossed from Ireland on missions to convert the Picts of northern Britain. Continuing their work, saints Aidan and Cuthbert began the evangelisation of Northumbria from Lindisfarne (see page 202).

Nevertheless, much of Anglo-Saxon Britain remained pagan and Augustine was sent from Rome by Pope Gregory I to preach the gospel to these people. According to the famous legend, the latter had in earlier times been captivated by some fair-haired slave boys he saw for sale in the slave market. *Non Angli, sed angeli* – 'not Angles, but Angels' – the future Pope is said to have remarked. At the time of Augustine's mission, the King of Kent was Ethelbert whose wife, Queen Bertha, was a Christian. The King allowed Augustine and his followers to preach freely and make conversions, and was himself duly baptised.

Bertha had previously rebuilt a Christian church which had existed since Roman times at Canterbury. It was here that, following his conversion of Ethelbert to Christianity, Augustine was permitted to establish his headquarters and become the first Archbishop of Canterbury. Ethelbert granted the new church land to build the first Canterbury Cathedral and the monastery that was later to become St Augustine's Abbey. Canterbury has been the ecclesiastical capital of England ever since, and its archbishops still occupy the Throne of St Augustine.

Augustine died in 604 and was buried in the abbey. However, he never attracted much of cult. Canterbury was not particularly a place of pilgrimage and probably never would have been but for the drama that followed a bitter quarrel between King Henry II and the 'turbulent priest', his former friend and Lord Chancellor now the Archbishop of Canterbury, Thomas Becket.

This culminated, of course, in Becket's murder in the cathedral on the night of 29 December 1170. Four of Henry's knights broke in and hacked him to death in the north transept. The assassins rode off, leaving the monks to attend to his body; to their amazement they found, under his fine archiepiscopal robes, a penitential shirt of horse-hair crawling with maggots and lice.

All of Europe was shocked by Becket's murder. Four year later the king famously came to Canterbury to show his grief and remorse, and to be flagellated at Becket's tomb by each of the monks in turn. By this time Becket had been canonised by Pope Alexander III and many miracles had already been reported after pilgrimages to his tomb and prayers asking for his intercession: the blind saw again, the lame walked, hideous deformities were healed and a boy drowned in the nearby River Medway had been restored to life.

In 1220, St Thomas's remains were moved to a glittering new gold-plated and bejewelled tomb. Over the subsequent centuries the pull of what became the most visited shrine in the medieval world, was to all classes and peoples across Europe. Various 'Pilgrims' Ways' were established, including from Portsmouth where pilgrims from the continent would travel via Winchester (see page 29) visiting the shrine of St Swithun *en route*. And, of course, there was the route from London down the Roman Road of Watling Street, described by Chaucer in his (fictitious) *Canterbury Tales*. It has been estimated that by the mid-15th century 100,000 pilgrims a year were visiting Becket's shrine. Monarchs including Richard the Lion Heart, French King Louis VII and Holy Roman Emperor Charles V, prostrated themselves before Thomas's tomb.

Another pilgrim was Henry VIII, so he would have seen for himself the gold, silver and jewels heaped at the shrine, donated by kings, emperors and nobles. He would also have been acutely aware that part of the appeal of this rather unlikely saint, was that he had resisted the authority of a king in church matters.

No wonder Henry was so relentless in his attack on the shrine at the Dissolution in 1538. It was reported that 26 wagons were required to transport the loot to the Tower of London. All traces of Becket were obliterated, so ending the age of pilgrimage to Canterbury. St Augustine's Abbey was destroyed, as were the city's priory and convent.

All that treasure which was heaped at the shrine accounts for the open expanse of empty flooring at the site today. Tourists in surprising numbers still stop and pause here in contemplation. No doubt some regard themselves as pilgrims.

The cathedral

The Precincts, CT1 2EH ✆ 01227 762862
⌂ www.canterbury-cathedral.org. Free access.
To enter Canterbury Cathedral through the main **South Porch** doors is one of the great architectural experiences of Britain. **The nave** is one of the last and greatest glories of English Gothic, vast in scale and with a grandeur reflecting its position as the core of the nation's spiritual life since the 7th century and the episcopal seat of the Primate of the Church of England.

The high altar is exactly that – raised, and reached by a broad stairway. There is a great sense of ceremony about the sweep from nave to choir. I was also keenly conscious that this is the way countless millions of medieval pilgrims would have processed.

However, amid all these glories I found myself inescapably drawn first to the **north transept** which is not only bare, but is an architecturally less interesting part of the cathedral. But this is the very soul of the place, because this is where Becket was martyred. For some reason, standing at this sacred and serene spot I could not get the gory details out of my mind.

The archbishop knelt on the flagstones as the four knights set on him with their swords, slicing off the crown of his head. Then one of their followers, Hugh of Horsea, flicked his brain out onto the ground. The very spot where the martyrdom took place is marked with a frightening-looking sculpture of the murder weapons.

Next to a single candle, a simple inscription etched into the stone floor reads:

The shrine of Thomas Becket Archbishop and Martyr stood here from 1220 until 1538.

St Augustine's Abbey and St Martin's Church

The abbey: Monastery St, CT1 1PF ✆ 01227 767345 ⌂ www.english-heritage.org.
uk/daysout/properties/st-augustines-abbey/; the church: North Holes Rd, CT1 1PW
⌂ www.martinpaul.org.
While Canterbury Cathedral survived the Dissolution by passing into the hands of the new Head of the Church of England, Henry VIII, the great **Abbey of St Augustine**, outside the city walls, did not. The Benedictine monastery had been founded by Augustine himself and was the burial place for the Anglo-Saxon Christian kings of Kent, from Ethelbert onwards. St Augustine himself was also buried there though no trace of his grave remains. Now a

ruin, the abbey is frequently overlooked by modern tourists and pilgrims to Canterbury.

So too is nearby **St Martin's Church**, on the site of the original Romano-British church restored as her private chapel by Queen Bertha before the arrival of Augustine. It may also have been here that Augustine baptised Ethelbert. Little remains of the Roman or Saxon structures, but it is probable that a square-headed doorway in the chancel is original. This gives the church a plausible claim to being the oldest Christian place of worship in Britain.

Canterbury Tales Visitor Attraction

12 The Friars, CT1 2AS ✆ 01227 479227 🖳 www.canterburytales.org.uk.

Towards the end of the 14th century, a group of travellers met at the Tabard Inn by the Thames in London. Among them was a knight down on his luck, a young 'lusty squire', a delicate prioress, a bawdy miller, a sea captain, a cook and 20 or so others. They were all about to ride to Canterbury on pilgrimage to the shrine of St Thomas Becket. The proprietor of the inn, Harry Bailey, suggested that they enliven the journey with a story-telling competition. Free lunch at the inn for the winner.

Such is the fictitious setting for Geoffrey Chaucer's rollicking *Canterbury Tales*. At times they are deeply moving, at others astonishingly crude and often laugh-out-loud funny. But collectively they give us an unparalleled amount of detail about pilgrimage to Canterbury in medieval England.

This visitor attraction, in a former church (St Margaret's) on St Margaret's Street a couple of minutes' walk from the cathedral, is no substitute for studying Middle English and reading the *Canterbury Tales* in Chaucer's original language. But it is a slick exhibition conjuring the atmosphere of 14th-century life and recounting a selection of the tales in a series of tableaux, enhanced by clever touches such as odour-enhancement!

Getting there

By **road** from London, the city is reached by the M2 and A2 and by **bus** on National Express (*0871 7818178; www.nationalexpress.com*). Canterbury has two **railway** stations, both of them near the city centre. From London, Canterbury West is reached from Charing Cross and Waterloo, and on a high-speed service from St Pancras. Canterbury East is reached from London Victoria.

Where to stay and eat

ABode Canterbury 30–33 High St, CT1 2RX ✆ 01227 766266 🖳 www.abodehotels.co.uk/canterbury. A swish, contemporary-style boutique hotel. Excellent restaurant.

Thanington Hotel 140 Wincheap, CT1 3RY ✆ 01227 453227 🖳 www.thanington-hotel.co.uk. An elegant, traditional-feeling hotel close to the city centre with an indoor pool, plus a bar offering a huge array of malt whiskies.

Thomas Becket 21 Best Lane, CT1 2JB ✆ 01227 464384. A rustic-feeling pub oozing olde-worlde atmosphere. Great choice of beers, and a more limited range of good-value food.

Tourist information
Canterbury Tourist Information Centre 34 St Margaret's St, CT1 2TG ✆ 01227 378100 🖱 www.canterbury.co.uk.

③ The Long Man of Wilmington
Windover Hill, Wilmington ✆ 01273 487188
🖱 www.sussexpast.co.uk. Free access.

While the carving of white horses into chalk slopes is known as leucippotomy (see box page 86), the rarer art of cutting hill figures in human form is sometimes referred to as gigantony. In Britain, there are only two of them of any size, note or antiquity. There is the mystifying Cerne Giant (see page 53) and there is this athletic fellow standing 235ft high on a steep South Downs incline in east Sussex, holding a staff in each of his outstretched hands.

The Long Man of Wilmington, also known as 'The Lanky Man' or sometimes 'The Lone Man', is said to be Europe's largest representation of a human. Local legend has him as prehistoric in origin – perhaps a warrior or a fertility symbol and akin to his sibling at Cerne Abbas. If this is true, maybe he was emasculated in a fit of Victorian prudery. One popular myth identifies him as Baldr, the Norse god of light, beauty, love and happiness. Other authorities have him as Bronze Age, or Roman. Some say he is Beowulf, or even St Paul. It has also been suggested that he may be the work of medieval monks from nearby Wilmington Priory.

In truth, The Long Man's identity remains a mystery though we do now have some clues as to his age. According to University of Reading archaeologists, who have carried out OSL (Optically Stimulated Luminescence) dating, the present Long Man was cut into the turf around 1545. However, this does not necessarily mean that this work did not replace an earlier figure, possibly an outline.

The first record of the figure appears in a 1710 survey, along with a drawing which includes eyes, nose and mouth, and something like a plume or helmet on his head. Another drawing, from 1766, shows him holding a rake in one hand and a scythe in the other. However, the Long Man's outline was relatively faint until 1874 when a group of antiquarians marked him out with yellow bricks. During World War II he was camouflaged with green paint so as not to be a landmark for enemy aircraft. The disguise remained in place until 1969 when it was replaced by today's white stone blocks which are still in good condition.

Life Cairn

On a clear day, and if he looks very carefully indeed, the Long Man of Wilmington can – from his position on a South Downs hillside – make out Mount Caborn in East Sussex. Just below the summit the first few stones have recently been placed of a 'Life Cairn', established in 2011 to commemorate all the species that have become extinct on earth as a result of human behaviour.

The embryonic cairn is of chalk and flint, reflecting the original state of many of the tumuli – or ancient burial mounds – found on the ridges of the South Downs. The instigators of the Life Cairn, including the BBC presenter and local clergyman the Reverend Peter Owen-Jones, hope that everybody who climbs Mount Caborn will add to the cairn by laying their own piece of chalk or flint. They ask visitors to spend a few moments reflecting on the fact that there are thousands of species on a United Nations 'Red List' (meaning that they are in imminent danger of extinction); and that every day 17 species – 200 times the natural rate – pass into extinction. The organisers also have an ambition that this Life Cairn will lead the way to there being an equivalent cairn in every country on earth.

As one of the first visitors, I laid my stone in the early morning as the world rushed to work below me. Doing so seemed to be a very ancient gesture expressing a very contemporary concern. This most recent sacred site in Britain brings together the past and the present in a way that I had not quite expected.

Getting there

The village of **Glyde** is near Lewes, reached on the A27 or by **train** to Glyde station. Opposite the village post office, there is a stile leading to a path up to the cairn.

The Long Man is now in the custodianship of the Sussex Archaeological Society, but is revered by an eclectic collection of devotees. A group of local Druids, for example, gather on top of the flat hill to the west of the figure at key dates such as the summer solstice when they mark the 'Feast of the Forgotten Sun'. Typically about 50 to 100 participants turn up for the ceremony during which actors wear masks depicting the sun, moon and earth. In February, a pagan Imbolc – the first celebration of spring – is held by Wicca adherents. And not to be outdone, on most summer weekends this sacred site is also worshipped with hats, sticks, bells and beer as the Long Man Morris Men dance at the giant's feet till their shadows lengthen.

There have, however, been a number of controversial incidents. In 2007 a television show called *Undress the Nation* presented by the fashion duo Trinny and Susannah pulled off the feat of giving the Long 'Man' a sex change. This they achieved by marshalling 100 women dressed in white on to the figure, where they used their bodies to add fulsome breasts, broad hips and pigtails. The stunt provoked a protest by Druids who accused the women of 'dishonouring an ancient pagan site of worship'.

Less subtle still, was the painting by pranksters of a 20ft phallus (a not unreasonable size, given his overall dimensions) onto the figure three days before the 2010 summer solstice. He was also given a smiling face. The decorating was done with football pitch line marking paint, and thus the figure was easily restored to his previous dignity.

Getting there

The Long Man is signposted off the A27 between Eastbourne and Lewes, 2 miles west of Polegate. There is a car park near Wilmington Prior, and a footpath to the figure's base. The nearest **railway** stations are Berwick and Polegate, both about 3 miles away. Taxis are available from both stations.

Where to stay and eat

Boship Farm Hotel Lower Dicker, near Hailsham BN27 4AT ☎ 01323 844826 ⌂ www.boshipfarmhotel.co.uk. A delightful, small hotel in rural Sussex with a 17th-century farmhouse at its core.

The Giants Rest The Street, Polegate BN26 5SQ ☎ 01323 870207 ⌂ www.giantsrest.co.uk. The nearest accommodation and watering hole to the Long Man. Fantastic location, OK rooms and food, great beer.

Tourist information

Lewes Tourist Information Centre 187 High St, BN7 2DE ☎ 01273 483448 ⌂ www.enjoysussex.info.

④ Winchester

Alfred the Great, King of Wessex, presides commandingly over Winchester's Broadway. With sword aloft, crowned head held in a stern, middle-distance gaze, the bronze statue was erected in 1901 to mark the 1,000th anniversary of his death in 899. (OK, so it was a couple of years late.)

Between the times of Alfred and Henry II, Winchester went from being capital of Wessex to capital of England and one of the most important cities in Europe. Today it is a fairly quiet cathedral town with a rich repository of English history. Kings from Alfred to Edward the Confessor were crowned here. So were William the Conqueror and Richard the Lionheart, in addition to their coronations at Westminster Abbey, just to be on the safe side.

The cathedral, founded in 1079 on the foundations of its predecessor the 7th-century Saxon Old Minster, houses the remains of numerous historical bigwigs from King Canute to Jane Austen.

Winchester Cathedral and St Swithun

1 The Close, SO23 9LS ℂ 01962 857200 🖥 www.winchester-cathedral.org.uk.
Free access.

There is no disputing the magnificence of the cathedral. Though occupying a low-lying position, its perpendicular Gothic arches rise above the highest point of the hilly town. The staggering dimensions and craftsmanship raise the answerless questions as to how architecture became so accomplished a science, centuries before man ever thought of comparatively simple inventions such as the steam engine.

From the inside, the soaring perpendicular arches pointing up to stone vaulting high above contribute to the sense of absolute vastness. It is one of the largest cathedrals in England, has the longest nave of any Gothic cathedral in Europe, and took some 300 years to complete.

Stone 'mortuary chests' (tombs containing remains originally buried elsewhere, but later 'translated' here) are perched high up on stone screens. There is King Canute, his son Hardicanute, William II ('Rufus') and at least half-a-dozen other kings of Wessex or England. The notable absentee is Alfred the Great whose remains were moved to nearby Hyde Abbey, a Benedictine monastery; his tomb was destroyed at the Dissolution, leaving no trace of Alfred.

William of Wykeham, Bishop of Winchester and architect of the cathedral's great nave, founded Winchester College in 1382 to provide an education for 70 impoverished boys and prepare them for the Church. He now lies in episcopal grandeur in a side chapel beneath a gilt effigy of himself, designed by him, and with three Benedictine monks praying at his feet. I noticed, however, that Jane Austen, in her much more discreet tomb, was receiving markedly more attention from visitors.

More revered than any of them, however, is St Swithun, the worker of miracles and tutor of Alfred the Great, to whom the cathedral is dedicated. Swithun was born in about 800, probably at or near Winchester. He was educated at the cathedral, became a monk, and in 852 was appointed Bishop of Winchester. There are few recorded facts about his life, other than that King Aethelwulf of Wessex entrusted to him the education of his young son Alfred, later to be known as Alfred the Great.

What is clear is that Swithun became renowned for his personal austerity, extreme modesty, and generosity and compassion for all humanity, particularly the poor. When he gave banquets, as bishops were expected to do, he went against all conventions by inviting the lowest in society rather than the rich and powerful. Nothing exemplifies his humility more than the instructions he left for his own burial. He felt unworthy to have his remains spend eternity within sacred walls and so asked to be buried outside. Not only that, he specifically wanted to lie near a door on the damp north side of the church, so that he would be trampled on as a constant reminder of his unworthiness.

On his death the monks apparently could not bring themselves to carry out this wish. Nevertheless, in deference to his humility they interred him in an inconspicuous side aisle of the Old Minster. This simple tomb began to attract increasing numbers of pilgrims, seeking his intercession on account of his undoubted closeness to God. In response to Swithun's burgeoning cult a new shrine was built for him behind the high altar and his remains were disinterred and carried there with due pomp on 15 July 971. He registered his disapproval by causing an almighty rainstorm which did not let up for 40 days.

In 1093, soon after construction began of the present cathedral, St Swithun was moved again to another shrine this time in the rectochoir. He continued to attract medieval pilgrims in their hundreds of thousands. After Becket's martyrdom, many would walk a 'Pilgrim's Way' from St Swithun's shrine in Winchester to that of St Thomas at Canterbury (see page 23).

Like so many others, the shrine was demolished after Henry VIII's Dissolution of the Monasteries. So too were the chapter house and cloisters of the cathedral's attached Benedictine monastery, the Priory of St Swithun. However, the cathedral survived and today the site of St Swithun's great medieval shrine is marked by a simple, modern memorial behind the high altar at the eastern end of the cathedral, surrounded by worn flagstones.

I paused at this revered spot, reflecting that from what we know of the man, this is a far more fitting commemoration of him. A few feet away is a small doorway leading to a narrow, dank passage which does not seem to go anywhere. This is the 'Holy Hole' through which pilgrims used to crawl in penance (perhaps it was once much longer) arriving immediately below the saint's healing relics. Above the door are nine beautiful Russian Orthodox-style icons installed between 1992 and 1996 including, in pole position, St Swithun.

The final word on Swithun, however, has to go to the proverb which that deluge he caused in 971 created:

St Swithun's day if thou dost rain
For forty days it will remain
St Swithun's day if thou be fair
For forty days 'twill rain nae mare

Or, according to a simpler, local version:

If on St Swithun's day it really pours
You're better off to stay indoors

A walk from Winchester to St Cross

Hospital of St Cross, St Cross Rd, SO23 9SD ☎ 01962 851375 🏠 www.stcross.f2s.com.
I began my walk at Alfred the Great's statue and strode down the wide Broadway, past the stately **Guild Hall** and on to the pedestrianised High

Street. Here, ancient and modern buildings are strikingly juxtaposed. A leaning, timber-framed medieval building faces a flickering wall of HD and 3D television screens; old-fashioned stone façades mask the familiar interiors of retail chains such as W H Smith; and tattooed and body-pierced young people hang around the 15th-century stone-sculpted **Butter Cross**.

The High Street seems to mark a boundary between old and new, with a multi-storey car park and modern blocks off to the right, and narrow alleyways of ancient, worn paving-stone leading down to the cathedral and historic Winchester on the left.

I stopped at **Great Hall**, one of Winchester's many historical superlatives. There was a hushed atmosphere in this vault of a place built for Henry III in the 13th century. Ancient oak beams, marble piers and panelled walls are adorned with heraldic records of the events the hall has witnessed during its 700 years: the first English parliament; the trial of Sir Walter Raleigh; the interrogations of the infamous Judge Jeffreys. Dominating the hall from high on the west wall is a round, oak table-top 18ft in diameter, depicting a splendidly robed and bethroned King Arthur, with the names of his knights around the circumference. The table has been dated to the 16th century, and so was not Arthur's after all.

A sharp left at the Butter Cross took me under a low archway, from where I threaded my way through the expanse of green outside the cathedral. **Jane Austen** is buried within the cathedral, but just behind, on College Street, is the small butterscotch-coloured house where she died. It is a private home, with just a discreet blue plaque above the front door recording that, '*In this house Jane Austen lived her last days and died 18 July 1817*'. Somehow this otherwise unremarkable cottage seems to have more significance than all the great tombs in the cathedral.

College Street passes the gates of William of Wykeham's Winchester College, the first of England's traditional 'public' (meaning 'private', paradoxically) schools with its stone quadrangles, courtyards, cloisters, chapels and schoolrooms aflurry with uniformed boys piled high with books, or changed for the sports field. The street leads down to **Wolvesey Palace** and the ruins of King Stephen's **Wolvesey Castle**.

Clear signs point the way to 'St Cross via Water Meadows'. The footpath turns left at another gateway to **Winchester College**, finds a grassy bank between two channels of the splintered River Itchen, and heads off in a straight line separated by the water from the college playing fields on one side, and the flood-prone meadows on the other. It is here that Keats is said to have been inspired to compose his 'Ode to Autumn'. When I visited the idea seemed entirely plausible. A gentle haze hovered a few inches above the limpid river and, although autumn was giving way to early winter and the newly bare trees swayed in the chill wind, there were still dense thickets of deep red, and rich golden hues around the river banks. '*Season of mists and mellow fruitfulness! Close bosom-friend of the maturing sun*'. Indeed.

This route of a little less than a mile to the village of St Cross seemed to belong to the waterfowl. Coots and moorhens paddled about in the slivers of channelled water, or scurried across the path; every now and then a flight of mallards circled overhead and splashed noisily on to the water.

The path crosses a road at an old pumping station, and then continues past a weir and along a track canopied with foliage to emerge in a broad, wet meadow. To the left is **St Cross Chapel** and its famous 'hospital', founded in 1132 by Henri de Blois, Bishop of Winchester, to provide shelter for *'13 men, feeble and so reduced in strength that they can hardly or with difficulty support themselves without another's aid'*. I had also read that 'Wayfarers' Dole'  of bread and ale can still be claimed free by travellers passing through.

There are currently 21 'Brethren', dressed in black gowns and bizarre hats rather like mortarboards, living in the old almshouses around a quadrangle. They are elderly, very respectable gentlemen – mostly retired widowers or bachelors – who live there today. One of them proudly showed me the chapel where they gather daily to worship. Then we went to the old kitchen with its huge old stone bread oven and hand-pump that draws straight from a stream beneath; and finally to the fine old 15th-century **Brethren's Hall** of ancient oak timbers and stained-glass windows.

On my way out I (slightly embarrassed) asked the gate porter if I might claim my 'Wayfarers' Dole'. 'By all means, sir!' he said enthusiastically, and fetched me a square of bread and a small glass into which he poured a measure of beer out of a supermarket chain's own-label plastic bottle. Thus sustained, I made my way back to Winchester – this time, for the sake of variety, along the path on the opposite side of the Itchen.

Getting there

Winchester is 65 miles southwest of London. It is reached by **road** via the M3 motorway and by **rail** from Waterloo station.

Where to stay and eat

Hotel du Vin 12 Southgate St, SO23 9EF ☎ 01962 841414 🖰 www.hotelduvin. com/hotels/winchester/winchester.asp. Small and intimate and housed in a 1715 Georgian townhouse. Lovely bistro, with the option to eat in the garden when the weather permits.

The Black Rat 88 Chesil St, SO23 0HX ☎ 01962 844465 🖰 www.theblackrat. co.uk. Delicious, modern British food. Only the name might put you off.

The Wykeham Arms 75 Kingsgate St, SO23 9PE ☎ 01962 853834

🏠 www.fullershotels.com. Fabulous old inn right at the heart of the city. Small but cosy rooms. Top-notch restaurant which needs to be booked well in advance.

Tourist information
Winchester Tourist Information Centre The Guildhall, The Broadway SO23 9GH 📞 01962 840500 🏠 www.visitwinchester.co.uk.

⑤ Stonehenge
Amesbury SP4 7DE 📞 0870 3331181 🏠 www.english-heritage.org.uk/stonehenge.
The titanic sarsen stones yoked by lintels, which comprise Europe's most mystifying and contemplated prehistoric monument, appear in silhouette from the A303 road which crosses the flat emptiness of Salisbury Plain. For millions, this first glimpse of something distant but unmistakeably ancient causes a frisson of excitement. Stonehenge!

What is Stonehenge? Strictly speaking, a 'henge' is a circular earth rampart and parallel internal ditch as at Avebury (see page 45), so Stonehenge is not really a 'henge' at all. Rather, this cluster of enormous stone circles is the centrepiece of the most significant prehistoric environment in Britain.

But on a recent trip to Stonehenge, I suddenly saw red. In consequence, here follows the only rant you will read in *Sacred Britain*. How on earth has this sacred monument been allowed to become so brutally divorced from its context?

After that initial frisson, the great majority of Stonehenge's 875,000 visitors a year pay an entrance fee to traipse through a concrete underpass from a car park to a remote viewing area near the noisy junction of the A303 and A344. Roads gash through the surrounding landscape. A Commons Select Committee has rightly described the situation as a 'national disgrace'.

An obvious solution, which has been proposed, would have been a tunnel taking the A303 underground. At best, this would have left Stonehenge in glorious open countryside allowing the site to embrace the sacred Avenue ritual pathway, long barrows, village sites and the new 'Bluehenge' discovery (see box, page 37). But this was too expensive, apparently, so the idea has been ditched in favour of an English Heritage 'visitor centre', 1½ miles away. Certainly a good interpretive exhibition is needed, but even after this new centre is completed, visiting the stones will remain, as Dr Andrew Lawson (see below) has put it, 'like entering a cathedral and looking only at the altar'.

History and legend
The first written record of Stonehenge was by the Welsh monk Geoffrey of Monmouth in his 12th-century *Historia Regum Britanniae* ('*History of the Kings of Britain*'). According to Geoffrey, Stonehenge was the handiwork of Merlin the Magician who transported the stones from Mount Killaraus in Ireland. He did so on the orders of King Arthur's uncle Ambrosius Aurelius,

to create a fitting memorial for noble Britons slaughtered by invading Saxons. It would also serve as a place of healing.

Fair enough, as theories go. However, since Geoffrey's time Stonehenge has been getting progressively older. Indigo Jones, the Court Architect visiting the stones with King James I in 1620, explained to his majesty that Stonehenge was in fact a Roman temple. Samuel Pepys, on the other hand, kept an open mind. Riding across Salisbury Plain in 1668, he pronounced the stones to be, '*as prodigious as any tales I ever heard of them and worth going this journey to see. God knows what their use was.*'

In the following century, antiquarian William Stukely decided that Stonehenge was built by Celtic Druids, and so was pre-Roman. In 'The Prelude', William Wordsworth wrote, after his wanderings among the stones in 1799:

> *... gently was I charmed*
> *Into a waking dream, a reverie*
> *That, with believing eyes, where'er I turned*
> *Beheld long-bearded teachers, with white wands*
> *Uplifted, pointed to the starry sky.*

Deeper and deeper into antiquity was Stonehenge shoved, so that by the beginning of the 20th century some archaeologists were postulating that the monument could have been constructed by a civilisation that flourished as long ago as 1000BC.

Modern radio-carbon dating indicates that the first earthworks in the site were in fact dug around 2800BC. The 82 bluestones, from the Preseli Mountains in Wales (Rolled? Dragged? Floated? ... nobody knows) probably arrived about three centuries later, at the beginning of the Bronze Age. The third phase was the bringing of giant, 50-tonne sarsen stones from the Marlborough Downs about 20 miles away a few centuries after that. By this time Stonehenge was joined by a ceremonial avenue to the River Avon. By about 1500BC Stonehenge had fallen out of use.

At least, that is the current archaeological orthodoxy. It will probably change; who knows, maybe future generations will revert to Geoffrey of Monmouth's Arthurian theory. Geoffrey was at least correct that the stones of Stonehenge arrived from the west by some seemingly magical means. Perhaps his story retained traces of some ancient folk memory.

Visiting the stones

Access to Stonehenge has been restricted since 1978. Yielding to the mounting pressure of growing visitor numbers, erosion and random acts of vandalism, the authorities decided to deny general contact with the stones. Since then, most visitors have had to make do with simply looking at the monument from a distance. They do not wander among the stones or touch them. There is no sense of intimacy. There is not even a museum to interpret Stonehenge and its significance, unless you count a few half-hearted exhibitions housed in temporary sheds.

Nevertheless, there are various ways of getting up close and personal with Stonehenge. By applying in advance and paying a fee on top of the normal ticket price, Stone Circle Access is possible in groups of up to 25. Requests are considered by English Heritage on a case-by-case basis, but typically these parties are of people with special reasons for being there: amateur archaeologists; Druids; believers in ley lines and dousing; or groups practising meditation or yoga, for instance.

I was fortunate enough to be among the stones shortly before dusk on a beautiful summer's evening. I was there with the former Director of Wessex Archaeology, Dr Andrew Lawson, who was helping me and a party of others to fathom the history and significance of Stonehenge. We were able to weave between the stones and run our fingers over the lichen-covered blocks that

have been here for 4,000 years.

I recalled how I once clambered over the stones as a child in the 1970s. Andrew told us: 'The fact that the outer circle is not complete is explained by the Victorians' penchant for taking away some of the stones to adorn their gardens. And incredibly, as recently as the early 20th century people were given hammers and chisels and actively encouraged to chip off a piece of Stonehenge to take home as a souvenir.'

So it is not really surprising that top-heavy stones were starting to fall down. The last to topple was in 1963, after which all those which had tumbled since 1747, when records began, were re-erected.

In fact, the history of vandalism and graffiti here is almost as old as the stones. The crude outline of a dagger etched on one of them may be about 2,000 years old. The just-discernable upper case letters L, I, V and E are clearly more recent. Some life-affirming moral message perhaps? Unlikely, says Andrew. 'The graffiti is quite new. I'm willing to bet that the artist had an interest in football and was interrupted before he could add R, P, double O, L.'

It took an expert like Andrew to illuminate details such us how the stones are aligned on both the axes of the summer solstice sunrise and winter solstice sunset. And how the massive lintels are bound to the upright sarsens using the same methods as a carpenter might. 'There is no other structure anything like Stonehenge from the same period. In fact, nothing on this scale till the Romans. I suspect the whole business might have been a bit too much like hard work, so they decided not to attempt anything similar again.'

Our expert archaeologist also cheerfully acknowledged that we really have very little idea about the purpose of Stonehenge. However, it is safe to conclude that it had a ceremonial and ritual function. Recent DNA testing on two skeletons unearthed near the site indicate that one was an adolescent boy from the western Mediterranean about 3,500 years ago; the other was from the foothills of the Alps about 800 years later. Clearly, then, Stonehenge has been a tourist attraction for a very long time.

The alignments show that the sun, and perhaps the moon, were important. We have no idea what gods were worshipped there, but the overwhelming impression is that Stonehenge was a focus of enormous power, meaning and spiritual inspiration. This is testified to by its enduring magnetism, still potent today particularly around the solstices. In the modern era these are the times of year when Stonehenge becomes a meeting place for people inspired by a broad spectrum of 'alternative' spiritual beliefs.

Getting there
Stonehenge is 8 miles north of Salisbury, near the intersection of the A303 and the A344.

Access to the stones
Andante Travels ☎ 01722 713800 🖥 www.andantetravels.co.uk. Offer archaeology tours of the area, including access to the stones with an expert and visits to the associated sites. See box below.

See also *Appendix 2* for other operators running tours in the area.

Where to stay and eat
Fairlawn House 42 High St, Amesbury SP4 7DL ☎ 01980 622103
🖥 www.fairlawnhotel.co.uk. A stone's throw (an ordinary pebble, not a sarsen

Sites nearby – Stonehenge's wider context
About two miles from Stonehenge, and about 500yds from one another, are the sites of Neolithic henges and settlements **Durrington Walls** and **Woodhenge**. They were identified after an aerial survey in 1925 and excavations revealed them to have been villages of wooden houses with clay floors and central hearths. These villages, it can be surmised, were the homes of the priestly astronomers responsible for building Stonehenge.

The most recent archaeological discovery is **Bluehenge**, just a mile from Stonehenge and the site of a 5,000-year-old circle of blue stones from the Preseli Mountains in Wales. Bluehenge appears to have been a smaller, earlier circle whose stones were moved and incorporated into Stonehenge. Excavations in 2008 and 2009 found chips of stone showing that these blue stones are of the same origin as those at Stonehenge. All that remains now are the indentations where the 27 megaliths stood.

or blue stone) from Stonehenge. Elegant, traditional, good meals in Cellar's restaurant.

The Antrobus Arms Hotel 15 Church St, Amesbury SP4 7EU ☎ 01980 623163 🖰 www.antrobusarmshotel.co.uk. As if all the archaeology was not enough history, The Beatles stayed at this old coaching inn while filming *Help!* on Salisbury Plain and have a suite named after them.

Tourist information
Salisbury and Stonehenge Tourist Information Centre Fish Row, SP1 1EJ ☎ 01722 334956 🖰 www.visitwiltshire.co.uk/salisbury.

⑥ Bhaktivedanta Manor

Dharam Marg, Hilfield Lane, Aldenham, Watford WD25 8EZ ☎ 01923 851000 🖰 www.bhaktivedantamanor.co.uk. Free access.

During the 1960s the International Society for Krishna Consciousness (ISKCON) – better known simply as the Hare Krishna Movement – suddenly found itself at the forefront of western spiritual consciousness. One reason for this was the interest in eastern spirituality expressed by The Beatles, and in particular George Harrison who became a Hare Krishna devotee. In 1973 Harrison bought Piggott's Manor, a half-timbered country mansion in 17 acres of Hertfordshire parkland which he donated to the movement and renamed Bhaktivedanta Manor (which means, roughly, 'devotion to the Vedic scriptures' in Sanskrit). The idea was that the manor should be, in Harrison's words, '*a guide to Krishna consciousness and a place for people to taste the splendour of devotional service to the Supreme Lord*'.

Sweeping up a long drive lined with rhododendrons, my first impression was of a rather fine, though unostentatious, mock-Tudor country house. I was

welcomed by Radha Mohan Das, also known as Richard Cole, dressed in white robes and with his head shaven except for a single, long strand. He looked similar to other Hare Krishna devotees I have seen chanting in city centres.

Richard, a former drama student from Bromsgrove, told me that he spent 15 years as a monk here before leaving a couple of years ago to marry a Hindu woman from Mauritius. However, he remains an employee of the manor as its Communications Secretary, and explained how this is a place of profound spiritual teaching, where tens of thousands of visitors a year come to absorb the culture and teachings of His Divine Grace AC Bhaktivedanta Swami Prabhupada, the ISKCON Founder and Spiritual Master who died in 1997.

Said Richard, 'The Hare Krishna philosophy is different in emphasis from other Hindu sects. For example, we are on good terms with, but not close to, the Neasden Mandir, rather like Catholics and Protestants'.

At the manor's front door we slipped off our shoes before entering a wood-panelled, almost unfurnished, spotlessly polished spacious hall. What I imagine was once a capacious drawing room is now the main temple with a vibrant triptych altar of shrines to a selection of Hindu gods including Rama, Hanuman (the monkey god), Sita and, of course, the flute-playing Krishna the central scriptural character in the Bhagavad Gita elevated by some to the position of Supreme Being.

'Darshan' ceremonies of devotion to the gods are held throughout the day in the temple, the first at 04.30 and the last at 21.00. Elsewhere around the house activities were going on, such as handicraft and theatre workshops, chanting, meditation sessions (despite a constant background hum) and talks for school groups.

There are about 30 monks and nuns and many more lay residents living at Bhaktivedanta, the majority of them British including several UK-born Hindus of Indian ancestry. The manor runs a bakery, a shop, the Krishna Avanti independent primary school and an 80-acre farm on adjoining land, bought in the 1990s with donations from the British Hindu community. A herd of 46 cattle supply an organic dairy, while oxen are used to grind grain for muesli.

Away from all the activity, the most peaceful part of Bhaktivedanta is the 'Woodland Walk' from the George Harrison Memorial Garden, through a broad-leafed copse and round a small lake. Between pauses at plaques quoting from the Bhagavad Gita, Richard told me how in the 1980s relationships with the local community and the manor became tense, leading to attempts by Hertsmere Borough Council to restrict their activities. 'In the end, compromise was the answer, and really these days Hare Krishna is no longer seen as a cult'.

All the same, after leaving Bhaktivedanta I walked through Aldenham village reflecting on the incongruity of a Hare Krishna community in a place like this. Falling into conversation with an elderly couple walking their dogs, I learnt that when the Hare Krishnas first arrived there had been great local consternation and fears of noisy weirdos imposing on the village's tranquillity. 'As it turned out', said the smiling lady, 'we could not have hoped for more peaceful and obliging neighbours.'

Getting there

The nearest **train** stations are at Radlett, just over 3 miles away, and Watford Junction, 5 miles away. **London Underground** stations Edgware and Stanmore, terminuses of the Northern and Jubilee lines respectively, are about 10 minutes away by **taxi**.

Visiting the manor

Bhaktivedanta Manor is open daily from 04.00 until 21.30 for tours of the house, grounds and farm, and for ceremonies in the temple. For courses and overnight stays, contact the manor directly.

Where to stay and eat

The Red Lion 78–80 Watling St, Radlett WD7 7NP ☎ 01923 855341
🖰 www.redlionradlett.co.uk. A gastro-pub and small hotel offering creature comforts which might feel like an antidote to the Hare Krishna temple.

⑦ Amaravati Buddhist Monastery

St Margarets Lane, Great Gaddesden, Hemel Hempstead HP1 3BZ ☎ 01442 843239
🖰 www.amaravati.org. Free access.

Hidden away in the Hertfordshire's Chiltern Hills there is a small, rather beautiful patch of woodland. The broad branches of ancient beech trees throw dappled shade over vivid birch saplings. Scattered oaks and ash tower above hazels, horn beams, white beams and cherry trees; in autumn, there are tiny sweet chestnuts to be harvested by those who know where to look.

My guide through these woods was Ajahn Amaro, Abbot of Amaravati Buddhist Monastery. I followed his saffron robes and shaven head under some low-slung branches and across a grassy glade as he explained how in 1984 the Sangha Trust, an organisation formed to found a Buddhist monastic order in Britain, acquired the former St Margaret's School in the secluded village of Great Gaddesden along with 32 adjoining acres.

The spiritual roots of Sangha monasteries are in Thailand, where the order is of the 'theravada' meditative tradition. Since forests are considered suitably calm and conducive to meditation, forestry and conservation have become woven into the tradition. A couple of camouflaged, single-room wooden huts where monks and nuns on retreat meditate are the only signs of humanity in the woods. The main monastery buildings are a few hundred yards away.

A tractor pulling a trailer-load of silage had passed the monastery gates just as I arrived. The farmer waved cheerily to one of the monks with whom he stopped to exchange a few pleasantries before rattling on past the sign announcing Amaravati Buddhist Monastery & Retreat Centre. Visitors are welcome to drop in at any time between early morning and 21.30; however, people who expect to find a riot of pagodas and gilded temples as they may have seen in Thailand might be disappointed. Much of the site is taken up by long, low buildings which were once schoolrooms.

The community currently comprises 46 monks, nuns, novices and lay residents. Some are from Thailand, Cambodia and Sri Lanka, but most are Europeans, including my broadly grinning and very urbane host Ajahn Amaro who has been a monk for 32 years. Previously he was Jeremy Horner from Kent, educated at an exclusive private school and London University before setting off for Thailand on the spiritual quest which was to result in his becoming one of the west's most eminent Buddhist teachers. The abbot is also a raconteur to be reckoned with. I particularly enjoyed the tale of how he once shared a train carriage with some aggressive West Ham fans who saw an easy target in his unorthodox garb. Somehow he gained their rapt attention, telling them how he rose for meditation at the 04.00 morning bell, ate nothing after midday and was celibate. It was the latter revelation that was met with the greatest incredulity, 'No way mate! ... yer mean you 'aven't 'ad it for 32 years?'

One group of buildings is set apart for meditation retreats. These are offered to outsiders, usually last for two or three days (sometimes longer) and are led by members of the community. Others of the monks and nuns travel widely, explaining the precepts of Buddhism to anyone who invites them. They ask for no money, but – in the tradition of 'alms mendicants' – live entirely on gifts and donations. They do not buy food; it is all given, either directly to the monastery, or to monks who take their bowls to the local towns of Hemel Hempstead or Berkhamstead and stand waiting for gifts 'in the traditions of our origins', as Ajahn Amaro puts it, adding that: 'I have never gone hungry yet, in fact we usually have surplus food, which we in turn donate to whoever needs it.'

The day is punctuated by meditation and chanting sessions, the first at 05.00 and the last at 19.30. These take place sitting in the lotus position on cushions in the main temple, one of only a very few new constructions at the monastery, built entirely of oak without even the use of nails. A huge gilt Buddha statue presides over proceedings. There is also a new rectangular cloister which has nothing to do with any Buddhist tradition, but was added as a mark of respect to Christian monastic traditions.

Walking over towards the woods, the abbot led me across a field with, in the middle, a large stupa – a copy of the famous Borobudur monument in Java. Then we strode over to a copse of young oaks which, Ajahn Amaro told me, has been planted to symbolically recall the sacredness which the Druids attributed to their oak groves. The grove has, however, been planted in the shape of a Celtic cross with, at the central wheel, a Buddhist stupa embedded with pieces of flint gathered from the surrounding fields.

After witnessing this extraordinary living emblem of inter-faith understanding, I was unsurprised to hear that regular monastic gatherings are held at Amaravati represented, amongst others, by Christian Benedictines and Muslim Sufis. It also seems natural that people of many faiths have chosen to scatter the ashes of their loved ones in this sacred grove. Perhaps the most moving memorial plaque is on a tree hung with a Star of David and dedicated to a little boy who '*was born and went to heaven on 7 December 2007*'.

Getting there

Great Gaddesden is 6 miles northwest of Hemel Hempstead, reached via the A4146. The nearest **train** station is Hemel Hempstead, from where there are Arriva **buses** to Great Gaddesden (*0871 200 2233; www.arrivabus.co.uk*).

Visiting the monastery

Day visitors are welcome without appointment and may share in meditation sessions, in the main daily meal at 11.00, and other light refreshments during the day. Any donations are voluntary. For overnight stays, retreats and courses, contact the monastery in advance.

Where to stay and eat

The Pennyfarthing Hotel 296–298 High St, Berkhamsted HP4 1AH ☏ 01442 872828 www.thepennyfarthinghotel.co.uk. A small, friendly hotel by the Grand Union Canal incorporating a Café Rouge restaurant.

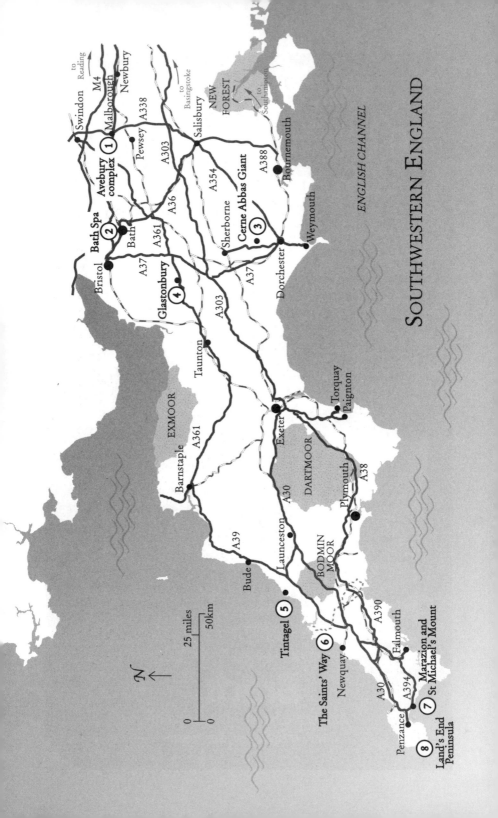

SOUTHWESTERN ENGLAND

ENGLISH CHANNEL

to Reading
to Basingstoke
to Southampton

Swindon
M4
Malborough
Newbury
Pewsey
A338
① Avebury complex
A303
A36
Salisbury
NEW FOREST
A354
A388
Bournemouth
Cerne Abbas Giant
② Bath Spa
Bath
A361
A37
A36
Sherborne
③
Weymouth
Bristol
A37
Dorchester
④ Glastonbury
A303
Taunton
A361
EXMOOR
Barnstaple
Exeter
Torquay
Paignton
DARTMOOR
A30
A38
Plymouth
A39
Launceston
BODMIN MOOR
Bude
⑤ Tintagel
A390
Falmouth
⑥ The Saints' Way
Newquay
A30
A394
⑦ Marazion and St Michael's Mount
Penzance
⑧ Land's End Peninsula

N

0   25 miles
0   50km

3. SOUTHWESTERN ENGLAND

England's far southwest is a palimpsest of ancient beliefs layered one upon another: the spine-tingling energies on St Michael's Mount; the Celtic magic seeping from the frondy wells and holed stone of Land's End peninsula; the cliffs of Tintagel falling into the sea and swirling with the legends of Arthur and Merlin. On to this sacred scene arrived stories of the mystical Jesus of Nazareth. Unravel the threads of these faiths, legends and mysterious earth forces and they all seem to lead to a town out in the marshy Somerset levels. Centuries on, Glastonbury is still the place where modern pilgrims can peruse a vast menu of spiritual sustenance.

Elsewhere, a city founded in ancient times by a swineherd-cum-king on the spot where he discovered some sacred springs, still draws visitors in great numbers seeking its healing waters.

① The Avebury complex

Free access.

A defining moment in the life of John Aubrey, the 17th-century 'Father of British Archaeology', is said to have come at the top of Silbury Hill, the largest prehistoric mound in Europe. Aubrey noticed that the Roman road between London and Bath (now the A4) swerved to avoid the hill. Suddenly he had a revelation: *The mound had been built before the Romans arrived!*

The 150ft hill sits like a giant Christmas pudding in a field just off the road, while a few hundred yards away, across the A4, is West Kennet Long Barrow, one of the largest burial chambers in Britain. These, along with the colossal sandstone boulders which comprise the largest stone circle in the world, are the main features of an astounding collection of prehistoric remains centred on the Wiltshire village of Avebury.

Aubrey's epiphany was the start of a life-long enthrallment with these prehistoric monuments shaped into the chalk downland of Wiltshire, which collectively comprise the greatest Neolithic site in Britain. I suggest that the Avebury complex is far more rewarding to visit even than Stonehenge (see page 34). Particularly more than Stonehenge, in fact, given the brutality with which the latter's stones have been divorced from their context.

Avebury and its surrounding monuments, by contrast, can be reveled in as a whole. The complex is a UNESCO World Heritage Site, in the care of the

National Trust and accessible free of charge. It is immense – easily big enough to absorb even bank-holiday crowds. I walked from site to site, gaining by degrees a feeling for their relationship and significance.

Avebury Stone Circle and Henge

The colossal sandstone boulders comprising a great circular henge and two intersecting stone circles lie within a massive earthwork rampart enclosing about 28 acres. The circles are the largest of their kind in Europe. I climbed up and walked round the rampart, which is about 30ft high from the bottom of the wide ditch. At one point I stopped to observe a man with a long, grey ponytail as he approached one of the megaliths carrying a parallel pair of wire coat-hangers bent into right-angled rods. Slowly and purposefully, as he walked towards a particular stone, the rods swung back and forth, crossing over. 'Ah, Avebury is on a ley line', dowser Viv Ball told me, adding that, 'the energies were enough to tap into the deepest impulses of the ancient, so that they dug and built the landscape into works of art. By comparison, making a bit of wire twitch is no big deal.' Put like that, I could see Viv's point.

The circle and earthworks are breached in four places by two roads leading into the pretty, though at first sight unremarkable, village, part of which is within the circle. Cottages are thatched or stone-roofed; there is a church, a National Trust shop, and the Alexander Keiler Museum of local archaeology. Avebury circle and two smaller rings within are, according to museum displays, thought to have been erected between 2800 and 2700BC and were probably the hub of a Neolithic power structure encompassing various satellite sites.

Continuing my circumambulation of the village, I noticed that several of the stones are missing. Thanks to William Stukely, the 18th-century President of the Antiquarian Society who continued Aubrey's work and charted the stones' positions, it is at least known where they stood. Vandalism of the stones probably started in the Middle Ages, when superstitions about the 'Druid circle' led people to crack them by lighting fires. The skeleton of a barber-surgeon, along with his lance and scissors was found, many centuries later, beneath one toppled stone. But Stukely recorded where many of the original stones had stood, and a concrete post now marks each gap.

Next I followed a signpost to a muddy track bordering a stream (the embryonic Kennet) for about a mile, which took me to the next enigma in the Avebury complex.

Silbury Hill

Conical Silbury Hill with its flattened top rises above the surrounding field, its base covering 5½ acres. And not to be out-done by Avebury on the superlatives front, Silbury wears the mantle of largest manmade mound erected in European prehistory.

Unfortunately, because of erosion damage, climbing the hill is no longer permitted, (although the occasional ambitious sheep seems to find its way half way up. (I wonder why, given the bountiful green grazing pastures all around?) I would have loved to have stood at the top, and looked out over the swerving Roman road as John Aubrey did.

Instead, I stopped far enough away to get some perspective, and read about the local legends that Aubrey unearthed and recorded. According to one of these, Silbury Hill was raised as a posset of seething milk; another story says that it was the burial place of ancient royals, and it contains the gold statue of a king on horseback.

There have been a number of archaeological probes into Silbury's interior over the years, but none have found evidence of any person or any treasure buried in or under it and so the purpose of Silbury remains a mystery. However, carbon dating and probes into the core show that the hill was built about 4,600 years ago, using nine million cubic feet of chalk, probably cut from the nearby Marlborough Downs and built up in steps like Egyptian pyramids. Only at the final stage was turf added to create its present profile. Perhaps it is only coincidence, but Silbury Hill is almost identical in size to Cheops, the smallest of the Giza pyramids.

This was something to ponder as I crossed the road and trudged up the chalk-flecked path to West Kennet Long Barrow.

West Kennet Long Barrow

This immense stone trapezoid is the largest prehistoric burial chamber ever found in Britain. The entrance is guarded by giant portal stones which were moved aside from the chamber mouth when the barrow was first excavated in 1859. It is now known that construction of the barrow was begun in about 3250BC, and completed in 2600BC with the sealing of the burial chambers and the erection of the portal stones. There is a small window of thick glass in the roof, added in the 1960s to the existing hole as if some official was keen that the ancient site should resemble a public convenience. This unnecessary embellishment aside, West Kennet Long Barrow is the earliest of the sites in the Avebury complex.

I flicked on a torch and crept inside to explore the crannies of the dank, empty tomb where various chambers are separated by sarsen stones linked with fine dry-stone walling. Here, at the 1859 excavation, the remains of 46 people were found resting not so much in peace as in pieces, their skeletons violently scattered around the chamber. Tools and other Neolithic paraphernalia were also found, including some faience beads that – to the excitement of archaeologists who see the comparable sizes of Silbury Hill and the Cheops pyramid as more than chance – could plausibly be Egyptian.

Returning to Avebury village I took a different route, completing a circular walk by descending from the Long Barrow to the village of West Kennet on the A4. From here I followed a path between two straight parallel lines of sarsens. This 'causewayed enclosure' is Windmill Hill and is the intriguing, if less-visited, fourth site of the Avebury complex.

Windmill Hill

Windmill Hill needs imagination and interpretation, otherwise it is merely a walk from A to B (Avebury to Barrow, or vice versa) with some stones to guide you. In fact, it is the largest example of a Neolithic 'causewayed enclosure' in Britain (well, isn't everything around here the largest example of something?), apparently enclosing an area of 92,650yds^2.

Early antiquarians believed Windmill Hill, along with other such causewayed enclosures, to be fortifications. However, because they cover a huge area, have such wide gaps, and existed at a time when there were only small populations, in the 18th century William Stukely looked for other explanations.

On Windmill Hill, Stukely found a series of pits apparently dug by an agrarian society, into which offerings such as pottery were placed. He realised that the way these pits are arranged, revealed unmistakable patterns on the ground. And so he concluded that they might have been a combination of ritual sites and trading centres.

Getting there

The Avebury complex is 7 miles west of Marlborough, on the A4. The nearest **train** station is at Pewsey on the London Paddington to Taunton line, from where the Wilts & Dorset Bus Company run services to Avebury (*01202 678291; www.wdbus.co.uk*).

Where to stay and eat

Ivy House Hotel 43 High St, Marlborough SN8 1HJ ☎01672 515333 ✈ www.ivyhousemarlborough.com. A friendly 3-star hotel in the centre of Marlborough, with rooms around a covered courtyard.

The Circle High St, Avebury SN8 1RF ☎01672 539514. In keeping with Avebury's New Age traditions, this is a vegetarian restaurant near the stones, next to the Alexander Keiller Museum and run by the National Trust.

The New Inn Winterbourne Monkton SN4 9NW ☎01672 539240 ✈ www.thenewinn.net. A cosy country pub with rooms, a mile's beautiful walk from the stones and Avebury village.

The Red Lion High St, Avebury SN8 1RF ☎01672 539266 ✈ www.red-lion-pub-avebury.co.uk. The world's only pub inside a prehistoric stone circle. The thatched building features on numerous lists associated with the paranormal. The bar and restaurant, by contrast, serve the normal sort of fare expected at a country pub.

Tourist information

Avebury Tourist Information Centre The Chapel Centre, Green St, SN8 1RE ☎01672 539179 ✈ www.visitwiltshire.co.uk/site/things-to-do/avebury-stone-circle-p134483.

② Bath Spa

Meditating with Zen monks submerged in a natural hot pool on Hokkaido Island while the Sea of Japan fades from tangerine to cobalt ... or swimming in a steaming stream gushing from a mountainside in the lee of looming Icelandic glaciers. What can sacred Britain offer, to compete in the premier league of Great Hot Bathing Experiences of the World?

The original Bath, that's what. Every day, more than a million litres of water bubble up from the bowels of the earth at a scalding 116°F, from three springs in what is now the centre of the city of Bath. These are the only hot springs in the British Isles and from prehistoric times have been sacred, with people placing faith in their curative powers.

Looking out across the World Heritage City of Bath, my vantage point was the open-air rooftop thermal pool at Thermae Bath Spa where I sat pensively poaching. This is the mother of all baths, I concluded, trying to imagine the hot rivulets coursing through the rolling English countryside, centuries ago when it was as pristine as the Icelandic wilderness.

What would the Romans or Georgians have made of all this modern spa gismology, I pondered. This is the place that, for me, provides the most powerful allure of Thermae Bath Spa. Looking out across the townscape, I was reminded how innovative was the technology that the Romans brought to the hot springs when they built the baths 2,000 years ago. Similarly, the Palladian architecture of Ralph Allen and John Wood was cutting edge for its time.

History and legend

Bath's story starts with Bladud, the legendary King of the Britons and father of King Lear, who in his youth was sent to study in Athens and returned with leprosy. As a leper he was banished from his position at court and left the royal palace disguised as a nomadic swineherd with a herd of pigs which were also victims of some dreadful pestilence.

Roaming the land, Bladud reached the Vale of Avon where his pigs rolled in some hot mud bubbling up from underground. When he saw how they seemed to have been cured from their scabs and sores, Bladud followed their example, bathed in the murky hot water and was also healed. He returned to court in rude health and duly inherited the crown. King Bladud founded a city at Bath, and dedicated the curative powers of the sacred hot springs to the Celtic goddess Sul.

For centuries the ancient Britons remained faithful to Sul, as did the Romans after their conquest of Britannia in the 1st century AD. The Romans raised a magnificent Classical temple on the site and named it Aquae Sulis. They used their technology to construct a full-scale bathing complex, which became a place of rest and recreation for legionaries fighting on the northern frontier. Soon, bigwigs arrived from all over the empire, and Bath entered its first phase as a major visitor destination.

After the disintegration of the Roman Empire, the baths fell to ruins and the springs silted up. Nevertheless, there is evidence of pilgrims to a medieval monastery that flourished in Bath, believing in the healing powers of the hot water. Following the Dissolution of the Monasteries, there was a brief period in which the infirm and other visitors were attracted to a cluster of guesthouses around the hot pools.

Then came the great revival. During the 18th century, Bath bloomed into the most fashionable city in the land, where the high-born and wealthy hob-nobbed in the imperious Grand Pump Room, took the waters and were carried around town in sedan chairs. This was the era in which the city first lent its name to the English lexicon both as a noun and a verb. We have bathtubs in our bathrooms. We bath and we bathe.

Novelist Jane Austen, a Bath resident, provided some caustic commentary on the foolish pomp of these times. However, her lesser-known contemporary Tobias Smollett observed the wealthy, poor and sick alike, taking the waters. In 1771 he wrote, '*There you see the highest quality and lowest tradesfolk, jostling each other without ceremony hail-fellow well met.*'

Either way, this was the era when a triumvirate of movers and shakers tore down medieval Bath and replaced it with a crucible of architectural splendour. Richard 'Beau' Nash, Master of Ceremonies in the city, controlled society; Ralph Allen was the money man, visionary and owner of the stone quarries; and architect John Wood (later, his son John Wood the Younger) built the crescents, arcades, squares, circuses and Palladian embellishments, using local, honey-coloured limestone.

On the therapeutic side, Bath Royal Mineral Water Hospital opened in 1739, and continued to treat patients with the natural thermal water until 1976. By this time, the concept of the spa as a serious source of cure and well-being had virtually disappeared in Britain – astonishing as this may seem to people from parts of the world where spas are a central feature of healthcare.

However, despite the fact that the global concept of the therapeutic spa hails from Bath, the water was off-limits for nearly 30 years. Bathing in the reconstructed Roman Baths, 2,000 years after their initial construction, finally ended in 1978 after a health scare. The springs which spawned the city and drew millions to Bath over the ages, were simply left to flow, like worthless effluent, into the River Avon. An instance if ever there was one, of throwing the baby out with the Bath water.

In part it may have been a feeling that the hot springs, wards of Sul and amniotic fluid of Bath's birth, had been treated with shameful disrespect, that led to the decision of the Millennium Commission in 1997, to fund the extravagant and forward-looking project which finally opened as the new Thermae Bath Spa in 2005.

The Roman Baths

Abbey Church Yard, BA1 1LZ ☎ 01225 477785 🖰 www.romanbaths.co.uk.

The Roman bathing complex, which was excavated and rebuilt at the end of the 19th century, remains the single most visited attraction in Bath. It is interesting to note that while Celtic and Druidic practices were savagely put down where they posed a political threat, the occupying Romans had a remarkably ecumenical attitude towards religion. Certainly, here in Bath the toleration of a native cult led to a fusion of beliefs.

The sacred springs had been a place to worship the native goddess Sul. So the Romans called it Aquae Sulis, while simultaneously identifying Sul with the Roman goddess Minerva and building a resplendent classical temple to the composite goddess. Around the spring there grew up a magnificent series of edifices connected either with worship or with healing, or both. Other echoes of the use of this place as a sacred site are the huge number of votive offerings thrown into the water by worshippers: coins in their thousands, alongside tablets of lead tossed in perhaps nearly two millennia ago to invoke the curses of the goddess on enemies.

The most prominent part of the complex to survive is the **Great Bath**, now open to the air but once, from the second century onwards, covered by a vast barrel-vault rising to more than 50ft, made of hollow tiles to lessen the weight. The altars and memorials show that visitors came from France and Germany as well as nearer to home for the solace and healing spirit which, despite the crowds of tourists who visit today, you can still feel beside the Great Bath.

Next door, in the elegant **Pump Room** which is now a restaurant, a string trio saw away on their cellos while the official 'pumper' in Georgian breeches and cravat, hand-pumps hot thermal water from beneath, for 50p a glass.

Thermae Bath Spa

6–8 Hot Bath St, BA1 1UP ☎ 0844 888 0844 🖰 www.thermaebathspa.com

The setting for the four-storey Thermae Bath Spa is a sublime urban landscape. The unabashedly 21st-century building rubs shoulders with architectural pearls such as the original Roman Baths, Bath Abbey and the gracious Royal Crescent. I took my debut plunge on a frosty winter's night, seeing Bath stripped to its elegant Georgian bones with the floodlit colonnades of Prior Park mansion commanding the heights of Combe Down.

By contrast, the curved glass façade of Thermae Bath Spa on Hot Bath Street just 100yds from the Roman baths, appears to run counter to the conformity embraced by Bath's Georgian traditions. Sheltered by walls of glass, the 14m² rooftop pool is of cutting-edge design with rounded edges and an assortment of whirlpool baths and airbeds which add to the sense that one is floating above the city. Even so there are nods everywhere to the traditional townscape.

For example, the interior is clad in Bath stone from the same local quarries that once belonged to Ralph Allen. Moreover, the multi-faceted project has involved the restoration of some of the smaller baths that survive from the 18th-century heyday.

One of these, the octagonal **Hot Bath**, originally built by John Wood the Younger, has been recreated as a pool for relaxation after treatment in one of 12 rooms, each with thermal water pumped in and offering therapies ranging from herbal wrapping to shiatsu. Another, the **Cross Bath**, has always been more recreational, and was reserved for Bath residents until it fell into disuse in 1978. Bathonian Mike Gray recalled, 'It was known affectionately as the "tuppenny hot". I learnt to swim here as a child in the 1960s.' In this tradition, the rebuilt Cross Bath has a separate entrance, and residents of the city can use this open-air hot bath at a 50% discount.

But the overall impression is one of high tech. At the main spa pool on the first floor of the new complex, it is easier to imagine yourself in a Star Trek film. Beam up to the next level and a series of steam rooms, each one offering a differently fragranced form of aromatherapy, are positioned around a fibre-optically illuminated central hot and cold water fountain. As you walk through, the fine mist on the outside becomes progressively heavier, as colours oscillate through the spectrum.

Getting there

Bath Spa is 100 miles west of London, reached via the M4 motorway. It is on the main **train** line between London (Paddington) and Bristol.

Where to stay and eat

Royal Crescent Hotel 16 Royal Crescent, BA1 2LS ☎ 01225 823333
🖰 www.royalcrescent.co.uk. Magnificent, luxurious and expensive. Superlative rooms, restaurant and spa on Bath's most famous crescent.

Springs Thermae Bath Spa, 6–8 Hot Bath St, BA1 1UP ☎ 0844 888 0844
🖰 www.thermaebathspa.com. Café and restaurant serving healthy snacks and dishes to spa users. Reasonable wines.

The House 17 Lansdown Crescent, BA1 5EX ☎ 01225 471741
🖰 www.bedandbreakfastbathuk.co.uk/the-house. The full Georgian experience in this beautifully styled townhouse offering up-market B&B.

The Pump Room 39 Stall St, BA1 1LZ ☎ 01225 444477 🖰 www.romanbaths. co.uk. Morning coffee, lunch and afternoon tea to the strains of stringed instruments in the neo-Classical salon where Jane Austen observed her fellow bathers. Open to all.

Tourist information

Bath Tourist Information Abbey Chambers, Abbey Churchyard, BA1 1LY
☎ 0844 847 5256 🖰 www.visitbath.co.uk.

③ The Cerne Abbas Giant

Free access.

Long may you exercise your right to silence,
I thought, as I stood watching the Cerne
Giant's vigorous, unabashed outline. The
ancient chalk figure, standing 180ft from
head to toe, was waving his club from the
hillside opposite. Particularly intriguing
me, were all the claims and counter-claims
I had heard about his age and origins.

So who did carve the giant into this hillside? And how
old is he really? The answer is that nobody knows for sure. Rather like
Gulliver in the land of Lilliput, the giant refuses to be pinned down. One
expert, Professor of Archaeology at Bournemouth University Dr Tim Darvill,
supports the theory that the figure is either prehistoric or a Romano-British
depiction of Hercules. He points to a scientific study which proved that a
comparable British hill figure, the Uffington White Horse in Oxfordshire (see
page 83), has been scientifically proved to be about 3,000 years old.

Historian Dr Ronald Hutton of Bristol University has also called the
Uffington White Horse as a witness. 'But you have to understand that it is not
actually white, but red. And far from being a horse, it is in fact a herring.' Dr
Hutton reckons the giant is more likely to be 17th century, the central point
being that while there are numerous references to the Uffington Horse from
across the ages, there are none to the Cerne Giant before 1694, when '*three
shillings for repairing ye giant*' was budgeted in the parish accounts.

It is quite inconceivable, Dr Hutton believes, that the 10th-century monk
Aelfric, who lived and wrote in Cerne Abbas, would have failed to mention
the giant had it been there. Or that John Aubrey, the 17th-century 'father of
British archaeology' would not have known about it.

'Oh he's much, much older than that', said amateur local historian Kathleen
Slocun, with all the wisdom and authority that comes with advanced years.
Infertile couples have been 'visiting' the giant on account of his sacred powers,
'since ancient times', she assured me. The giant has been credited with
numerous conceptions including, apparently, the Marquess of Bath's daughter
Silvy Cerne, born in 1958. 'And anyway, he might have been buried under
vegetation for centuries.'

'If only the giant could talk, we would know for sure. But really this
speculation is all a bit tasteless', Mrs Slocun continued. 'I mean, we all know
what it is about the giant that gets everybody excited, don't we?'

Indeed we do. On account of his renowned, oversized phallus, ribaldry
and innuendo inevitably attend the figure, and village sensibilities have been
upset in the past when commercial interests have tried to hijack him for
publicity stunts. Among the guilty are Heineken, Raleigh, Durex and The
Simpsons which, in 2008, created a temporary Homer Simpson chalk giant

on the adjacent hillside. 'It's all a question of dignity and respect for the giant,' chirped a young man with a pierced lip in the New Inn pub, as I bought him a pint.

Theoretically, it would be possible to date the giant fairly accurately, using the Stimulated Luminescence Dating technique which has produced a definitive date for the Uffington White Horse (see page 83), but perhaps the giant deserves some anonymity; certainly, the enigma surrounding the figure is part of his allure.

So let a thousand theories blossom. My favourite comment came from another villager, when I asked for her opinion on the age of the giant. 'Well' she said, cocking her head, 'by the look of him I would say about 18, or in his early twenties at most. And he has been since time immemorial.'

The village

Cerne Abbas is as twee a huddle of thatched and ivy-clad cottages as nestles in any Dorset dell. In the Middle Ages it was an important centre for leather and brewing but it was left out when the railways were built in the 19th century, and industry withered. Today tourism fuels the village economy, its fortunes lying squarely with the manly giant.

So, prim little shops sell postcards, mugs, sweatshirts and tea towels glorifying his priapic image. Dear old ladies cheerfully peddle pornographic souvenirs as if they were lace doilies. In teashops, families daintily nibble round the private parts of shortbread giants.

From Long Street at the heart of the village, Abbey Street leads past a duck pond and through a graveyard skirting the ruins of a 10th-century Benedictine monastery. Those who doubt the giant's prehistoric provenance number the monks among its suspected creators, and one theory suggests that the monks' early Christianity was entwined with a pagan fertility cult. A counter theory has it that the figure was the work of anti-Papists at the time of the Dissolution of the Monasteries, intended to satirise monkish habits.

Giant Hill

From the monastery ruins, a muddy track leads up to the hill into whose steep, chalk, western flank the giant is carved. A barbed-wire fence frames the figure in about five acres of smooth, green turf, though a sign requests visitors not to climb the fence. However, having secured permission from the National Trust, I entered this exclusive member's enclosure and climbed the hill to find myself at the top of the giant's left hand.

I walked along the scoured, brilliantly white paths, each about a foot wide, that form the arm's outline and meander off in parallel, one trail joining his torso at a T-junction. His nipples are roundabouts, his ribs, cul-de-sacs. It was like being an ant on a child's comic book maze.

The top of Giant Hill is crowned with ancient earthworks, probably Iron Age, which may or may not be contemporary with the giant. One fact that struck me from here, sitting in solitude, is that the giant enjoys stupendous views over Cerne Valley as he whiles away the centuries. I watched a pair of graceful roe deer emerge from a copse and wander nonchalantly across open farmland to drink from the Cerne River.

Getting there

Cerne Abbas is just off the A352 in Dorset, 11 miles south of Sherborne towards Dorchester. The giant is about a quarter-of-a-mile northeast of the village. The best view is from a lay-by at the convergence of the A352 and Duck Street, just north of Cerne.

Where to stay and eat

Abbots 7 Long St, DT2 7JF ☎ 01300 341349 🖰 www.abbotsbedandbreakfast. co.uk. Basic but friendly B&B with tearoom.

The New Inn 14 Long St, DT2 7JF ☎ 01300 341274 🖰 www.thenewinncerneabbas.co.uk. A 16th-century coaching inn with simple, comfortable rooms, cask ales and good food prepared with fresh, local ingredients.

Tourist information

Cerne Abbas Sub Post Office and Shop 9 Long St, DT2 7JF ☎ 01300 341513 🖰 www.cerneabbasvillagestores.co.uk.

④ Glastonbury

From miles away across the flatness of the Somerset Levels, it was not hard to understand why some people see Glastonbury Tor as the breast of a sleeping goddess. The crowning Tower of Archangel Michael certainly makes a credible nipple. Or is this 500ft cone the earth's navel, linking the planet to a universal womb of knowledge? Or a mere detail in the galaxy of images that make up a sign of the zodiac on a cosmic scale?

My head was swimming with myths, legends and stories as I climbed up the steep, terraced track to the Tor's summit. Below me was the Somerset market town, which was once an island surrounded by marshes and water with the greatest monastery in England at its heart. From my vantage point the remains of the abbey church resembled a child's toy smashed in anger. Beyond was a 360° panorama over expanses of pasture speckled with cattle. It all felt immeasurably tranquil. Then I let my eye follow the road six miles out of town to Pilton village and Michael Eavis's fields, where upwards of 100,000 revellers gather for the annual Glastonbury Festival.

The idea of multitudes raving to rock music seemed inestimably distant. Yet the notion of crowds being drawn here is ancient. The mystical associations with Glastonbury are numberless, as are the varying beliefs that this is a place of unique 'spiritual energy'. And so in an age – a 'New Age' – in which such beliefs are free to flourish outside the constraints of conventional religions, modern Glastonbury has become home to an astonishing concentration of Druids and dowsers, witches and trance dancers, pagans and Green Man followers, Buddhists and Goddess devotees, Sufis and Christian mystics, karmic astrologers and Sea Princess worshippers, alchemist and healers. In fact, some 400 holistic healers of various descriptions. Nowhere in sacred Britain is there a place remotely comparable with Glastonbury.

The usual pattern for visitors seems to be first to wander down the High Street, through Market Square to Magdalene Street, inhaling the wafts of incense from shops with psychedelic façades selling glistening crystals and spell-casting ingredients. Next come the two main sacred 'sites': the abbey and the Chalice Well, the latter being at the foot of the Tor visitors climb as an energy-expending climax.

I approached Glastonbury from the other direction, taking my perspective from the Tor before descending into town to the disorientating juxtaposition of shops such as 'Man, Myth & Magic' and 'The Psychic Piglet', cheek by jowl with the Co-op and a branch of Boots. The contrast, I soon found, has parallels in terms of the tensions which exist between the 'alternative' (for want of a better name) communities who account for about 35% of this town of some 10,000 souls, and the indigenous 'Glastonburgers' (still in want of a better name, I've invented one). The former camp are far from homogenous, as I discovered in the Glastonbury Pilgrim Reception Centre, brainchild of investment banker turned 'spiritual counsellor', Barry Taylor.

Said Mr Taylor: 'Glastonbury is a market town running side-by-side with what we might call a pilgrimage town. The latter is the element within the town which is perceived as having special spiritual energies. We know that in excess of 40% of all visitors to Glastonbury might be called pilgrims as they are attracted by these energies. The Pilgrimage Centre was established to supply the information and support needed by these visitors.' In other words the Pilgrim Reception Centre is an 'alternative' tourist information centre (of which the 'mainstream' version is round the corner in the Town Hall).

And it was in the Pilgrimage Reception Centre that I learnt of one particular chasm which divides the two sides of Glastonbury: the abbey. 'The grounds are a place of sacred geometry, of fantasies and myth, which is why people are unhappy that it is protected for Christians', said Paul Fletcher, a dapper-looking fellow who looked quite the man about Tor, but who was drawn here as an 'Esoteric Soul Healer'. 'It should be free for any form of worship, a sacred place open to all.'

Later I wandered the grounds of this very place with Katherine Gorbing, Director of Glastonbury Abbey. Katherine explained, 'We reach out to the whole community, and of course anybody can come here on an individual basis. But religious ceremonies? This is ecclesiastical ground and a living church so we cannot allow Pagan or Druid ceremonies.'

History and legend

So many strands of myth and fable are woven into the history of Glastonbury that it is hard to find a starting point. Various traditions have it that Glastonbury had been a place of religious tradition long before the Christian era. According to some of these beliefs, it is precisely because Glastonbury is on an intersection of ley lines, or is for other reasons a place of timeless and irrepressible spiritual energy, that mystical happenings have always occurred here. Among these happenings are the events that gave rise to a pair of intertwined legends at the core of Glastonbury's identity, both of them intimately connected with the sacred associations that have drawn millions over the millennia.

First we have the story about St Joseph of Arimathea, a member of the 'Sanhedrin' Supreme Council of Jews and man of influence mentioned in all four gospels, who asked Pontius Pilate for Christ's body after the Crucifixion. It is likely that he would have been a family acquaintance, and possibly a relative, of St Joseph the Virgin Mary's carpenter spouse. If so, an ancient belief preserved by miners in southwest England gets quite a fillip.

According to this legend, Joseph of Arimathea had been a trader in metals in the 1st century AD and made regular expeditions from the eastern Mediterranean, landing in Cornwall and travelling up to Somerset where lead was mined in the Mendip Hills. On one such voyage he brought with him a young lad from Nazareth with good carpentry skills (and about whom the scriptures are silent from the time of his exploits in a temple aged 12, till the start of his ministry 18 years later). Jesus on his gap year, if you like.

'Sure as our Lord was at Priddy', is an old Somerset saying that survives today and just as surely alludes to the ancient lore that Christ visited the lead-mining village of Priddy in the Mendips, on the journey which naturally also had the party drawn across the marshes to the ancient hallowed Isle of Glastonbury. But it was William Blake who gave fulsome voice to the legend with his 1804 poem 'Jerusalem!', these days sung to music composed in 1916 by Sir Hubert Parry and sung as a sort of unofficial English national anthem at patriotic occasions such as the Last Night of the Proms. Certainly, the song succeeds in mining seams of emotion that 'God Save the Queen' will never reach.

Chapter Two of this same legend has Joseph of Arimathea returning to Britain after Christ's Crucifixion. With him, he had the cup used at the last supper in which he had caught drops of Christ's blood from the wound in his side as he hung on the cross. This time Joseph came not on a trade mission but to bring the new Christian faith to Britain. Again he landed at Cornwall – according to some at St Michael's Mount (see page 66). This connection between the mount and Glastonbury has special significance for those who set store by idea of a ley lines connecting the two. Making their way to Glastonbury, the last stop was Wearyall Hill where Joseph thrust his hawthorn staff into the ground, whereupon it burst into bloom.

Joseph then chose the site where the abbey ruins now stand to build, from wattle and daub, the first Christian church in Britain. And, somewhere at or around Glastonbury, he buried or otherwise hid the cup containing Christ's blood. Which, of course, is the direct connection with the second legend, that of King Arthur and his Knights on their quest for the Holy Grail.

Folklore surrounding the legendary King Arthur goes back to the 5th or 6th century AD, when the 'Protector of Britain' against Saxon invaders on who the fables are based, may have lived. Glastonbury had long been identified as the Isle of Avalon – the island in the marshes renowned for its delicious apples – where Arthur was carried by a trio of black-robed queens after being mortally wounded at the Battle of Camlann. This association received a massive boost when in 1191 the monks of Glastonbury Abbey unearthed an oak coffin bearing the inscription, '*Here on the Isle of Avalon lies buried the famous King Arthur*'. Inside were the skeletons of Arthur and Queen Guinevere, whose blond tresses turned to dust in the hands of a monk.

We need to rewind to the early 7th century for the first archaeological evidence of a monastery founded by Celtic Britons on the site where legend claimed Joseph of Arimathea founded the first church. Glastonbury Abbey subsequently fell into Saxon hands and the first stone church, whose foundations still form the west end of the nave, was begun in 712. Tradition maintains that Patrick and David, patron saints of Ireland and Wales respectively, had both been visitors to the site. A key figure in the history of the abbey was St Dunstan, Abbot of Glastonbury in the 10th century. Dunstan took the monastery into the Benedictine fold, became Archbishop of Canterbury and used his power and influence to enlarge the abbey church on a huge scale, building extensive new cloisters and other monastery buildings.

The expansion continued after the Norman Conquest with the 1086 Doomsday Book recording Glastonbury as the largest and richest abbey in England. Then in 1184 a great fire destroyed the monastic buildings. It was in the course of reconstruction that, two years later, King Arthur's coffin was unearthed. Cynics have suggested that the then Abbott, Henry de Sully, must have been a bit of a PR supremo, turning disaster into glory by ordering a search for Arthur's bones after the fire. The find bathed a burnt-down monastery in a blaze of publicity that was to see pilgrims in untold numbers visit the enshrined remains of Arthur. When, in 1278, King Edward I and his mother Queen Eleanor attended a magnificent ceremony in which Arthur's remains were reburied at the foot of the high altar in the abbey church, the two legends were finally fused.

The abbey's fortunes continued to prosper, with Glastonbury coming second only to Westminster Abbey in size, power and riches with monastic estates spreading over a swathe of southwest England. Royalty would visit, including Henry VII, father of the king whose Dissolution of the Monasteries a generation later was to visit a fury of destruction on the abbey on a scale commensurate with its influence and wealth. In 1539 treasures were plundered, fires burnt and the last abbot, Richard Whiting, was taken up to the Tor summit where he was hung, drawn and quartered.

While the abbey spent 400 years quietly decaying and crumbling into today's ruins, Glastonbury's associated legends faired rather better. The Holy Thorn tree which grew from Joseph of Arimathea's staff, or at least its descendant, still flowers at Christmas time; a spray even joins the holly at the festive lunch table of today's royal family. And the spot where Arthur's and Guinevere's bones were discovered remains a sacred place on the grassy floor of the ruins, which are now the property of the Church of England diocese of Bath and Wells.

As G K Chesterton wrote after his 1910 visit, '*In Glastonbury, as in all noble and humane things, the myth is more important than the history.*'

Glastonbury Abbey

The Abbey Gatehouse, Magdalene St, BA6 9EL ☎ 01458 831631
🌐 www.glastonburyabbey.com.

The abbey today is part visitor attraction, part religious site. It is best to start with the small museum just past the entrance, where to a background of soft Gregorian plainchant as might have been sung in the pre-Reformation era, you can read the history and look at scale models of the abbey as it once was. Then allow yourself to be enveloped in the aura of the abbey as it now is.

Of all the ruins brought about by the Dissolution of the Monasteries, none have induced in me such powerful pangs as the scattered fragments which remain in this area of grassy parkland. In part, it is the sense of the staggering scale: I pictured glories such as Westminster Abbey (see page 2) and Durham Cathedral (see page 121), then tried to imagine what Glastonbury Abbey might have been like had it survived the devastation of the Dissolution.

There is enough left of the **Lady Chapel** with its stone-carved depictions of the Annunciation, and the soaring transept piers, for it to be evident that a stupefying building had once existed here. Some ancient ruins acquire an overpowering feeling of romance, but this site seemed more to shriek with the pain of the terrible violence done to the traditions of medieval monasticism.

The site of **Arthur's and Guinevere's tomb**, marked on the grass in the choir, is another poignant reminder of what has been lost. The 14th-century **Abbot's Kitchen**, on the other hand, has survived almost intact. It is the only monastic building to have done so, with its lantern ceiling and four gigantic corner fireplaces. Back in museum mode, tableaux of hogs roasting on the spit re-create the picture of bon-viveur abbots and their guests.

The Chalice Well and gardens

Chilkwell St, BA6 8DD ☎ 01458 831154 ⊕ www.chalicewell.org.uk.

The 12th-century Chalice Well, set in a lush water garden at the foot of the Tor, has become a place of quiet contemplation where twice daily a bell is rung asking visitors to pause in silence for a while.

Countless attributes have been, and still are, associated with the red-tinged, iron rich water that spills out of the ground here – about 125,000 litres a day. The story which gives the spring its name is that this is the place where Joseph of Arimathea hid the Holy Grail. It has also been known as the 'Blood Well' and 'Red Spring'. The pinkish tinges in the water are seen as everlasting reminders of Christ's spilt blood carried in the chalice, while the water has for centuries been held to have healing powers.

The well head is protected from over-zealous grail hunters by a wrought iron mesh. However, you can drink the irony-tasting spring water from a lion's head spout, soothe your feet in the pools it fills, or listen in silence to it trickling along rills through the gardens.

Glastonbury Tor

Free access.

Even though the surrounding marshes are drained to dry farmland by canals and ditches, the conical hill does (as well as resembling a breast) still give the impression of insularity – especially on a misty day.

Once upon a time it was considered a penance to climb to the summit, particularly with sharp stones in your shoes, purposefully placed there to lacerate your toes. No doubt it was excruciating, but comfortably shod the spiral footpath winding up to the summit is invigorating. The crowning tower is all that is left of the burnt medieval church dedicated to the Archangel Michael in common with St Michael's Mount in Cornwall (see page 66) and Mont-St-Michel in Brittany. The connection between the three is especially affirming to those who set store by the idea of a 'St Michael's ley line' connecting a string of churches dedicated to the archangel, on the former sites of the Celtic god, Lug. St Michael was, of course, the vanquisher of evil which is something to think about as you reach the summit where Richard Whiting, the last Abbot of Glastonbury, was butchered in 1539.

Certainly, there is a sense up here of rising above the troubles of the world, past and present.

A **Glastonbury Tor Bus** runs between the abbey car park in the town centre, to outside the Chalice Well. The climb up the Tor starts near here.

Getting there

Glastonbury is 21 miles southwest of Bath and is reached via the A37 and A361. The nearest **train** station is 10 miles away at Castle Cary from where there are **taxis**, but no buses.

Where to stay and eat

Café Galatea 5a High St, BA6 9DP ☎ 01458 834284 🖰 www.cafegalatea.co.uk.
Vegetarian and vegan food, organic wines and beers. **The Apple Tree Guest
House** 27 Bere Lane, BA6 8BD ☎ 01458 830803
🖰 www.appletreeguesthouse.org.uk. A delightful guesthouse serving sumptuous
breakfasts with plenty of vegetarian options.
The George and Pilgrims 1 High St, BA6 9DP ☎ 01458 831146
🖰 www.georgeandpilgrims.activehotels.com. You follow in the footsteps of
medieval pilgrims when you stay in this 15th-century inn. There's 21st-century
dining at the restaurant.

Tourist information

Glastonbury Tourist Information Centre 9 High St, BA6 9DP ☎ 01458 832954
🖰 www.glastonburytic.co.uk.
The Glastonbury Pilgrim Reception Centre 10 High St, BA6 9DU ☎ 01458
835 572 🖰 www.glastonbury-pilgrim.co.uk.

⑤ Tintagel

If, as I did, you approach from the north along the Southwest Peninsula
Coast Path, the outline of a romantic castle comes into view from a long way
off, perched on a projecting headland. However, as you near this Victorian
monstrosity, called the Camelot Castle Hotel and built to cater for the 19th-
century Arthurian boom, it becomes more of an eyesore. Tintagel today is, of
course, famous mainly for its association with King Arthur and the Knights
of the Round Table. This explains why the clifftop village has become one of
Cornwall's chief tourist honeypots, spawning the King Arthur's Arms, King
Arthur's bookshop, and souvenir shops named after Celtic legends peddling
Merlin masks and plastic Excalibur swords.

The Old Post Office (*Fore St, PL34 0DB; 01840 770024; www.tintagelweb.
co.uk/OldPostOffice.htm*) is an anomaly amid all the tat. This 14th century
yeoman's cottage has survived the ravages of developers (largely because it
was taken over by the National Trust in 1903) and offers a rare glimpse of
life in a medieval dwelling. In the 19th century it was briefly a centre for mail
distribution, hence the name.

The other attraction worth a visit in Tintagel village is **King Arthur's
Great Halls** (*Fore St, PL34 0DA; 01840 770526; www.tintagelweb.co.uk/
KingArthursGreatHalls.htm*).This museum and homage to Arthurian
legend was created in the 1920 by a millionaire mustard magnate with the
magnificent name of Frederick Glasscock, who had become obsessed with all
things Arthurian. It is a good place to brush up on the history and legends
surrounding Tintagel, before heading down into the chasm in the coastline
below the village, to explore the castle and island.

History and legend

The first settlement here was probably a Celtic monastery founded around AD500. Little is known about when or why it was abandoned, or what became of the monks. However, it is easy to imagine why they chose this wild headland peninsula pounded by frothy waves, attached to the mainland by a narrow rocky passage. As at other Celtic monasteries such as Iona (see page 181) and Lindisfarne (see page 105), the margins of the sea had spiritual significance.

More historically certain is the fact that the first castle was built here in the 13th century by Richard Earl of Cornwall, a son of King John. The castle buildings spanned the island and the facing mainland, so the medieval builders would doubtless have been aware of the monastery's remains.

But what about Arthur? Is he based on a real historical character? If he did exist, he was probably a 5th or 6th century Romano-Celtic warrior who led defences against Saxon invaders. The earliest connection made between King Arthur and Tintagel was by the 12th-century court chronicler Geoffrey of Monmouth in his fanciful *Historia Regum Britanniae* ('*History of the Kings of Britain*'). Quite possibly, the embellishment of Arthur was a deliberate piece of nationalist propaganda, attempting to unite the English around a folk hero. Whatever the truth, Monmouth certainly provided the bones of Arthurian legend complete with Arthur's father Uther Pendragon, Merlin the Wizard, Queen Guinevere, the sword Excalibur, Arthur's final battle against Mordred, and his burial at Avalon (see page 55). In addition, of course, to his birth at Tintagel.

Arthurian poems and stories thrived in the early Middle Ages when, by degrees, Sir Lancelot, various other knights and a circular table were added. Enter also the Holy Grail, further beefing up the connection with Avalon.

After that, Arthurian legend seems to have waned somewhat. However, in the 19th century it caught the imagination of romantic poets, most notably Alfred Lord Tennyson who believed that the morals and integrity of an English gentleman have their roots in the ideals of chivalry epitomised by the legendary King Arthur.

It was Tennyson who, while poet laureate, popularised the Arthurian legends in his twelve 'Idylls of the King' poems which he wrote between 1856 and 1885. In this re-telling of the legends he elaborated on the position of Tintagel as the stronghold of Gorlois, Duke of Cornwall and his wife Igraine when Uther, King of the Britons, invaded Cornwall. Merlin used his magical powers to make Uther resemble Gorlois. The king then entered Tintagel Castle and seduced Igraine. Gorlois died and King Arthur was born to Igraine at Tintagel.

Meanwhile back in the 19th century the medieval castle, which had fallen into ruins, became the target for an increasing number of visitors, many of them venerating King Arthur. In 1935 a thorough archaeological investigation was carried out by C A Ralegh Radford who decided that, '*no evidence whatsoever has been found to support the legendary connection of the castle with King Arthur.'* However, the lack of evidence did little to dampen the appeal of Tintagel. This seems to me to be because it is one of the most evocative places on the British coast, and a perfect setting for one of the world's great legends.

Tintagel Castle and the island

Bossiney Rd, PL34 0HE ☎ 01840 770328 🖰 www.tintagelcastle.co.uk.

Either side of a gash in the coastline, paths from the village and headland lead down to the ticket office and site entrance. I was shown around by Robert Tremain, site supervisor for English Heritage. Robert told me, 'Today everything looks calm but believe me, we are regularly battered by storms so there is constant erosion. You can see why nothing is permanent here.'

Certainly, wind and waves have chiselled away at the structures leaving crumbling ramparts, and listing stone walls and doorways. First, however, we followed the path down to a sandy inlet to scramble along a sea-surged natural tunnel through the rock beneath the castle ruins. This, of course, is **Merlins's Cave**. According to most versions of the legend the wizard lived here and became teacher to the boy Arthur as he grew up in the castle.

Flights of wooden stairs curl up the cliff to the **Main Courtyard**, still on the mainland, which is the outermost part of Earl Richard's medieval castle. It's Robert Tremain's opinion that, 'Richard built the castle here because he was aware of all the Cornish legend about Arthur, and wanted a look in on some of the glory himself.'

A vertiginous footbridge spans the deeply eroded passage dividing island from mainland. Here you reach the ragged and timeworn ruins of the **Inner Courtyard**, which would have been the heart of the medieval castle. Parts of the ruin have fallen down the cliff. Recalling Robert's remarks about the constant battering and erosion, it is easy to understand why.

Beyond are the high sea cliffs and sensational views across the Bristol Channel to Lundy Island and to Hartland Point in Devon. The true history of Tintagel seemed almost incidental, as I stood breathing salty air and watching seabirds soaring on the up-currents.

Getting there

Tintagel is 17 miles west of Launceston, reached via the A39 and A395.

Where to stay and eat

Bossiney House Hotel and Cedar Tree Restaurant Bossiney Rd, PL34 0AX
☎ 01840 770240 🖰 www.bossineyhouse.com. A family-run hotel just outside
Tintagel. The restaurant is very popular locally.
Camelot Castle Hotel PL34 0DQ ☎ 01840 770202 🖰 www.camelotcastle.com.
Kitsch it may be, but this hotel enjoys location, location and location.
King Arthur's Arms Fore St, PL34 0DA ☎ 01840 770831
🖰 www.kingarthursarms.co.uk. If you can't beat 'em, join 'em at this Arthurian-
themed pub, restaurant and B&B.

Tourist information

Tintagel Tourist Information Centre Bossiney Rd, PL34 0AJ ☎ 01840 779084
🖰 www.tintagelweb.co.uk.

⑥ Walking The Saints' Way

Resting my back against St Breock's Longstone, a Bronze Age menhir, I stopped
to munch my sandwiches while gazing over the wind-harassed uplands of
central Cornwall. I couldn't help wondering: Did St Petroc also stop here for
his lunch in the 6th century AD? Or bands of medieval pilgrims a millennium
later?

I was hiking – over three days – 'The Saints' Way', a 30-mile waymarked
trail from Padstow on the north Cornwall coast to Fowey in the south. The
route meanders through a captivating collection of prehistoric standing stones,
Celtic crosses, shrines and holy wells that have gathered along the way.

Over the centuries these paths has been trodden for many different purposes.
Winds and tides carried Petroc's coracle across the sea to Padstow in AD513,
and from here the saint set about converting the Cornish to Christianity.
However, we need to fast-forward to the Middle Ages for tales of pilgrims
from Ireland and Wales following his footsteps over moors and through the
valleys of central Cornwall, so as to cut out the treacherous sea passage round
Land's End. From the Fowey estuary, boats took them on the next leg of their
journeys to Rome or Santiago de Compostela.

The Saints' Way is one of several long-distance footpaths to have been
waymarked along ancient pilgrimage routes in recent years. Would those
hiking them be comfortable with the 'pilgrim' label, I wondered?

Pilgrimage is, of course, the oldest form of organised travel, and there are
many accounts, from Chaucer onwards, of fun and games along the way. And
it was, admittedly, in this less hair-shirted spirit that I paid my respects to the
revered Rick Stein, by dining and overnighting at The Seafood Restaurant on
the harbourfront.

With lingering aftertastes of scallops with hazelnuts and coriander butter, I
climbed to hillside St Petroc's Church, to take directions from the first discreet

wooden post pointing the way with a stylised Celtic cross. The first few hours were among the most beautiful on the entire Saints' Way, as I marched up the estuary of the River Camel with the screech of seabirds filling the air. The sun and tide were out, exposing creeks glistening and bubbling with what looked like a giant version of one of Stein's puddings.

In **Little Petherick** village I found a strange 14th-century church, also dedicated to St Petroc and built into a hillside. Then I made a short detour to an even older chapel, dedicated to St Issey – daughter of 4th-century Welsh King Brychan – who accompanied Petroc to Padstow. Both places felt serene, holy and lonely. If I was a pilgrim, I was the only one.

The ascent of **St Breock Downs** took me into wilder country where prehistoric burial mounds and monuments such as the Longstone share the exposed moorland with futuristic wind turbines. Eventually I dropped into the shelter of Tregawne Valley and isolated Tregolls Farm B&B, where a steaming plate of beef in ale pie cooked by my hostess, farmer's wife Marilyn Hawkey, awaited.

Next day was rather different. Instead of striking out across open terrain, The Saints' Way took me through dappled woods, over ancient stiles and stone bridges, and through farmland and hamlets. Deliberately, and somewhat circuitously, it threads together the chapels, Celtic crosses and holy wells dating from the golden age of pilgrimage.

Route notes guided me to arcane carved stone Celtic crosses, forgotten for aeons along waysides. The wheel-headed **Reperry Cross**, for example, is near the busy A30, but hidden by a hedge. I had to inspect the tall, broken cross in the churchyard at Lanlivet very carefully, to make out the mysterious, carved figure of a man with a tail.

I felt a particularly peaceful and soothing aura at **St Bryvthth's Well**, a little seeping, moss-covered shine in a shady glade reached via a footpath near the Crown Inn at Lanlivery, where I stopped for the second night. The well is actually just off the Saints' Way, but I chanced on it because I added a few miles to my day by walking to another holy well, in the neighbouring village of **Luxulyan**. I think it must have been the seductive-sounding name that drew me there.

'So, are you pilgrims?', I asked a group of four walkers, when we met at the tiny stone chapel covering the **Holy Well of St Cyor**, in the village. They had leather boots, hiking poles and Saints' Way route notes. 'Well, we are certainly enjoying some Cornish saints with our fresh air', beamed Bryan Bailey, from Bristol.

As local historian and Cornish Bard Carol Vivian said, 'I doubt that many of today's walkers are pilgrims in the traditional sense, but I can imagine people deriving some spiritual sustenance from special places such as these.'

The final eight miles got me to **Fowey** in time for lunch (excellent *bouillabaisse* at Sam's fish restaurant), along trails that curiously mirrored the start of The Saints' Way. I crossed some more high upland, and wove through woods above the emptying River Fowey estuary while glassy creeks flicked tantalisingly in and out of sight.

Fowey, huddling in Cornwall's softer underbelly, has been a harbour town for centuries. Scallop shells, the pilgrims' emblem, are embedded in the façades of medieval building, while records show that great numbers sailed from here to Compostela. The last leg of the Saints' Way threads through the back streets to the **Church of St Finnbarrus**, named after the 7th-century Bishop of Cork who landed at Padstow and walked across central Cornwall to Fowey, pausing to build the original church here *en route* for Rome. Further proof then, that I had truly walked a saint's way. Although unexpectedly, I had also eaten like royalty.

Walking The Saints' Way

Encounter Cornwall ☎ 01208 871066 🖰 www.encountercornwall.com.
Encounter Cornwall organise self-guided Saints' Way walks including B&B or inn accommodation, daily luggage transfer, transport between the start and destination, maps and route notes.

Where to stay and eat

The Seafood Restaurant Riverside, Padstow PL28 8BY ☎ 01841 532700 🖰 www. rickstein.com. Rick Stein's restaurant serves perhaps the best (you guessed it) seafood in Cornwall. There are also lovely bedrooms overlooking the harbour.
Sam's 20 Fore St, Fowey PL23 1AQ ☎ 01726 832273 🖰 www.samsfowey.co.uk. Celebrate the end of the walk with seafood fit for a saint.
The Crown Inn Lanlivery PL30 5BT ☎ 01208 872707 🖰 www.wagtailinns.com. An old inn with comfortable rooms and food ranging from hearty to fancy in the popular restaurant.
Tregoll's Farm St Wenn, near Bodmin PL30 5PG ☎ 01208 812154
🖰 www.tregollsfarm.co.uk. The place to spend the first night if you are walking The Saints' Way north to south in 3 days.

Tourist information

Visit Cornwall Pydar House, Pydar St, Truro TR1 1EA ☎ 01872 322900
🖰 www.visitcornwall.com.

⑦ Marazion and St Michael's Mount

TR17 0EF ☎ 01736 710507 🖰 www.stmichaelsmount.co.uk.
'Everything is so *sacred* here', declared Orange Trevillion at the front desk of her hotel, the Mount Haven in Marazion. Since she had no idea her guest was researching a guidebook to 'Sacred Britain', this was an encouraging start.

Marazion is the small town facing St Michael's Mount, a dramatic, castle-crowned tidal island of craggy slate and granite that rears 260ft out of the

Atlantic. For approximately two hours either side of every high tide, waves roll in over a causeway disconnecting mount from mainland. The island seems to have been regarded as a place of sanctity forever, which is precisely why my hostess and her husband Mike moved here to set up their boutique hotel. 'You can feel the energy if you have a mind that responds to such things', says Orange (so named on account of hair which in younger days was carrot-coloured).

I felt a shiver down my spine, when Orange told me softly, liltingly, that Marazion is 'beautiful, but at the same time quite frightening. It even has its own weather, different from the rest of Cornwall. There were ghosts in the old, dark coach house which we took over in 2001.' Happily these were sent packing by the late Hamish Miller, a famous dowser attuned to, 'the four ley lines which intersect on St Michael's Mount and account for the extraordinary spiritual energy of this place.'

Walls and windows went the way of the ghosts, as the Mount Haven Hotel was reincarnated as an 18-room sanctuary with a distinctly oriental feel, reflecting the owners' fascination with Eastern spirituality. Unusually for a Cornish seaside hotel, I found myself among mandalas and Buddhas; silk hangings from India; and caskets from Bhutan. There are open spaces and expanses of plate glass.

I sat on my balcony, sipping a (distinctly occidental) glass of chilled Pinot Grigio and gazing across to the tidal island. St Michael's Mount seems to take on completely different bearings, depending on the point from which you view it. For example, from the village seafront it had looked like a fortress; but from where I was sitting, it was pure fairytale. Rapunzel might have let down her hair from one of the turrets. I let my senses drift over the centuries to St Michael appearing to fishermen, and to medieval monks chanting. Then I saw a man walking on water.

At least, that is what it looked like. The man was followed by a string of other souls and a golden retriever, as the sea sunk to the causeway's level allowing them all to trot from the island back to Marazion.

Next day it was my turn to stroll the few hundred yards across the paved granite causeway. I did so in the company of James St Aubyn who lives in the castle, as his ancestors have done since 1660. Understandably enough, it is the history of the castle since this time which mainly seems to interest him. James showed me round the castle, the chapel and the gardens recounting with gusto anecdotes from this era and the part his family played in it.

As simply a historical site it is a wonderful and romantic place. It is no surprise that upwards of 200,000 visitors a year find their way here. A few of them are Christian pilgrims, a few more are fascinated by straight lines carrying special energy and power – 'ley lines' – between sacred sites.

So I felt I needed to ask James about the island's more ancient stories; about the legends and the ley lines. 'Well, I am not entirely sceptical', he conceded, and offered to take me up to the place where the four lines of energy intersect. The precise spot was shown to him some years ago by Hamish Miller (the dowser and ley line expert who banished Orange's ghosts). Despite his smart suit and polished brogues, James bounded like a mountain goat up the precipitous southern face of the island, and I followed him to a small grassy plateau. 'This is it, one of only 27 points on Earth where four ley lines cross. One of which is the St Michael Alignment which connects us with Glastonbury and Avebury and God knows where else. It is a very sacred place.'

History and legend

Leaving geological theories to one side, the hunk of rock on a tidal island was created in antiquity by the Cornish giant Cormoran who lived here in a cave on the island. At low tide he used to wade ashore to terrorise local people, stealing sheep and cattle to feed his gluttonous appetite. Fortunately, he was slain by 'Jack the Giant Killer' – a local lad whose own mythology is entwined with a venture up a beanstalk.

There is evidence that tin was stored on the island, known to the ancient Greeks as *Ictis*, and traded with Phoenicians in Marazion in the centuries leading to the birth of Christ. St Joseph of Arimathea may have been one such trader who, according to varying stories, brought with him his young relative Jesus of Nazareth and/or, later, the cup used by said relative at the Last Supper. Thus is a link with Arthurian legend established, and the connection with Glastonbury (see page 55) strengthened.

The association with St Michael dates from AD495 when the Archangel (who, rather unusually for a non-human, is also styled as a saint) appeared, standing on a rocky ledge, to a group of fishermen. A chapel was built at the place of apparition and became a pilgrimage shrine in the Middle Ages. St Michael is the vanquisher of evil and has numerous sacred places dedicated to him, including the ruined church tower at the summit of Glastonbury Tor and Skellig Michael island (from the Gaelic *Sceilig Mhichíl* meaning 'Michael's rock') off the coast of Kerry in Ireland, as well as Mont-St-Michel (see below).

Celtic hermits and monks (about whom little is known since there was no Cornish equivalent of the Venerable Bede to record the era; see page 113), inhabited the islands from at least the 8th century. In 1044 Edward the Confessor (see page 3) gave St Michael's Mount to the Benedictine monks of Mont-St-Michel – an uncannily similar tidal island connected by a causeway to the Normandy coast, where apparitions of St Michael were also recorded in the 5th century. The Benedictines built the present church and founded a dependent priory. However, in the early 15th century when King Henry V declared war on France, the priory was seized as enemy property. In 1425

King Henry VI made the island over to Brigettine nuns (an order founded by St Bridget of Sweden) who remained until the Reformation when the island was reclaimed by the Crown.

Since then the island has been in secular hands despite its sacred associations. During the English Civil War, Royalists held St Michael's Mount against Roundhead forces and stored arms here. At the restoration of the monarchy in 1660, it was acquired by Colonel John St Aubyn whose descendants still make their home in the castle. In 1954 however, ownership was transferred to the National Trust, under an arrangement which allows the family to live there and manage the estate.

Today, about 20 people employed by the St Michael's Mount Estate live in the cottages scattered about the harbour. There is also a booth where you can buy tickets for the castle or to tour the gardens (or both).

The castle

A cobbled path leads up to the castle which is a place to dwell on the island's more recent history, rather than its ancient sacredness. Armour, antique furniture and hunting scenes hang from the walls of halls and passages, as you walk from the stained-glass windowed Chevy Chase to a Garrison Room stuffed with weaponry and other reminders of all the battles fought here.

There is an intriguing collection of cartography, and a model of the mount made out of champagne corks in the Map Room. In 'Sir John's Room' there is an ingenious 'tidal clock' made in 1780 to help the resident family time their crossings. The 15th-century chapel has a tower with a turret, which for centuries was used for the guidance of ships. Don't miss **The Terraces** atop the castle walls, from where there are commanding views over the gardens, Marazion and, on a clear day, right across to The Lizard peninsula.

The gardens

Sub-tropical plants, which would struggle to survive anywhere in Britain other than Cornwall, cling to rocky slopes and terraced beds tumbling down to the water's edge. Steep trails wind among them. Gardeners can occasionally be seen abseiling down the cliffs, in search of the remotest targets for their green fingers.

Getting there

Marazion and the causeway to St Michael's Mount are 3 miles east of Penzance.

Where to stay and eat

Mount Haven Hotel Turnpike Rd, TR17 0DQ ☎ 01736 710249
☞ www.mounthaven.co.uk. Superb and unusual hotel and restaurant, with oriental flourishes (see above).

The Island Café St Michael's Mount TR17 0EF ☎ 01736 710507. Serves the best of

traditional Cornish fare from pasties to clotted cream teas.
The Kings Arms The Square, TR17 0AP ☎ 01736 710291. A traditional pub with good food, on the waterfront facing the mount.

⑧ Land's End Peninsula

Surrounded by dramatic seascapes, this granite peninsula – also known as Penwith – rises up to expanses of high, wild moorland. Up here, amid quickly changing conditions of light and atmosphere, are some of Britain's most intriguing links with sacred prehistory.

Men-an-Tol
Free access.

The walk alone is good enough reason to find your way to this very strange megalithic structure. I reached Men-an-Tol after a bracing hike across sheep-cropped moors. Somehow this monument felt very far flung; it was scarcely believable that it had taken me just 20 minutes to get here from the nearest metalled road.

Men-an-Tol means, in Cornish, 'holed stone', although it is also known locally – and rather more disturbingly – as 'the Devil's Eye'. The Flintstones came to mind as I approached the giant wheel-like stone with an almost perfect circle at its centre. Or perhaps a giant's doughnut turned to stone and on to its side, then embedded in the turf. In addition to this central feature, the monument consists of three other stones: an upright megalith on either side of the holed stone, plus a fallen stone at the foot of the western upright.

Needless to say, there is a vast amount of myth and legend surrounding this stone. Archaeological studies have suggested that Men-an-Tol may have been a component part of a burial chamber and, intriguingly, that the hole had a ritual significance as a window between one life and the next. But that is guesswork. What is clear is that the site has been a place of ritual healing for aeons.

There are stories going back several hundred years, of women who believed themselves to be infertile crawling through the hole in the stone at full moon to cure their barrenness. The stone has also been credited with the power to heal various ailments in children, particularly rickets, by passing the youngsters through the hole.

Another piece of Cornish folklore has it that if you place a pair of brass pins as a cross on top of the round stone, you can ask it any 'yes' or 'no' question. The question is answered by the upper pin swinging right for 'yes' and left for 'no'. Or perhaps it was the other way round. Anyway, I had clean forgotten to bring any pins, brass or otherwise, and it would have taken me ages to go through the whole field of the 3.15 at Market Rasen, asking the 'will x win?' question for each in turn.

Getting there

There is a lay-by on the B3306 between Madron to Morvah, with a signpost marking the track to the stones. Parking and access are free and unrestricted.

Chun Quoit

Free access.

A 'quoit' sounds as if it might be a circular object, like Men-an-Tol; a large one, perhaps, suitable as a recreational game for giants and ogres. But in Cornish prehistoric archaeology a 'quoit' is a cluster of large standing stones supporting a heavy capstone. Elsewhere, similar structures are known as dolmens or cromlechs. This one, Chun (pronounced 'choon') Quoit is one

of the best preserved and most spectacular, and probably dates from the early Neolithic period – somewhere between 3500 and 2500BC.

Chun Quoit stands high on a hump of the West Penwith Moors. It comes into view as a silhouette on the horizon like a giant mushroom, from the B3318 beyond Pendeen before this road joins the A3071 to Penzance. There is a small parking area next to this road, from where I followed a track up the hill to the site, marvelling at its sheer scale. The capstone is vast – about 11.5ft long by 10ft wide – supported by four huge megaliths. The monumental feat that getting it up there must have been, told me that it surely had some weighty purpose. Just how did they manage it? Certainly, its commanding position suggests intent to define a territory, or perhaps bring a community together.

I was able to creep into the interior through a hole in one side, and I found myself in a dark, chilly cavity where ancient bones might have been left.

Getting there

Chun Quoit is on open ground and easily reached from the car park on the B3318.

Madron Well

Free access.

Scraps of cloth, hundreds of them of knotted to shrubs shading a reedy pool fed from this holy well, testify that this sacred Celtic site still projects its power in the 21st century. The practice of tying multi-coloured 'clouties' to branches dates back to early Celtic times when pilgrims made journeys to the well. They dipped the rags brought for the purpose in the sacred water as part of a healing ritual or as an offering to the nature spirits that dwell in the well, especially Modron, the Celtic goddess of Fates.

In Christian times, Modron morphed into St Maderne and similar practices continued with the offering of a petitionary prayer for healing. In particular, mothers would bring sickly children and plunge them into the water. Sometimes a strip of cloth was torn from clothing covering the part of the body afflicted. The idea was that as the cloth decomposed, so the hurt would by degrees disappear. Not an instant cure, then. (And certainly a warning against non-bio-degradable 'clouties'!)

The walk to the well felt enchanted, as if I had entered some fantastical story. I twisted along a dappled lane flickering with shadows. The atmosphere was haunting, strangely discomfiting even, especially when I was suddenly surprised by shimmering colour on reaching the 'clouty'-festooned pool. The original well head dating from Celtic times is within a dilapidated circular stone enclosure overhung with rowan bushes and thorn trees. Water was trickling out of the trough into a bog of moss and ferns where innumerable frogs the size of my thumbnail were frolicking.

Don't leave without pausing at the nearby ruined, roofless 14th-century well-chapel about 100yds on. Here another spring, presumably from the same source, seeps into a stone basin. There is also a low stone altar against the eastern wall.

Getting there
From the village of Madron 2 miles north of Penzance, take the narrow, nameless **road** north and turn right down the lane towards Boswarthen. A short way along here from the car park follow the (often muddy) path through the trees to the well and chapel.

The Merry Maidens
Free access.
I drove past the Merry Maidens twice on the B3315 between Newlyn and Treen, before I spotted them. I must have been expecting something a little more obvious than the simple lay-by giving access to a field where this smallish circle of granite megaliths has stood for thousands of years.

There is a lot of legend, though precious few facts, known about this almost perfect circle approximately 65ft in diameter. The stones number 19 in all, evenly spaced though of differing shapes and sizes. Nineteen has been noted as the number of megaliths which originally comprised various other circles around Cornwall. Was the number important, as some 18th-century antiquarians believed, meaningful to people guided by lunar cycles?

Dates and astronomical significance might remain unresolved, but I did get out my compass to confirm that some of the most prominent stones are pretty much exactly on the cardinal points. Does this suggest some sort of calendric function, perhaps relating to the agricultural year? The commonly accepted interpretation of Neolithic standing stones is that they fulfilled some ritual purpose. However, I felt that the real draw of this place was the very fact that we know so little about the people who erected the circle: their beliefs, language and myths, for example.

On the other hand, there are few local people who disagree that the stones are girls transmogrified for profaning the Sabbath by dancing. The Cornish name for the stones is *Dans Maen*, meaning 'dancing stones'. Nearby is a pair of megaliths known as 'the pipers' which, according to the legend, are the petrified remains of musicians who led these Neolithic It-girls astray one Saturday night. But when the pipers heard the church bells at St Buryan strike midnight, they realised that they were breaking the Sabbath, and fled leaving the maidens still dancing. Result: everybody got turned to stone!

Do these stories contain echoes from across the ages of rituals that took place here? Or are the stories more recent attempts by the Christian Church to impose its morality on pagan practices? We don't know.

Getting there

The Merry Maidens are adjacent to the B3315 Newlyn to Treen Road. Access is from a lay-by at the western corner of the field.

Where to stay and eat

The Abbey Hotel Abbey St, Penzance TR18 4AR ☎01736 366906 www.theabbeyonline.co.uk. An excellent, slightly zany hotel in a Georgian townhouse painted a striking shade of blue.
The Cornish Range 6 Chapel St, Mousehole TR19 6SB ☎01736 731488. Wonderful seafood restaurant, in this tightly huddled little village south of Penzance.
Whitesands Hotel Sennen, near Land's End TR19 7AR ☎01736 871776 www.whitesandshotel.co.uk. A family hotel by the beach at Sennen Cove, just a mile from Land's End. Conventional rooms or (in summer) a choice of teepees or yurts if you prefer.

Tourist information

Penzance Tourist Information Office Station Rd, TR18 2NF ☎01736 362207 www.purelypenzance.co.uk.

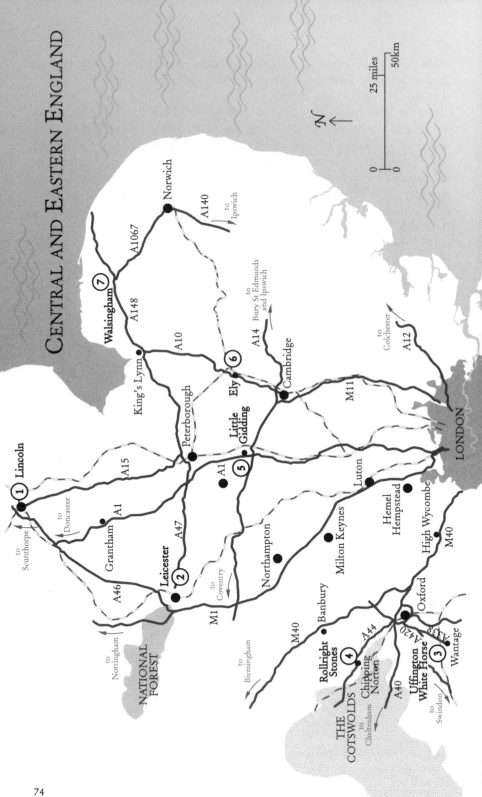

CENTRAL AND EASTERN ENGLAND

N

25 miles
50km
0
0

to Ipswich
A140
Norwich
A1067
Walsingham ⑦
A148
to Bury St Edmunds and Ipswich
A10
King's Lynn
A14
⑥ Ely
Cambridge
to Colchester
A12
Peterborough
Little Gidding
M11
Lincoln ①
A15
A1
⑤
LONDON
to Scunthorpe
to Doncaster
Grantham
A1
A47
Luton
Hemel Hempstead
Northampton
High Wycombe
M40
Leicester ②
to Coventry
Milton Keynes
Oxford
A46
M1
Banbury
M40
A44
A420
A338
Wantage
to Nottingham
NATIONAL FOREST
to Birmingham
Rollright Stones ④
Chipping Norton
Uffington White Horse ③
A40
to Swindon
THE COTSWOLDS
to Cheltenham

4. CENTRAL AND EASTERN ENGLAND

Geographically speaking, Leicester is at the heart of Middle England. Culturally, however, this city has over the last few decades become the centre of Britain's south Asian communities, pulsing with the sounds, scents and colours of India. Eastern promise without leaving the East Midlands.

Sites saturated with spiritual yearnings are scattered across this region of England. Visitors find their emotions stirred in great cathedrals rising out of the Fens, where dauntless saints are still revered; and at tiny chapels where poets have spoken of 'the intersection of the timeless moment'. And they discover pilgrimage to medieval shrines flourishing in the 21st century, with south Asians again among the faithful.

① Lincoln

A few hundred years ago the Devil tossed two little imps into the wind, instructing them to make mischief wherever they landed. A gust took them through the portals of Lincoln Cathedral where they harassed the Dean and leapt about the transepts and altar, mocking the carved stone angels in the choir. When the angels warned them not to go too far, one heeded their advice and went off to frolic elsewhere, while the other persisted in his mischief-making until finally the angels' patience ran out and they turned him to stone.

The tiny fellow is only just visible high up in the Angel Choir, but by putting 20p in a slot a special spotlight will pinpoint him as he sits there cross-legged with his horns and wicked grin. In the glory and vastness of the cathedral, which dates back nearly 1,000 years, the miniature statue and the legend surrounding it does rather steal the limelight; the imp clearly had the last laugh over the angels.

Lincoln Cathedral and St Hugh

Minster Yard, LN2 1PX 📞 01522 561600 🖰 www.lincolncathedral.com.

This cathedral has as good a claim as any to being the richest and fullest work of Gothic architecture anywhere in Britain. However, Lincoln's original cathedral was one of the Normans' crowning glories, drawing comparisons with its counterpart at Durham (see page 121). Work began in 1072 on the orders of Remigius, the first bishop, and was for the most part complete within an astonishingly hasty 20 years.

But fire ravaged the cathedral in 1141, after which it was rebuilt by the third Bishop of Lincoln, the so-called Alexander the Magnificent, in a style intended to be commensurate with his sobriquet. Pride seems to have augured the fall that was to come, because in 1185 a very localised, but evidently powerful, earthquake toppled it. This time the task of overseeing the second rebuilding fell to a bishop whose hallowed presence is still felt in the cathedral. Bishop Hugh (earlier Hugh of Burgundy and later Great St Hugh of Lincoln) began a massive reconstruction that was to make this cathedral the third largest in Britain after York Minster (see page 136) and St Paul's in London.

Hugh was a Carthusian monk from Avalon in the foothills of the French Alps, who was sent to England in 1179 to found Witham Priory in Somerset at the request of Henry II, as part of his penance for the murder of Thomas Becket. Hugh proved to be as strong-willed and capable as he was learned and holy. He initially refused to carry out many of the king's wishes until local people had been compensated for the land and materials they had sacrificed for the building of the priory. And he became renowned for the way in which he treated everybody equally, irrespective of wealth or position. He even admonished the king – a regular visitor to Witham – for keeping bishoprics vacant so that the crown could profit directly from their income. Perhaps he was heeding this reproach when, in 1186, Henry appointed Hugh himself as Bishop of Lincoln, a position which had been vacant since the earthquake.

In Lincoln, Hugh rebuilt and expanded the cathedral. He also established himself as strongly independent from the king, again frequently refusing to carry out royal instructions when he disagreed with them. In particular, he opposed the royal hunting and forestry laws which had been imposed after the Norman Conquest and gave noblemen unfettered rights on any land. This frequently resulted in the destruction of crops and even whole villages, leading to starvation among the peasantry.

But the bravery for which Hugh is most renowned was his protection of the rights of Jews who were mercilessly persecuted after Henry II's death and the accession to the throne of Richard I. As in York when Jews took refuge in Clifford's Tower (see page 140), there were anti-Semitic riots and attacks on Jewish property. With its synagogue and sizeable population in the Jewish quarter, similar atrocities might easily have taken place in Lincoln, but Bishop Hugh personally confronted anyone who threatened Jews, and offered Jews sanctuary in the cathedral.

Hugh died in 1200 and two decades later was canonised. His cult grew rapidly, with pilgrims making the journey to Lincoln to pray at his tomb in the cathedral, which was adorned with the emblem of a swan in reference to the bird said to have been his companion and guard. In time, and for a variety of reasons, he became the patron saint of sick children, shoemakers – and, of course, swans.

Pilgrims would enter the cathedral through the Judgement Porch, kneel before the gold-lined and jewel-encrusted tomb which held St Hugh's body, and ask for healing, forgiveness or guidance. For some reason, his head was detached from his body and was venerated separately on a plinth. Although the shrine was damaged and stripped of its treasures following the Dissolution of the Monasteries, it was not completely destroyed. The tomb is still there in the Angel Choir, and is a place to pause and remember a man not afraid to stand up to the rich and powerful, on behalf of the poor and oppressed.

A walk around Lincoln

I began outside the cathedral in **Minster Yard**, on the south side at the foot of three massive towers, in the heart of 'Uphill', as Lincoln folk refer to the old part of their historic city. The Romans made the hilltop one of their key garrisons in Britain, on account of its defensive position. To explore some of their remains, I made my way under the great stone arch of **Exchequergate** (nothing to do with cover-ups at Number 11 Downing Street – it was built in 1320) and made my way along Bailgate where lines of

'Little St Hugh'

Lincoln's other 'St Hugh' is not really a saint at all – in the sense that he was never formally canonised. Nevertheless, there is tragedy and touching poignancy in the story of 'Little St Hugh', and his shrine in the south aisle of Lincoln Cathedral.

Little Hugh was a nine-year-old boy who went missing in July 1255; his body was found in a well 29 days later. A local Jew named Jopin was accused of the murder and, under torture, confessed to the crime and to the fact that it was a Jewish custom to kill a Gentile child every year. Jopin was hanged, as were other Jews – upwards of 18, accounts vary – as fear of ritual Jewish killings spread.

The wee victim whose murder had sparked the episode, meanwhile, was becoming something of a Christian martyr. He was buried in the cathedral and his tomb became a shrine to be visited by pilgrims, alongside that of his revered namesake. Lincoln's stock as a pilgrimage destination undoubtedly benefitted from this additional attraction. Various ballads and scraps of folklore attribute miracles to Little Hugh, and Geoffrey Chaucer in the *Canterbury Tales* refers to him in 'The Prioress's Tale'.

Today, a plaque marks the site of Lincoln Cathedral's second shrine.

black circles mark the places which once were the bases of Roman columns. At the end is **Newport Arch**, said to be the only Roman structure in Britain that you can drive under.

Other remains in the thick of the Roman quarter are more vestigial, such as the base of a wall and a carefully excavated well. I left the Romans behind at the **corner of Westgate and Union Road** which run along two sides of Lincoln Castle, passing a pub called **The Strugglers Inn** where, until the 18th century, prisoners were read The Last Rites before being hanged publicly outside.

Leaving the centrepiece of 'Uphill' till last, I completed my circle of the castle by returning to Exchequergate, just a few paces from the entrance. The formidable fortress was built in 1068 on the instruction of William the Conqueror, incorporating remains of the original structure which once crowned the hill; various towers and embellishments have been added over the centuries.

The castle remained a prison up until 1878 and **Cobb Hall**, a 13th-century defensive tower, is the place to see cells and dungeons of unspeakable medieval torture. More depressing still, I felt, was the stark Victorian chapel where prisoners were locked in high-sided, coffin-like individual pews from where they could see only the pulpit and the chaplain preaching his repentance-demanding sermons.

The **Observatory Tower**, the castle's highest point, was more uplifting. To reach the top I climbed a steep stone staircase narrower in places than I am, to emerge into a cold, blustery wind. The views took in the Trent Valley and, to the southeast, the endless Lincolnshire fields stretching to the pimple-like Boston Stump rising out of the flatness with The Wash beyond.

Lincoln's most characterful street, known simply and accurately enough as **Steep Hill**, leads from outside the castle down to the lower part of town ('Downhill'), which historically has been the quarter of tradesmen and industry. 'Uphill' used to be reserved for gentry and clergy, and is still the most fashionable residential area. Making my way down the cobbled, pedestrianised hill, I stopped for a pint of beer and a bite under the low ceiling of the timber-framed 14th century **Wig and Mitre**, Lincoln's most famous pub named, apparently, because of its equidistance from the cathedral and the law courts.

A little further down I passed the ornate carved façades and arched Norman doorways of the **Jew's House and Jew's Court**, dating from the 12th century when Jewish merchants, traders and moneylenders were the richest and most influential citizens of Lincoln. The house is now a restaurant.

I followed the road on down to **The Strait**, which is lined with timber-framed buildings and is one of Lincoln's busiest shopping streets. I continued under an archway through the great 15th-century **Stonebow** that marks the southern entrance to the old town. Just beyond, I reached the carved stone bridge over the River Witham where I turned right down a narrow alley called **Glory Hole**, to **Brayford Pool**.

From Roman times the area round this small lake was the fulcrum of Lincoln's trading activity, being the junction of the River Witham up which ships sailed from the North Sea, with the Fossedyke Canal connecting to the River Trent. Nowadays it is leisure craft which use the pool, river and canal.

After tracing my footsteps the short distance back to **High Bridge**, I followed a waterside path which emerged at wide Broadgate at the edge of the city, leading back to 'Uphill'. A right fork took me on to **Lindum Hill**, from where I climbed the steep south side back to the cathedral, by means of the ancient, well-worn **Greestone staircase**.

Finally, I reached the hilltop through a stone gateway into Minster Yard on the cathedral's exposed south side, to be greeted by a ravaging wind, which I had been sheltered from downhill. It was easy to understand how a strong gust could have tossed a couple of free-floating imps up there.

Getting there
Lincoln is 81 miles southeast of York via the M18 motorway and the A15. It is 142 miles north of London via the M1 motorway and the A46. There are direct **trains** to Lincoln from London King's Cross and Cambridge.

Where to stay and eat
Hillcrest Hotel 15 Lindum Terrace, LN2 5RT ☎ 01522 510182
🖰 www.hillcrest-hotel.com. Exceptionally friendly, centrally located family-run hotel in a former rectory. Homely food served in the restaurant.
Jews House Restaurant 15 The Strait, LN2 1JD ☎ 01522 524851
🖰 www.jewshouserestaurant.co.uk. Reasonable, well-priced restaurant in this historic, 900-year-old building.
The Strugglers Inn 83 Westgate, LN1 3BG ☎ 01255 535023. Great selection of ales. A good place to have your last pint.
Wig and Mitre 30–32 Steep Hill, LN2 1LU ☎ 01522 535190
🖰 www.wigandmitre.com. Famous pub and a good stop for traditional fare.

Tourist information
Lincoln Visitor Information 9 Castle Hill, LN1 3AA ☎ 01522 545458
🖰 www.visitlincolnshire.com.

② Leicester's Hindu, Sikh and Jain temples

Leicester is an industrial city in the East Midlands, founded by the Romans as a garrison town at the northern end of the Fosse Way. Richard III is buried in the Anglican cathedral's nave. King Lear and Lady Jane Grey were born here. So were Simon de Montfort; Thomas Cook, founder of the package tour; England footballer Gary Lineker; and the fictional Adrian Mole. In the

19th century the city prospered as a stronghold for the footwear and hosiery industries.

However, I was here because modern Leicester has become one of the most 'Indian' cities anywhere outside India. As a result of immigration from the sub-continent, mostly in the latter decades of the 20th century, perhaps as many as 25% of Leicester's inhabitants are Hindus, Sikhs or Jains.

In consequence, there are scores of temples and holy places strewn around the city. My guide to a selection of these was Nimisha Mehta of Leicester Shire Promotions who was born in Leicester and, as her name reveals, is of Indian heritage. Nimisha's parents emigrated from the Punjab, via east Africa, before the birth of the daughter who would be taken to worship at the Shree Sanatan Mandir temple, earn a degree at Durham University, and return to Leicester to live with her parents before marrying a suitable boy (also of Indian parentage).

So, it was a very typical young 'Asian' Englishwoman I met on Leicester's Belgrave Road, otherwise known as 'The Golden Mile', before exploring the city's exotic temples. Immediately, I found that the scents of incense and spices alone were enough to transport me to Amritsar or Varanasi. Pavements are lined with Indian goldsmiths and jewellers, sari boutiques, Indian travel agents, music stores and sweet stalls, curry houses, lassi bars, and numerous shops selling all manner of groceries imported from India. Here I began my day's immersion in six of the best sacred sites in Indian Leicester.

I had hoped to make this a walking tour through the city, but the layout of England's eighth most populous settlement argued against the idea. So instead we leapt into a whining auto-rickshaw (OK that's not *quite* true, it was an ordinary taxi) and headed for the south end of the city in search one of only a handful of Jain temples anywhere in the world outside India.

Jain Centre
32 Oxford St, LE1 5XU ✆ 0116 254 1150 🖥 www.jaincentre.com. Free access.
Jainism has several million adherents in India and is possibly the world's oldest religion, with a history stretching back about 5,000 years. I was met by Dr Ranesh Mehta, a retired Leicester GP and devout Jain who shows visitors round while explaining the basics of Jainism. His starting point was that Jainism means 'victory' (over the self) and is essentially a way of life and thought, based on science and logic in a universe that is eternal. Non-violence and reverence for life are Jainism's core principles.

The temple is a former congregational church with a white marble façade which Leicester's 1,000-strong Jain community acquired in 1979, in part because they were keen that their temple building should have history as a place of worship. Inside there are one or two echoes of this era such as chandeliers and modern stained-glass windows illustrating Jain stories, in place of their Christian counterparts. (Stained glass has no tradition in Jain temples.)

But these are tiny details amid the magnificence of 44 yellow sandstone and marble pillars hand-carved at Jaiselmere, transported across the Rajasthan desert by train and shipped from Mumbai. Each one depicts a piece of symbolic Jain art or lettering etched into the rock. On an upper level there are four main shrines dedicated to manifestations of the deity, while overhead a strikingly beautiful domed ceiling is decorated with traditional Jain symbols.

'John Major was particularly fascinated by the ceiling, and also asked many searching questions', smiled Dr Mehta, showing me a plaque recording a visit by the then prime minister.

Guru Nanak Gurdwara and museum

9 Holy Bones, LE1 4LJ ✆ 0116 262 8606 ⊕ www.thesikhmuseum.com. Free access.

We walked along Vaughan Way passing Jewry Wall, then up a side street mysteriously called 'Holy Bones' (apparently in reference to a Roman temple dedicated to the God Janus, to whom beasts were sacrificed). If this is true, then like the Jain Centre, Leicester's foremost and longest-established Sikh temple is also on the site of a former place of worship. However, it is housed in a building which was more recently a hosiery factory.

As at the Jain Centre, a plaque was on display confirming that a high-ranking dignitary had preceded me – this time The Queen. In the museum adjoining the temple, Her Majesty may have learnt that while Sikhs make up not much more than 1% of the population of British-ruled India, they accounted for more than half the casualties in the anti-colonial resistance. And that the first Sikhs to settle in Leicester were demobbed soldiers from World War II who had been given British passports after fighting for Britain.

While walking through several different prayer rooms, a Mr Singh explained to me the tenets of the Sikh faith and the symbolism of its five articles: Kes (unshorn hair), Kangha (comb), Kara (bracelet), Kirpan (dagger) and Kachhera (soldier's shorts). Then he took me to the dining room where sari-clad dinner ladies were doling out crispy samosas and fiery plates of *pakora* – a potato and vegetable curry. Simple meals are served here every day, without charge, as an act of charity to anybody who enters the temple, regardless of creed. For some of Leicester's homeless and down-and-outs, the Gurdwara is a lifeline.

Shree Swaminarayan Temple

139–141 Loughborough Rd, LE4 5LQ ✆ 0116 266 6210. Free access.

Another rickshaw ride (OK, OK another taxi) took us north to this small temple dedicated to Swaminarayan Pampradaya – a sect of Hinduism which was established by Lord Swaminarayan two centuries ago. He did so to fulfil a promise made by Lord Shree Krishna in the holy Hindi scripture the Bhagavad Gita, that 'wherever and whenever there is a decline in religious practice and wicked actions predominate, I descend myself and assume a form.'

There was nothing to suggest '*wicked actions*' of any description on the noisy Loughborough Road cutting through a Leicester suburb. But nor was there much to suggest a life beyond the mundane, save for the three pink spire-like 'shikaras' crowning the former low-rise office that is now a temple.

A trio of women, two of them Gujarati-born, were offering devotions at Swaminarayan's shrine, and perhaps wondering how Krishna's promise applies to modern secular Britain.

Shree Ram Mandir

Hildyard Rd, LE4 5GG ☎ 0116 266 4642 ⚓ www.rammandirleicester.org.uk. Free access.

Back in the vicinity of the Golden Mile, this rather nondescript rectangular, red-brick building hides a panoply of garish shrines to Hindu deities. They include elephant-headed Lord Ganesh; Hanuman the Monkey God; and Sai Baba of Shirdi, the revered guru and yogi who died in 1918 and is regarded by his followers as an incarnation of Shiva.

Here in the commercial heart of the Asian community's commercial district, the temple is very evidently a place where people come for a moment of calm amid the daily noise and haste. While I was there a businessman in a suit breezed in and, leaving his laptop on a chair next to him, closed his eyes in meditation for five quick minutes, then rose and left as quickly as he had arrived.

Sri Siva Murugan Temple

Unit 3b, Abbey Mill, Ross Walk, LE4 5HH ☎ 0116 251 0625 ⚓ www.leicestersrimurugantemple.org.uk. Free access.

A noisy *puja*, complete with fire and plangent cymbals, performed by bare-chested priests with torsos streaked with paint and ash, was in progress behind what looked from the outside like a garage door. More than at any other temple in Leicester, I felt instantaneously transported to somewhere very far from the East Midlands. This temple is dedicated to the God Muruga, also known in Tamil as Kadavul, and is one of the main places of worship for Leicester's South Asian Tamil Community.

One of the priests explained to me how fire in the ceremony signified the Lord Muruga's vanquishing of evil. 'These are days of darkness, and evil takes the form of temptations and pressures and tensions in everyday life', he said.

Shree Sanatan Mandir

84 Weymouth St, LE4 6FQ ☎ 0116 266 1402 ⚓ www.sanatanmandirleicester.com. Free access.

And so to one of the most prestigious Hindu temples in Britain. In 1969 a renowned preacher and holy man named Ram Bhakta arrived in Leicester. At that time the hundreds of Hindus already living in the city had only their homes in which to pray. Ram Bhakta resolved to help create a temple which would also serve as a meeting place for the community (which is what a 'Mandir' means).

Today, the temple has evolved into a huge centre of worship for thousands of Leicester's Hindus. Beautiful marble shrines house the deities, while the temple is adorned with intricate patterns, designs and symbols telling the story of Hinduism.

While candle flames flickered and a medley of scents seduced my nostrils, the strains of flutes and sitars floated over from the adjacent community centre as a young persons' music group limbered up.

Getting there

Leicester is 100 miles north of London, just off junctions 21 and 21A of the M1. Direct **train** services to the main station just south of the city centre, operate from numerous cities including London (St Pancras) and Birmingham (New Street).

Where to stay and eat

Bobbys, 154–156 Belgrave Rd, LE4 5AT ☎ 0116 266 0106 🖰 www.eatatbobbys. com. Vegetarian curries on the Golden Mile, mouthwatering enough to convert even a committed carnivore.

Hotel Maiyango 13–21 St Nicholas Pl, LE1 4LD ☎ 0116 251 8898 🖰 www.maiyango.com. Stunning 14-bed boutique hotel with highly imaginative Asian-influenced touches to the décor. There is a cocktail bar and excellent, if rather pricey, restaurant.

Spindle Lodge Hotel 2 West Walk, LE1 7NA ☎ 0116 233 8801 🖰 www.spindlelodgehotel.co.uk. Good value, small 3-star hotel in a Victorian townhouse on a leafy street near the railway station.

Tourist information

Leicester Tourist Information Town Hall Sq, LE1 6BF ☎ 0844 888 5181 🖰 www.goleicestershire.com.

③ Uffington White Horse

Free access.

This strangely seductive, big-eyed beast has been loping across the Berkshire Downs for some 3,000 years. In common with the other two mysterious, giant figures carved in antiquity into the chalk hills of southern Britain, there are myths and legends galore about its origins.

However, unlike Dorset's Cerne Giant (see page 53) or the Long Man of Wilmington in Sussex (see page 27), we do have a pretty good idea about how old this creature is. In 1994 a new technique – Stimulated Luminescence Dating, which reveals the date that buried soil was last exposed to sunlight – was used. Archaeologists were staggered to discover that the carving was at least a millennium older than any of them had previously guessed. Tests confirmed that the figure had been constructed by digging a trench in the shape of the creature and then backfilling with chalk blocks. They also indicated that the shape is in a position almost identical to when it was built, which was between 1200 and 800BC. In other words, the white horse dates back to the Bronze Age.

None of this detracts in the slightest from its sense of mystery, or from its beauty. I glimpsed the figure from miles away across the green fields spangled with chunks of chalk which overlay the Vale of the White Horse. Its elongated, arched form and energy-pulsing sense of an animal in movement, reminded me of the wild creatures painted on southwest France's Lascaux caves. But the scale is vastly greater. It is 370ft from head to tail and etched into the grass just below the top of an escarpment followed by the Ridgeway, the ancient road which may be 2,000 years older than even the horse itself.

But is the Uffington White Horse a horse at all? Just below the figure, the ground drops away steeply to a small, round knoll with a bare, flat top. This is Dragon Hill on which, according to legend, St George slew a dragon. Blood, spewed by the dying creature, poisoned the ground forever. (This is, of course, why even today no grass grows on the hill's scarred plateau.) So is the 'horse' perhaps a dragon?

The first record of the figure as representing a horse seems to be an 11th-century register written on vellum by monks of Abingdon Abbey, which refers to the ritual scouring every seven years, of *mons albi equi* – the 'white horse hill'. But the origins of this practice are as lost to history as the figure's original purpose. Perhaps it was the emblem of a local tribe, cut as a territory-marking totem. Very possibly it had a religious significance. If the intended form is indeed a horse, then there might be a connection with Epona, the horse-goddess worshipped by the Gaulish Celts whose counterpart in Britain was known as Rhiannon. Another theory is that the figure is the work of worshippers of the Celtic sun god Belinos, who was frequently depicted on horse-back.

What history does record, is that the seven-yearly grooming of the horse remained a ritual observed right through to the late 19th century. It strikes me as astonishing that local people kept a practice such as this alive, through ages when 'pagan' earth carvings would have been regarded with deep suspicion if not downright hostility by Christian authorities. Moreover, it seems as if the custom took place as part of great fairs held on the hill. Perhaps it is simply the powerful and mysterious atmosphere of this place, which carried its customs through the ages.

White Horse Hill

I drove up to the Uffington White Horse car park, to walk first to the ridge on White Horse Hill overlooking the figure and Dragon Hill. To the west, just below the horse, is a dramatic, precipitous valley known as **The Manger**. One legend has it that the horse is a mare with an invisible foal on the hill beside her, and at night the pair come down to feed here. Certainly, the swathes of lime-green grass looked suitably nourishing.

Above the horse is a series of humps known, descriptively enough, as the **Pillow Mounds**. These are Neolithic and Bronze Age although, unusually, excavations have found that they were reused for Romano-British and Anglo-Saxon burials. **Uffington Castle**, an Iron Age fort consisting of a rampart and ditch, crowns the hill. The fort is virtually on the Ridgeway, the oldest continually used road in Britain, perhaps in Europe.

A mile-long grassy stretch of the Ridgeway, cut with ruts reaching down to the chalk, leads to **Wayland's Smithy**. This long barrow, or burial mound, takes its name from Veland, the Saxon god of the forge. Hidden away in a copse of beech trees, it is an eerie place with the tomb entrance guarded by a cluster of boulders. According to one legend, Veland rode a white stallion and would shoe your horse if you left it by the smithy with a coin in its mouth. Another story has it that the Uffington horse itself is Veland's mount and that once every 100 years it gallops across the sky to be re-shod in his smithy.

Getting there

The Uffington Horse can be seen from a wide swathe of the Vale of the White Horse, below the ridge. Take the B4507 through the valley, between Ashby and Wantage from where the car park is signposted. The figure is a few minutes' walk from here.

Where to stay and eat

The White Horse Woolstone, near Faringdon SN7 7QL ☏ 01367 820726
🍴 www.whitehorsewoolstone.co.uk. This particular white horse is a pub with rooms and a restaurant. Thatched and 16th century, it is still nothing like as old as its counterpart etched onto the hillside. A 2-hour circular walk from here takes you on to White Horse Hill and the Ridgeway.

Other hill figures

There is a word for the art of cutting white horses into hillsides – leucippotomy – coined, with a touch of mischievous humour, by authority on the subject Morris Marples in his definitive 1949 book *White Horses and Other Hill Figures*.

Wiltshire's white horses

According to expert Bill Daly, whose website ✆ www.wiltshirehorses.org.uk is the definitive source of contemporary information, 'Wiltshire is the county for white horses'. Some have been neglected and disappeared back into their hillsides, but several others are good as new.

There is only one known prehistoric white horse. It is not in Wiltshire, and is perhaps not even a horse. Nevertheless, it is the **Uffington White Horse** that inspired a wave of leucippotomy (these figures unmistakeably equine) across the chalk downland of Wiltshire, most of them in the 18th and 19th centuries.

The 1812 **Alton Barnes Horse** on Milk Hill, about a mile north of the village of the same name in the Vale of Pewsey above the Kennet and Avon Canal, can be seen from the A345. The **Hackpen Hill Horse**, probably carved to commemorate Queen Victoria's coronation in 1838, is two miles southeast of Broad Hinton village and can be seen from the A4361. The **Cherhill Horse**, on Cherhill Down near the Lansdowne Monument obelisk comes into view on the A4 and is the second oldest in Wiltshire, having been originally cut in 1780, then completely restored in 2002.

The sedate **Westbury Horse** dates from 1778 and so is the oldest and also the best positioned, high on Bratton Down and visible between Bratton and Westbury. Climb to the top of the escarpment for sensational views across west Wiltshire.

The Mormond Horse and Stag

Scotland's solitary white horse, probably late 18th century, is carved on Mormond Hill in Grampian and filled with local white quartz. On the other side of the hill is a stag, cut and filled in the same way. The horse can be seen from the B9093

Tourist infomation

Wantage Tourist Information 19 Church St, Wantage OX12 8BL ✆ 0845 722 3344 ✆ www.wantage.com.

④ Rollright Stones

Long Compton OX7 5QB ✆ www.rollrightstones.co.uk. Open year round from sunrise to sunset.

On certain nights of the year these limestone rocks break from the almost perfect circle they form, and rush down a hill to drink from a nearby spring.

Holy isles

'Thin places, where only a tissue separates the material from the spiritual.' (George McLeod)

Twice a day the rising tide uncouples St Michael's Mount from the mainland. (main image: P & below: DL/D)

St Aidan settled on Lindisfarne (Holy Island) in AD635 and today it remains a place of spiritual solace. (P)

The Avebury stone circles are the largest of their kind in Europe. (P)

Southwestern England

'England's southwest is a palimpsest of ancient beliefs layered one upon another.'

A vast menu of spiritual sustenance is on offer at Glastonbury. (EL/A)

EMMA HOWE
Visionary
α Seer Ω
ANCIENT WISDOM FOR A
CONTEMPORARY WORLD
Unique Personal
Readings
DELTA EQUILIBRIUM
△ MANTRAS △
Achieve Self-Mastery with
DIVINE METHODOLOGY
Identify your
Life Purpose
CALL FOR A CONSULTATION -
01458 834286

A moment of calm in the Glastonbury gardens fed by red-tinged water from the Chalice Well. (EL/A)

'Clouties' are tied to a tree at Madron Well in hope of healing various afflictions (pictured left). Meanwhile, crawling through the Men-an-Tol holed stone at full moon is a cure for barrenness (below). (both MS)

Marked with ancient Celtic crosses, The Saints' Way follows St Petroc's footsteps from Padstow to Fowey. (MS)

People have held faith in the curative powers of the hot springs at Bath Spa since prehistoric times. (P)

Recent times have seen a resurgence of pilgrimage to the medieval Marian shrine at Walsingham. (P)

CHAUCERS CANTERBURY PILGRIMS

In his 14th-century *Canterbury Tales*, Geoffrey Chaucer wrote of high jinks among the hair shirts. (P)

On Bardsey Island, where the first monks settled in the 5th century AD, you not only unwind, but rewind through the centuries. (MS)

St Peter's at Bradwell-on-Sea is possibly the oldest church in Britain still in regular use. (P)

The 'field of flowers' outside Kensington Palace where pilgrims petition a 20th-century princess and unofficial 'saint'. (P)

Pilgrimage

'A sense of the mystical is waiting to be discovered in destinations of pilgrimage. Travel to sacred places is, after all, the world's oldest form of tourism.'

The Witness Cairn at Whithorn commemorates St Ninian's arrival from Ireland in AD397 while present-day pilgrims place stones for lost loved ones. (KB)

Pilgrims pray to St Winefride at Holywell while abandoned crutches are displayed as evidence of miraculous curings. (both MS)

Shree Sanatan Mandir is a centre of worship for thousands of Leicester's Hindus. (MS)

Central and eastern England

'Sites saturated with spiritual yearning are scattered across this region.'

The saintly Bishop Hugh oversaw reconstruction of Lincoln Cathedral, Britain's third largest. (BL/A)

Hand-carved sandstone pillars were transported from Rajasthan to the Jain Temple in Leicester. (MS)

Dragon Hill, below the Uffington White Horse, site of St George's legendary heroics. (W/D)

Poet and mystic T S Eliot was moved to transcendence at Little Gidding which is still a pilgrimage site to this day. (S&J/A)

Myths, legends and a powerful aura attend Oxfordshire's Rollright Stones. Legend has it that a king (pictured here) and his knights were turned to stone by a mischief-making witch. (P)

The crucifixion of St Andrew on a diagonal cross inspired the Scottish Saltire. (WC)

St Etheldreda attracted multitudes to her shrine at Ely. (WC)

Saints

'Tombs of saints and martyrs have always had the power to draw pilgrims.'

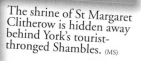

The shrine of St Margaret Clitherow is hidden away behind York's tourist-thronged Shambles. (MS)

The spirit of Thomas Becket remains palpable in the cathedral where he was murdered. (HH)

Modern pilgrims place doves at the feet of St Aidan's statue in the ruins of Lindisfarne Priory. (P)

between New Pitsligo and Strichen; the stag from the A92 just north of New Leeds.

The Kilburn Horse

Yorkshire's only white horse was cut into the Hambledon Hills north of York in 1857, near the village of Kilburn, and whitened with lime. At more than 300ft long, the Kilburn Horse is visible from several miles of the A19, south of Thirsk towards York.

The Whiteleaf and Bledlow Crosses

A white cross 246ft high is cut into a steep Chilterns escarpment on Whiteleaf Hill in Buckinghamshire, about a mile northeast of Princes Risborough. A few miles southwest a similar cross is cut into Bledlow Ridge. The origins of both remain mysterious, with medieval monks and Cromwellian troops prominent on the list of suspected artists. For Whiteleaf Hill take the A4010 southwards from Aylesbury and turn left at Monks Risborough. For the Bledlow Cross take the B4009 towards Chinnor; the cross is on the hillside to the left.

20th-century carvings

More recent times have seen a blossoming of new ideas for chalk carvings, such as the **crown** cut in 1902 just east of Wye on the Kent North Downs to mark the coronation of King Edward VII. Although this was a year before the dawn of aviation, it is nevertheless one of several best appreciated from the air. Another, much more aptly, is the **aeroplane** which was cut into the chalk below the north side of Dover Castle after Louis Blériot's cross-Channel flight in 1909. The 240ft-long **Kiwi** bird covering Brecon Hill, near Bulford on Salisbury Plain was cut by New Zealander troops during World War I. Of a similar age are **military badges** cut into the downs at Fovant, Wiltshire and visible from the A30.

The largest British hill figure of all is a 600ft lion carved in 1933 into the hillside at Whipsnade Wild Animal Park in Bedfordshire.

They are '**The King's Men**', tricked and turned to stone by a witch because their regal master had ambitions to conqueror all of England.

Said the witch, '*Seven long strides thou shalt take, and if Long Compton thou canst see, King of England thou shalt be!*'

The king's band of knights huddled into a circle to discuss the challenge, while the king himself fell into the trap of taking seven paces as commanded, and placing himself at the foot of a mound which blocked his view of Long Compton

'*As Long Compton thou canst not see, King of England thou shalt not be! Thou and thy men hoar stones shall be, And myself an elder tree!*' cackled the hag. Then she turned the lot of them to stone, but before taking the form of an elder, she was set upon by four of the knights who had not been part of the original huddle. In the *mêlée* they also became petrified.

The spring where they drink, those knights on the nights when the spell is temporarily broken, is at nearby Little Rollright Spinney. But anybody who witnesses them doing so, will die or go mad. Other legends have it that a terrible fate lies in wait for anybody who tries to move, or in any way damages, the stones. There is a story about a man from a nearby village who chipped a bit off one of the stones, and returned to his cart to find that the wheels were immovably locked. This may not sound too terrible in the big scheme of things; however, another local chap – a young soldier during the time of the British Raj – took a chip of one of the stones with him to India. On arrival he promptly died of typhoid. So beware!

An alternative version of the legend insists that anyone who cuts a flower from the witch-elder will be stained with her blood. Another has the stones not drinking, but joining hands and dancing at the witching hour. Other accounts reckon that one day the spell will be broken for good and that the whole pack of them, king and all, will come back to life and continue their conquest of Britain.

A fact not in dispute is that nowhere in England between Cumbria and Wiltshire is there anything like this complex of oolitic limestone megaliths near Long Compton and Chipping Norton in Oxfordshire, near the county's border with Warwickshire. Broadly, the Rollright Stones consists

of 'The King's Men' stone circle; **'The King's Stone'**, a nearby single monolith just across a lane; and about 40m away the remains of a burial chamber guarded by four standing stones known as **'The Whispering Knights'**.

From the lay-by on the lane between the A44 and the A3400 I noticed first the King Stone, its rather odd, top-heavy shape making it appear likely to topple over. However, considering it has been there since between 1800 and 1500BC, when it was probably first erected as a marker stone for a Bronze Age burial site, this is actually rather unlikely. About 8ft tall, it is protected by a circle of iron railings, and decidedly does not enjoy a view of Long Compton.

'The King's Men', back across the road, is a monument on a much greater scale. I approached through a turnstile in the hedgerow said to contain the witch-elder. There seemed to be plenty of elders among the hawthorns and brambles, so it was hard to know which one it was that would bleed if cut while in bloom. Next to the information board there is an 'honesty box' requesting donations of £1 per visitor.

At the entrance to the circle is a pair of stone portals which have been identified as an astronomical 'sightline' aligned with the rising moon at midsummer. Then there you are, astonishingly, in the very monument where rites which we really know very little about, were first performed at least 4,000 years ago.

Reaching the closely spaced, almost perfect circle about 30m across, what struck me most was how delightfully free of officialdom they are. The stones are weathered and hacked at by centuries of passers-by who – despite the foreboding legends – believed that a chipping would act as an amulet. '*Corroded like worm-eaten wood, by the harsh jaws of time*', was how the 18th-century antiquarian William Stukely saw them.

A couple of my fellow visitors were attempting to count the stones because, in common with other circles such as Long Meg and her Daughters in Cumbria (see page 126), one of their tricks is to defy enumeration. I made it 77, but by the time I got to the end I could not remember whether I had included the two entrance portals; then, before I could start again I was distracted by the arrival of a tall woman with purple hair and a pair of wire coat-hangers straightened into divining rods. In this strange environment of warped myths, legends and strange energies, it somehow did not seem the slightest bit odd that she should be following their weaving directions.

The forceful aura of this place remained palpable as I followed the grassy path at the edge of a ploughed field, leading to the tight cluster of four upright and one fallen stone. These are that band of the king's followers petrified as 'The Whispering Knights'. In fact, archaeological evidence points to this monument being older than either 'The King's Men' or 'The King's Stone'. They are part of a Neolithic long barrow about 5,000 years old, of which the lone fallen pillar was probably the capstone. On the other hand, one glance at this huddle, now rather cruelly corralled by some modern railings, does seem to substantiate the idea of a group leaning conspiratorially inwards.

Getting there

The Rollright Stones are located 3½ miles northwest of Chipping Norton in Oxford-shire, on a minor road between the A34 and A44 (closest to the A34). From either road, turn at a sign for the Rollrights. Park along a signposted lay-by and enter via a path that leads past the small warden's hut.

Where to stay and eat

The Falkland Arms Chipping Norton OX7 4DB ☎ 01608 683653
www.falklandarms.org.uk. An old Cotswolds inn with 5 rooms and a sunny beer garden.

The Fox Hotel Market Pl, Chipping Norton OX7 5DD ☎ 01608 642658
www.thefoxatchippy.co.uk. An enticing 16th-century inn with pub-style bar and contemporary restaurant.

The Red Lion Inn Main St, Long Compton CV36 5JS ✆ 01608 684221
🖢 www.redlion-longcompton.co.uk. A lovely old pub with rooms and a good-
value restaurant. Roaring log fires in winter.

Tourist information
Chipping Norton Tourist Information Centre The Guildhall, Chipping Norton
OX7 5NJ ✆ 01608 644379 🖢 www.chippingnorton.net.

⑤ Little Gidding
The Church of St John, Little Gidding, Huntingdon PE28 5NX ✆ 01832 293417
🖢 www.littlegiddingchurch.org.uk. Free access.
This tiny hamlet secluded in the Cambridgeshire countryside can be pretty
hard to find. Nevertheless, a steady stream of 'pilgrims', as quite a few people
describe themselves in the visitors' book, are drawn to Little Gidding's utterly
unforgettable little **St John's Church** next to a red brick manor house and a
deep, shaded pond.

On a misty autumn morning I parked between the church and the house, at
the same time as three Episcopalian couples from Topeka, Kansas – a US state
bordering Missouri, birthplace of T S Eliot. 'Little Gidding' is the title of the
last of Eliot's *Four Quartets* which he published in 1942, and it is the intense,
mystical and uplifting verse by the 20th-century American poet, that entices
so many people here.

So, what was it about Eliot and this far-flung little church – more of a chapel,
really? It must have been some extraordinary, transcendental happening that
moved him to begin the second stanza with these words:

> *If you came this way,*
> *Taking any route, starting from anywhere,*
> *At any time or at any season,*
> *It would always be the same: you would have to put off*
> *Sense and notion. You are not here to verify,*
> *Instruct yourself, or inform curiosity*
> *Or carry report. You are here to kneel*
> *Where prayer has been valid.*

And in direct consequence of these words, an eclectic assemblage of people,
from across a wide spiritual spectrum, do make their way to Little Gidding.
They start from anywhere and (unless they have a better satnav than mine)
take any route, particularly over the last few miles.

According to Eliot's biographer, Peter Ackroyd, the poet and mystic first
came to Little Gidding on a bright spring day in 1936. An ancestor of his
hailed from a nearby village which may be one reason why he was familiar with
the area. He was also an honorary fellow of Magdalene College, Cambridge.

But the initial allure for Eliot was doubtless his interest in Nicholas Ferrar, the scholar, parliamentarian, traveller, businessman, and partner in the Virginia Company which was established in the American colony in 1607.

A combination of factors, including financial disasters and an outbreak of the plague in London, seem to have been the cause of Ferrar leaving the capital with his extended family, a community of about 30 people. They settled in Little Gidding where Ferrar bought the manor house but otherwise renounced worldliness in favour of godliness. Ferrar became a Church of England deacon and, with various members of his family, turned part of the manor into an almshouse, started a school, and restored the church which was abandoned and being used as a barn. They founded a highly unusual community whose fame for prayer, craftsmanship, spiritual healing, compassion and sanctity spread throughout England. Word of the works going on in Little Gidding reached King Charles I who visited the village and demanded that Ferrar make him copies of the *Gospel Harmonies* – a form of cutting and pasting of gospel lines to create an easily digestible narrative – that Ferrar had devised.

Ferrar died in 1637. However, in May 1646 as the English Civil War raged and atrocities were being committed across the land, the king returned to Little Gidding in secret. Risking his own life, Nicholas's brother, John Ferrar, hid the king from the Cromwellian forces after the Battle of Naseby before he moved northwards in the ultimately unsuccessful game of cat and mouse that ended on the scaffold at Whitehall. Later that year Cromwellian soldiers came to the village to ransack and deface the chapel in revenge.

'If you came at night like a broken king', wrote T S Eliot in the second stanza of 'Little Gidding', clearly referring to the royal visit two years before Charles's bloody end. The year of his writing was 1941, after he had himself witnessed the horrifying effects of human brutality, while serving as an air-raid warden in Blitz-ravaged London. Perhaps he saw echoes in World War II of the vengeful violence and destruction by Cromwellian troops of Ferrar's enlightened religious experiment at Little Gidding.

The grassy field below the manor house is still known as King's Close in honour of Charles's connection. The churchyard is strewn with cherry trees, crosses and gravestones, some broken, while Nicholas Ferrar's flat-topped 'altar tomb' is immediately in front of the church entrance. The stone slabs leading up to the church door are the tombstones of members of the extended Ferrar family who constituted the Little Gidding community. Eliot wrote:

They can tell you, being dead: the communication
of the dead is tongued with fire beyond the language of the living

The interior is simple. There is no electricity, only candles. There are some stained-glass windows dedicated to Charles Ferrar and to King Charles I. A chandelier hangs over the chancel where Eliot knelt. He described it as the *'intersection of the timeless moment'* suggesting that in this place he had touched a state of consciousness transcending time. He wrote of being divested of the characteristics of family, personality and reputation which identified him with the world.

Just as the facts of Eliot's visits here can be known but not experienced, so there is no way of understanding what it was about this place that moved him to such transcendence, and to pen 'Little Gidding' as the last words of poetry he published, perhaps the last he wrote. However, the power to draw people from Topeka, Kansas and beyond, lies in the mystery of his solitude at this sacred place.

Getting there

Little Gidding is only minutes from junction 15 of the A1(M). In Great Gidding, take the turning east by the Fox and Hounds pub along Mill Lane (signposted Little Gidding).

Where to stay and eat

Ferrar House Little Gidding PE28 5RJ ✆ 01832 293383 🖱 www.ferrarhouse. co.uk. A small retreat centre opposite the church, offering accommodation and meals.

Fox and Hounds 80 Main St, Great Gidding PE28 5NU ✆ 01832 293298. Traditional pub serving good bar snacks.

The Old Bridge 1 High St, Huntingdon PE29 3TQ ✆ 01480 424300 🖱 www.huntsbridge.com. An atmospheric townhouse hotel by a medieval bridge over the Ouse. Superb restaurant offing modern twists on traditional dishes, and an extensive list of wines for tasting.

Tourist information

Huntingdon Tourist Information Centre The Library, Princes St, Huntingdon PE18 6PH ✆ 01480 388588 🖱 www.ukinformationcentre.com.

⑥ Ely

Staggeringly in scale and incomparable in its ship-like shape, the **Cathedral of Ely** rose out of the eerie Fenland in a scene of drama that made my jaw drop. How on earth could it be that a small town in the emptiness of East Anglia is dominated by such an enormous and dazzling work of architecture?

The answer is easily traced to one woman, the Saxon St Etheldreda. And Ely's failure ever to burgeon into a sizeable city is explained by the fact that until the draining of the Fens in the 17th century it was an island, a hump of clay slightly raised above the River Ouse and its marshy surroundings. Rather like the Isle of Avalon, (also known as Glastonbury, see page 55) it was accessible only by boat, although a causeway was built to help pilgrims reach Ely in the

Middle Ages. The name is said to mean 'Eel Island' after the abundance of the snake-like fish in the waterways and marshes. At one time, the monks and nuns of Ely used eels as a currency to pay their taxes to the crown.

Driving across Cambridgeshire towards my looming, tower-crowned target, the drainage canals and watery meadows still looked plausibly eely. The cathedral's aspect changed with the angle of my approach, increasingly looking as if it was afloat. It was obvious why it has long been known as the 'Ship of the Fens'.

Ely, the city of some 15,000 souls, is a huddle of medieval streets lined with half-timbered tearooms and antique shops, plus some fine Georgian façades along walkways beside the River Ouse. It would be just one more rather charming, small Fenland town, were it not for the all-pervasive presence of the cathedral, and the resonant history it represents.

Ely Cathedral

Ely CB7 4DL ☎ 01353 667735 🖰 www.elycathedral.org.

The twin monasteries flourished until 869, when waves of marauding Danes swept through East Anglia in their customary orgies of rape and pillage. Many of Ely's monks and nuns were slaughtered, while the remainder fled for their lives as buildings were destroyed by fire. However, the following century saw a revival in monasticism when a new (monks-only) Benedictine monastery and abbey church were rebuilt on the Saxon ruins under the patronage of the Bishop of Winchester. There are records of King Canute, the Danish-born English King, visiting Ely Abbey and commenting on the beauty of its music.

Ely was one of the last pockets of resistance to the Normans, holding out against the invasion till 1070 under Hereward the Wake. Soon after this, England's new rulers took over the isle and the monastery. In 1083 work began on the church, which became a cathedral on its completion in 1189. Some of the crowning glories, however, are Gothic additions. The **Lady Chapel**, for example, is the largest of its kind anywhere in Britain; a separate building joined by a cloister, it was completed in 1349 during a period of intense devotion to the cult of the Virgin Mary. Etheldreda, however, eclipsed even the Mother of God with huge numbers of medieval pilgrims making the journey to Ely to pray at her shrine.

Henry VIII's Dissolution of Monasteries in 1539 was the end of monasticism at Ely, but like many others (and unlike the monasteries which were not also the seats of bishops) the cathedral survived with a handful of monks remaining to form the new Dean and Chapter. Statues of saints, particularly those of the Virgin Mary and others in the Lady Chapel, were decapitated. Etheldreda's shrine was desecrated.

St Etheldreda

Etheldreda (also referred to variously as Æthelthryth, Ethelthrith or Audrey) was born in AD630, one of King Anna of East Anglia's four daughters. This somewhat effeminate-sounding monarch was in truth a powerful warrior. He fought battles with the Kingdom Mercia, converted to Christianity and was described by the Venerable Bede as 'an excellent man'.

Accordingly, Princess Etheldreda and her three sisters were brought up in a pious household. From an early age Etheldreda resolved to take monastic vows and enter a convent. However, politics and peacemaking required her to marry neighbouring King Ecgfrith of Northumbria, which she agreed to on condition that she be allowed to keep her vow of perpetual virginity and live as a nun. Accounts vary about how this arrangement played out, but one of the more generally accepted is that her husband complied for the first 12 years.

However, in 672, following repeated attempts to persuade her to leave her cloistered life, his self-restraint failed him and King Ecgfrith tried to kidnap his wife.

With a few loyal nuns Etheldreda fled to Ely, the island that had been her dowry. Here she established a double monastery – one for monks, another for nuns – and became the first abbess of the latter in 673. She had built a magnificent church on the foundations of an earlier one founded by St Augustine that had been destroyed by war. There are records of extensive lands and wealth attached to the convent, presumably in consequence of Etheldreda's royal connections. And yet, despite these connections she seems to have been quite a radical, setting free all the feudal serfs within her fiefdom, while herself living a life of austerity and self-denial.

After her death from a huge and unsightly tumour on the neck in 679, word of Etheldreda's holiness spread and a cult of devotion to her rapidly took hold. People made journeys to Ely to ask for her intercession with God; to pray for healing; to ask forgiveness for sins; to seek God's guidance; and to give thanks for prayers answered.

Clues to the former importance of Etheldreda's shrine remain. A Gothic extension round the choir was added in the 13th century, creating an ambulatory for pilgrims to reach the shrine without disturbing the monks in the choir, and enlarging the area around it.

The sole fragment surviving from the Saxon period is **Ovin's stone**, the base of an 8th-century memorial cross in the south aisle of the nave; there is no record of who Ovin was, though the inscription translates as, 'To Ovin – give your light, O Lord and rest Amen.'

There is a small chapel dedicated to St Etheldreda in a quiet corner at the far east end of the cathedral, with a rack of votive candles burning in front of a modern statue of her. The cathedral official leaflet and map guides visitors to

Fifteen years after her death it was decided, by popular demand, to remove her remains from their simple grave to the more fitting tomb in the abbey which was to become her shrine.

Etheldreda's body was exhumed and, in evident confirmation of her saintliness, was found to be in a perfect state of preservation according to witnesses including her physician Cynefrid. Furthermore, the wound to her neck where Cynefrid himself had cut out the tumour was healed. More miraculously still, the next time her remains were disturbed – 450 years later by Norman architects as they began work on the present Ely Cathedral – they were reported to be still incorrupt. The Normans built a new shrine to Etheldreda behind the high altar, centred on a tomb in which the remains of her sisters, saints Sexburga and Withburga, and her niece Erminilda were also interred.

Meanwhile, the story surrounding Etheldreda's neck became a central feature of her cult. While alive she had accepted her terrible tumour as a divine punishment for the vanity of her younger days when she had loved to wear necklaces. But in death the healing of the wound was proof of the exalted state she enjoyed in heaven, in consequence of her later purity and self-denial. Necklaces became the enduring symbol of devotion to Etheldreda, or 'St Audrey' as she had been become by medieval times.

Nobody knows for sure what happened to Etheldreda's remains after the desecration of her shrine during the Dissolution of the Monasteries (see below), though it is claimed by some that a jewelled casket at the Roman Catholic St Etheldreda Church at Ely Place in London (where the bishops of Ely formerly had their London residence) contains one of her hands.

Even after the Reformation, an annual 'St Audrey's Fair' continued to be held in Ely on her feast day, 17 October, at which necklaces, neckerchiefs and later other silk or lace were sold. Over the years these became cheap and of poor quality, hence 'St Audrey' silk and lace became contracted to 'tawdry'. Alas, poor Etheldreda. After a life of chastity, self-denial, austerity and humanitarian works, her linguistic legacy is a by-word for showy tastelessness!

this place, suggesting that they may wish to, 'think about what you are seeking from God today.'

Curiously, though, the same official literature makes no mention of the more poignant memorial to the woman but for whom there would be no cathedral here at all. '*Here stood the shrine of Etheldreda, Saint and Queen, who founded this house in AD673*' reads the inscription on a slab of black slate behind the choir, guarded by four large candles mounted on tripods. Here I met a woman wearing a clerical collar who, after we had both stood in silence for a while, murmured to me, 'You know, Etheldreda held a higher position in the church than any woman in England does today. So why are we getting our knickers in such a twist about Church of England women bishops?'

Getting there

Ely is on the A10, 13 miles north of Cambridge. As a major **rail** junction, Ely can be reached by direct services from many places including London King's Cross, Liverpool and Cambridge.

Where to stay and eat

Cathedral House 17 St Mary's St, CB7 4ER ☎ 01353 662124 ☏ www.cathedralhouse.co.uk. Small, delightful B&B a stone's throw from the cathedral.

Riverside Inn 8 Annesdale, CB7 4BN ☎ 01353 661677 ☏ www.riversideinn-ely. co.uk. An elegant Victorian townhouse on the Ouse. Rooms with river views.

The Boathouse 5–5a Annesdale, CB7 4BN ☎ 01353 664388 ☏ www.theboat houseely.co.uk. Some of the finest food in Ely, in a magical setting on the Ouse.

Tourist information

Ely Tourist Information Centre Oliver Cromwell's House, 29 St Mary's St, CB7 4HF ☎ 01353 662062 ☏ http://visitely.eastcambs.gov.uk/tic/contact-us.

⑦ Walsingham

This flinty, far-flung village of half-timbered medieval cottages, five miles from the north Norfolk coast, holds the power to astonish in ways unlike any other sacred place in Britain.

Over the centuries leading to the Reformation, the **shrine** at Walsingham was on a par with that of Thomas Becket at Canterbury (see page 25). For this was the greatest Marian shrine in medieval Christendom, the Lourdes of its time. Millions made pilgrimages to 'England's Nazareth' for the miracles that took place at the 'Holy House', a replica of the house at Nazareth where the archangel Gabriel announced to the Virgin Mary that she had conceived. '*When you look in you would say it is the abode of saints, so brilliantly does it shine on all sides with gems, gold and silver*', noted the Dutch Renaissance scholar and writer Desiderius Erasmus after his visit in 1513. Little was Erasmus to know that Henry VIII's Dissolution was round the corner, and that within 25 years the shrine would be desecrated and Walsingham abandoned as a place of pilgrimage.

The truly astonishing chapter in this story, however, was still to come. I refer to the 20th-century regeneration of Walsingham as a sacred place with the magnetism to attract pilgrims in huge numbers. Yet, as a place of pilgrimage it bears painful scars from the violation that took place in 1538. I am not referring to the solitary arch, which is just about all that remains of the great priory which grew up around the medieval shrine. I mean the fact that today there are two Shrines of Our Lady of Walsingham in the town. One is Anglican, the other Roman Catholic.

History and legend

The story starts in 1061 with the Lady of the Manor of Little Walsingham, Richeldis de Faverches, praying that she might undertake some special work in honour of the Virgin Mary. The prayer was answered through Mary appearing to her in a vision. Richeldis was whisked away in spirit to Nazareth, shown the house where the Annunciation occurred, and commanded to build its precise replica in her home village, to serve as a perpetual memorial of the miracle of Mary's conception. The vision was repeated twice more, lest any detail of the house should escape her memory.

Taking craftsmen with her, Richeldis set about looking for a place to carry out the Virgin's command and observed, in a meadow just outside the village, a rectangle next to a spring where the dew had left dry a rectangular space. As instructed, she had the replica built. William of Worcester, on pilgrimage some centuries later, recorded it as being '*7 yards 30 inches long and 4 yards 10 inches wide*'.

Snippets of precision such as this aside, historical facts about the intervening centuries are sketchy. However, it is known that after Richeldis's time the 'Holy House' came into the care of the Augustinian Canons, a monastic order who were given papal approval to build a priory on the site. Walsingham's reputation was mushrooming, with bountiful offerings left before the Virgin's image and numerous miraculous healings and other works of wonder attributed to her. The shrine's allure gained a further fillip with the gift, from a crusader back from the Holy Land, of a phial of 'Mary's milk' – in fact, quite likely it was a solution of chalk dust from the floor of a Bethlehem grotto known as the 'Cave of Our Lady's Milk'.

Medieval pilgrims came from across Europe to 'England's Nazareth', while the country as a whole became known as the 'Dowry of Mary' when Richard II 'presented' his Kingdom to her in thanksgiving for the grace she had bestowed on Walsingham. The Milky Way became known as 'The Walsingham Way'; in addition to the obvious association with Mary's motherhood, it is easy to picture the starry road of our galaxy guiding pilgrims on their way. Less predictably, the favour of the Virgin was also particularly sought by lovers. In an early, anonymous ballad consisting of questions and answers, a love-struck pilgrim plaintively appeals to the Virgin:

As you came from the holy land
Of Walsingham,
Met you with my true love
By the way you came?

To which the Virgin replies assuringly:

Such a one did I meet, good sir,
With angel-like face;

*Who like a queen did appear
In her gait, in her grace.*

Kings and queens also made the pilgrimage. In fact, every monarch from Henry III (in 1226) visited the shrine, many of them several times during their reigns. The prize for persistent pilgrimage probably goes to Edward I who is recorded as having come at least 12 times. Henry VIII, the last English monarch seen in Walsingham, was a particular devotee having prayed here for the health of his infant son Prince Henry, by his first wife Catherine of Aragon. How differently the history of England might have turned out had this prayer been answered.

After Henry VIII's marriage to Anne Boleyn, Walsingham Priory was one of the first religious houses to sign the Oath of Supremacy recognising Henry as the head of the church. Dissenters, including sub-Prior Nicholas Mileham were hung, drawn and quartered. The king's commissioners sacked the priory church and smashed the 'Holy House' to smithereens. The wooden image of the Virgin Mary was taken to Chelsea and ceremonially burned along with other statues, in the presence of Thomas Cromwell, the king's chief minister.

However, despite the desecration and closure of the shrine, belief in the sacredness of 'England's Nazareth' was never completely stamped out. Not quite. A trickle of pilgrims still made their way to Walsingham, including Elizabeth I in 1578; and John Wesley who came in 1781 to preach in the Methodist chapel and surprised many in his congregation by lamenting the shrine's destruction.

But by the end of the 19th century it would have been hard to make out even the faintest embers still glowing of the flames which had once lit up one of the greatest shrines in Christendom. This is why it is so remarkable that – on the eve of a century that was to witness a dramatic decline in religious observance and the corresponding rise of secularism – Walsingham was on the cusp of an extraordinary revival as a place of pilgrimage. The rebirth was to take the form of a pair of parallel impulses, fuelled by adherents of the Roman Catholic Church on the one hand, and the Anglican on the other. The consequence is that today Our Lady has two shines dedicated to her in Walsingham.

The Slipper Chapel and the Roman Catholic Shrine

Roman Catholic National Shrine of Our Lady, Houghton St Giles, Walsingham NR22 6AL ☎ 01328 820495 🖰 www.walsingham.org.uk. Free access.

In Walsingham's medieval heyday, pilgrims arrived from every direction. There were inns along the main routes and, as with the paths to Canterbury, chapels where prayers would be offered. Pilgrimage was, after all, as much about the journey as the destination. The last of these was the alluring little '**Slipper Chapel**', built in the 14th century at Houghton St Giles a mile

from Walsingham. Here, penitents would slip off their shoes so as to walk the final winding stretch of the road barefoot.

The first pilgrimage of Walsingham's modern era was to the Slipper Chapel. Accordingly I too began my visit at Houghton St Giles, a hamlet rather beautifully set in low, wooded hills. The setting – in this county famed for its flatness – was my first surprise.

After the Reformation, the chapel was abandoned and for centuries used as a barn and cowshed. In 1896 it was bought by Charlotte Pearson Boyd, a pious lady who had converted to Catholicism. With the approval of Pope Leo XIII, she placed a statue blessed by him in the now-restored chapel, and the following year a group of Catholics made the first public pilgrimage to the chapel and to the abbey ruins. Other pilgrimages followed, numbers grew, and in August 1934 Cardinal Francis Bourne led a pilgrimage of the bishops of England and Wales plus some 10,000 others to the Slipper Chapel. Mass was celebrated here for the first time since the Reformation and the cardinal declared the chapel to be the National Shrine of England.

The idea of tens of thousands of people converging here seemed to me a rather bizarre notion, as Shrine Manager Tim McDonald led me across the cloistered area which joins the building of the modern shrine complex, to the tiny Slipper Chapel. At my estimation, 30 people in here would be a squash. There is an unremarkable altar and some stained-glass windows, but it is the striking deep blue, red and gold of the statue of Mary with the infant Christ that drew my eye. It reminded me of a god in a Hindu temple. Tim told me: 'When John Paul II came to Britain in 1982, the statue was taken to Wembley. The pope ordered it to be placed on the altar during the mass, which is completely out of order, canonically speaking. But hey, if you are the pope you can do what you like!'

Tim turned out to be a fountain of anecdotes. He had, for example, a candidate other than the obvious for why the chapel where pilgrims left their footwear is so named. The medieval word *slipe*, apparently meant 'next to' and this was the chapel next to Walsingham. More intriguingly, he told me about a recent Australian visitor, who had read in his great-grandparents' diaries of their having prayed at the 'holy barn at Walsingham' in the mid-18th century before emigrating down under. So here, claimed Tim, was written evidence substantiating folk-tales of people asking the local farmer if they could pray in the disused Slipper Chapel.

The shrine complex includes a well of holy water and font, a shop, a café and a church whose doors behind the altar can open out on to the central courtyard where at times hundreds gather for mass. This central area is enclosed within a square punctuated with the 14 Stations of the Cross, each station marked with a giant crucifix. These had arrived at the shrine in 1948, after being carried across England from different starting points, by 14 groups of World War II servicemen in a mass pilgrimage of Peace, Penance and Prayer.

The shrine was quiet during my late-autumn mid-week visit, with perhaps a dozen or so people milling around. But Tim McDonald was keen to emphasise that they host upwards of 80,000 pilgrims a year. Many come in busloads from their parishes, particularly around the three main feast days associated with Mary: The Mystery of the Annunciation (25 March), the Feast of the Assumption (15 August), and the Feast of Our Lady of Walsingham (24 September).

There are thousands-strong youth groups in summer, annual pilgrimages by Britain's Polish community, and Caribbean Catholics who come with steel bands. African drums resonate across north Norfolk during the annual Nigerian and Ghanaian pilgrimages. But for sheer numbers, none of these match the annual summer gathering here of about 7,000 Tamils of Indian and Sri Lankan origin. Mass in the Syro-Malabar rite (one of the Eastern churches in communion with Rome) takes about two-and-a-half hours.

I left the shrine via the Chapel of the Holy Ghost which is ablaze with votive candles placed here by pilgrims in such numbers that it takes shrine staff all year to get through them.

Little Walsingham and the Anglican Shrine

Anglican Shrine of Our Lady of Walsingham, The College, Knight St, NR22 6EF
📞 01328 820255 🖥 www.walsingham.org.uk. Free access.

The walk into the small town centre from the Slipper Chapel took me past pubs, the post office, sandwich bars and gift shops. Rosaries and statues are for sale, but there is no parallel with the brash consumerism which attends Marian shrines such as Lourdes, or Fatima in Portugal. Or indeed with Walsingham as described by Erasmus with its charlatans '*peddling bottles of Mary's milk*' or scraps of '*Christ's robe*' to the gullible. Instead, this is a pilgrimage town firmly within the tradition of British understatement. Even the name contains one of those typically British contradictions: the village is 'Little Walsingham', as distinct from the tiny hamlet a mile on, 'Great Walsingham'. ('*So the last shall be first, and the first last*' Matthew 19:30.)

First impressions of the Anglican shrine complex, is of a slicker operation than the Catholics are putting on up at the Slipper Chapel. Visitors are greeted at a reception area where there are audio-visual displays and a little cinema showing, in the manner of a modern museum, a film about the shrine and its history.

To take up the 20th century thread, the key figure was Father Alfred Hope-Patten, appointed Vicar of Walsingham in 1921. An Anglo-Catholic by inclination, it was his vision to re-establish a shrine to Our Lady of Walsingham and to re-awaken the dormant tradition of pilgrimage in England. First, Hope-Patten found an old seal showing an image of the original shrine statue of the

Virgin, the one that was burnt at Chelsea; he had it copied as accurately as he could and placed the new figure in the parish church. From the very first night local people gathered around it asking Mary to pray for them.

Over the next ten years a trickle of pilgrims swelled to a torrent, for whom a hospice (meaning, in its original sense, 'a place of hospitality for pilgrims') was opened. Father Hope-Patten chose a spot next to a well to have a copy of the 'Holy House' built and had the statue of Mary moved there. Later encased within a much larger church, the 'Holy House' remains the inner sanctum of the new Shrine of Our Lady of Walsingham. Since then a large guesthouse, a refectory ('fully licensed', hooray!) and various other chapels have been added.

Before making my way to the 'Holy House', I walked the Serpentine Path through the shrine gardens which are landscaped around a raised 'Calvary' dramatically topped by a trio of crosses. I was on my way to meet Bishop Lindsay Urwin, the Shrine Director, and was burning to ask him what his views were about the denominational divide here at Walsingham. But, as if already sensing my disquiet, my host immediately brought the subject up himself.

'It is a searing wound that we have two shrines in Walsingham. God does not want two shrines, and I can tell you that Our Lady will not allow ecumenical divisions', said Bishop Lindsay. I had already discovered at the Catholic shrine, that a bit of formal ecumenical cooperation takes place: some shared services; a joint procession on the night before the Feast of the Assumption; and the two shrines' respective websites linked under a single URL. But that is not what Bishop Lindsay meant at all. Rather, he was referring to the fact that visitors to Walsingham, whether 'intentional pilgrims' or 'people who just find themselves here', make light of the distinction. They visit both shrines. (I note, however, that the Anglican shrine claims 300,000 pilgrims a year, more than three times that of their Catholic brethren.)

Bishop Lindsay continued, 'For many people, going on a pilgrimage is a sort of gentle protest against the secular world. In medieval times, making a pilgrimage was normal. Now it is to swim against the tide.' He regrets, however, that 'we are seen sometimes as more the destination than the journey. When this is the case we lose something.'

And then, matter-of-factly, Bishop Lindsay said: 'Some while ago I met a father and his daughter here at the shrine. The girl had had an incurable illness and was in hospital in a coma. Her priest had sent a petition to us asking for prayers for her. The girl emerged from her coma one day, and announced "I've been to Walsingham". As far as we know she had never even heard of Walsingham. Anyway, she was cured in defiance of all medical expectation and she and her father are devotees of the shrine.'

Before leaving, I walked over to the shrine church where the daily 'sprinkling' ceremony at which pilgrims are blessed with holy water at the well, was taking place. Then I entered the hushed, empty 'Holy House'.

'*Our Lady stands in the dark at the right side of the altar … a little image, remarkable neither for its size, material or workmanship*', wrote Erasmus after pausing for reflection at this spot, in 1513. His tone had certainly taken a turn for the more approving, after his less complimentary comments about the gold, silver and gems at the shrine, not to mention the hangers-on outside the gates, selling pious tat.

I have a feeling that the gentle sceptic Erasmus might have looked favourably on the shrine today. Certainly, this curious little chapel standing in the middle of the nave of the much larger Shrine Church is adorned with gilt, statuary, candles and other religious artefacts of a kind which would have puritans, then or now, throwing up their hands in horror. But I found a place glowing with peace and devotion, as the strains of *Ave Maria* wafted on the air.

Walsingham Abbey

Walsingham Abbey Grounds and Shirehall Museum, Common Pl, NR22 6BP
📞 01328 820510 🔗 www.walsinghamabbey.com.

In the centre of Little Walsingham there is an imperious gatehouse leading into the expansive grounds of Walsingham Abbey. This is the site of the original 'Holy House' destroyed at the Reformation, and the Augustinian priory and church which fell into ruin thereafter and was eventually almost entirely demolished. The ruins and surrounding farmland passed through various hands before it was acquired by the aristocratic Lee-Warner family who built a large country house on the estate in the early 18th century. Only since then has it been known as an 'abbey'.

The estate still belongs to the Lee-Warner's. The house is private, but the public can buy tickets to a small museum and to the grounds in which the ruins stand. All that remains of the great priory church is the east end, where a pair of tall towers are joined by an arch over what was once a vast stained-glass window. A plaque on the grass marks the '*site of the 11th-century shrine of the Holy House of Nazareth (excavated 1961).*'

The same excavation unearthed some remains of the refectory, crypt and monks' bathhouse. Many visitors to Walsingham complete their pilgrimage by wandering among these sad, lovely ruins, and ambling through the meadows and woods, and along the banks of the River Stiffkey in the 18-acre park.

Getting there

Little Walsingham is 27 miles northwest of Norwich, reached via the A1067 to Fakenham. The nearest main line **train** station is at Norwich and from here there are **buses** operated by Norfolk Green to Walsingham (*01553 776980; www.norfolkgreen.co.uk*).

Where to stay and eat

Elmham House Friday Market Pl, NR22 6DB 📞 01328 820217

www.walsingham.org.uk. This is the pilgrim guesthouse run by the Roman Catholic shine, though in Little Walsingham village rather than at Houghton St Giles. Inexpensive B&B accommodation, most with shared bathrooms.

The Anglican Shrine (see details above). A wide range of accommodation at or near the shrine, ranging from smart, spacious rooms with en-suite bathrooms, to dormitories. Reasonably priced food and drink, including wines and beers.

The Bull Inn Common Pl, NR22 6BP ☎ 01328 820333 www.walsinghambull. co.uk. A half-timbered 16th-century inn which has been hosting pilgrims since before the Reformation. Small, but deeply atmospheric rooms with low ceilings. Good pub food and local beers.

The Victoria at Holkham Park Rd, Holkham, Wells-next-the-Sea NR23 1RG ☎ 01328 711008. A delightful hotel and restaurant near the sea, 10 minutes' drive north of Little Walsingham. Excellent fresh fish.

Tourist information

Walsingham Tourist Information Centre Common Pl, NR22 6BP ☎ 01328 820510 www.allattractions.co.uk/attraction/15590. At the heart of the village, opposite the Anglican Shrine.

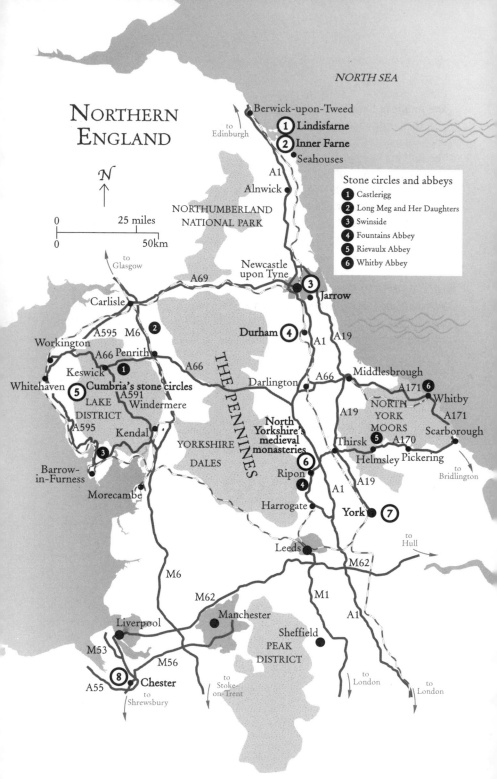

NORTHERN ENGLAND

NORTH SEA

to Edinburgh

Berwick-upon-Tweed

(1) **Lindisfarne**

(2) **Inner Farne**

Seahouses

A1

Alnwick

NORTHUMBERLAND NATIONAL PARK

N

| 0 | | 25 miles |
| 0 | | 50km |

to Glasgow

Newcastle upon Tyne

A69

(3)

Jarrow

Carlisle

A595   M6

(2)

Durham (4)

A1   A19

Workington

A66   Penrith

Keswick

Middlesbrough

A171 (6)

Whitby

Whitehaven

(1)

A66

Darlington

A66

NORTH YORK MOORS

A171

(5) **Cumbria's stone circles**

A591

LAKE DISTRICT

Windermere

A19

Scarborough

A595

Kendal

Thirsk (5)   A170

Helmsley   Pickering

YORKSHIRE DALES

North Yorkshire's medieval monasteries

(6)

Barrow-in-Furness

(3)

THE PENNINES

Ripon

(4)

to Bridlington

Morecambe

A1   A19

Harrogate

York (7)

to Hull

Leeds

M62

M6

M62

M1

A1

Manchester

Liverpool

Sheffield

PEAK DISTRICT

M53

M56

to Stoke-on-Trent

to London

to London

(8) **Chester**

A55

to Shrewsbury

Stone circles and abbeys

1 Castlerigg
2 Long Meg and Her Daughters
3 Swinside
4 Fountains Abbey
5 Rievaulx Abbey
6 Whitby Abbey

5. NORTHERN ENGLAND

A giant and strangely beautiful sculpture on an exposed hill appears fleetingly to road and rail passengers as they approach Tyneside. Contemporary it may be, but the *Angel of the North* opens its wings in embrace over landscapes and cities sculpted in all kinds of ways by the radical new religion that arrived from Iona in the 7th century. The Northumbrian saints succeeded in subduing the visceral violence between local kingdoms with, instead of weapons, extraordinary messages of pacifism, meekness, meditation and forgiveness. Today their cells, shrines and stomping grounds are sacred testaments to the monks' astonishing feats.

Further south in Yorkshire, monasticism was still alive and well 500 years later when monks with ideals similar to their Northumbrian predecessors sought far-flung refuges from worldly temptation; there is a tingling melancholy and hushed sanctity to the ruins of the great abbeys they raised. Meanwhile, across the Pennines lies the magical allure of Lakeland, where an innate sense of the sacred attends prehistoric stone circles abandoned in the watery fells.

① Lindisfarne (Holy Island)

Twice daily a narrow, mile-long neck of land sinks beneath the North Sea for five hours, uncoupling Lindisfarne (also known as Holy Island) from the Northumberland coast. You need to consult the tidal chart before choosing between two ways to the island (see below). Most visitors cross by car or walk along the three-mile cutlass-shaped causeway, at either end of which an alarming picture of an almost submerged vehicle illustrates a sign warning bluntly that, 'This Could Be You.'

The other option is the shorter '**Pilgrims' Route**' across the mudflats, marked by wooden stakes. This is the final leg of the 62-mile St Cuthbert's Way long-distance footpath starting at Melrose in the Scottish Borders. Barefoot and with boots laced together and hung round my neck, I tackled this squelching approach via what looked like an infinity of shiny chocolate pudding, but whose fetid odour mingled with a salty zephyr wafting off the sea.

The liquid call of countless curlews floated across the emptiness. Through binoculars I watched them dip their long, curved beaks into the mud, pulling out wriggling lugworms. The mud popped and whistled. As I progressed,

Lindisfarne's monolithic, castle-crowned rock encircled by sand dunes, green farmland and the silhouetted remains of a great priory, appeared out of the mist. There is a village of huddled white houses, a harbour, and rows of upturned boats with their hulls cut crosswise to make sheds for lobster pots and fishing tackle.

I arrived shortly before a single, shallow wave raced in, engulfing acre after bubbling acre, faster than most people can run. 'These Mudflats Disappear More Quickly Than You Would Believe Possible' that blunt sign might helpfully have explained.

Thank goodness for the tide. As the last crossing time approached, day visitors hurried to their cars to join a single-file migratory route back to the A1. Soon after, Lindisfarne turned back into an island and its singular atmosphere re-emerged. As my host on the island, Brother Damian Kirkpatrick put it, 'There is something holy about the ground, on an island that has produced so many saints. Here there is beauty, history, sanctity. Lindisfarne is St Aidan's island, St Cuthbert's island. It is the cradle of Christianity in England.'

Brother Damian is the vicar of St Mary's, Lindisfarne and also – unusually – an Anglican Franciscan friar. As such, he follows in a (much broken) tradition of monasticism on the island, stretching back nearly 1,500 years. I followed his brown habit and sandals through the priory ruins to the haunting statue – a sculpture really – of St Aidan gazing into the middle distance. Toy doves of peace and CND badges were among the offerings placed at his feet.

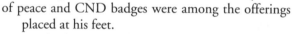

'Aidan was single-minded in living the gospel message through love. He is a role model for the 21st century', mused Brother Damian. 'For those who have a sense of the numinous, Lindisfarne is a splendid place.' But what about non-believers, I asked him. Does he feel that Lindisfarne's sense of the sacred rubs off on them? 'Well, love does not impose on where it is not wanted.'

History

In AD635 St Aidan, an Irish-born monk, was sent from St Columba's settlement on Iona (see page 181), to found a monastery on Lindisfarne. In the tradition of Celtic monasticism, the far-flung speck of land was to be his base for converting the powerful warrior heathens of Northumbria to an alien religion demanding peace and contemplation. The king of Northumbria at the time was St Oswald, who gave his blessing to the preaching of the gospel among his people.

Within a century, according to the Venerable Bede, the great chronicler of this era, *'many Northumbrians, both noble and simple, laid aside their weapons, preferring to take monastic vows rather than study the art of war.'*

The missionary work of Aidan's protégés, particularly sibling saints Cedd and Chad, carried the faith further afield into England. The holiness and miracle-working of Aidan's successor as Bishop of Lindisfarne, St Cuthbert, made him one of the most venerated saints in medieval England and the island a pilgrimage destination. During the late 7th or early 8th century, Eadfrith – and possibly other monks of Lindisfarne – produced the sublime 'illuminated' (ie: illustrated in minute and intricate detail) Latin gospels of Matthew, Mark, Luke and John, known as the *Lindisfarne Gospels*.

Was it the Christian message – and practice – of non-violence that left Lindisfarne defenseless against the marauding Vikings in the following century? The monastery was repeatedly attacked from 793 onwards, with monks butchered or captured for sale as slaves. In 875 they finally left, carrying with them the *Lindisfarne Gospels* (now in the British Museum) and the miraculously uncorrupted corpse of Cuthbert.

Monks returned to Lindisfarne in the 11th century, after the Norman Conquest. Benedictines from Durham Cathedral (see page 121) built the priory on the foundations of Aidan's original abbey, and stayed until 1536 when Henry VIII dissolved the monasteries. Later, in the 16th century, stones from the crumbling priory were taken to build Lindisfarne Castle as part of the war effort against the Scots. The castle was converted into a private residence in 1903.

In recent centuries the islanders have been fishermen and farmers. Nowadays there is a better living to be made in cafés and bed and breakfasts. The island is a centrepiece of Northumbrian tourism and draws throngs of visitors, along with pilgrims at the end of the St Cuthbert's Way long-distance footpath, and others seeking spiritual solace.

Lindisfarne Priory and museum

TD15 2RX ☎ 01289 389200 🖥 www.holy-island.info/englishheritage/lindisfarnepriory. The roofless ruins of pinkish sandstone walls, arches and windows are all that remain physically of the 1,000-year-old **priory**. Yet, so intense is the atmosphere here in the heart of the village that this should be a place to pause and reflect on the sacredness of Lindisfarne.

The very spot where St Cuthbert was buried for 11 years, before the monks of the first monastery carried him away in 875, is on the green turf at the heart of the ruins. And it was from his eventual resting place, Durham Cathedral, that Benedictine monks returned more than 200 years later. The priory was built in the mid-12th century, in a style strongly influenced by Durham. The famous 'rainbow arch' – a vault rib – is still intact and an example of the richly decorated style borrowed from the cathedral.

The small **Lindisfarne Priory Museum**, next to the ruins, has some relics of the original Celtic monastery, and a commendably approachable interpretative centre covers the life of St Cuthbert and the priory's history. Adjoining the priory ruins and museum (though not subject to the entry ticket) is the **church of St Mary the Virgin**. This parish church was also built by the monks in the 12th century, although since then it has been added to considerably. It was established on the site of St Aidan's original 635 wooden church and has been an Anglican parish church since the Reformation, and so survived the looting of the priory buildings to construct the castle.

The gaunt, but beautifully serene **statue of St Aidan** in the churchyard, by 20th-century sculptress Kathleen Parbury who is also buried here, is much visited by pilgrim devotees of the 7th-century saint.

Lindisfarne Heritage Centre

Marygate, TD15 2SD ☎ 01289 389004 ⧉ www.lindisfarne.org.uk/hicdt/museum.htm. This museum in Lindisfarne village, put together by islanders, gathers together various exhibitions charting the island's past, present and natural history. However, the main reason to visit is to see an electronic reproduction of the *Lindisfarne Gospels*, at the place where they were created 1,200 years ago.

In a wonderful coming together of ancient and modern, 40 of the most beautiful pages of the *Lindisfarne Gospels* are immaculately reproduced in electronic form. The exhibition is the creation of the British Museum (where the originals reside despite a campaign to have them relocated here or to Durham) and is operated by interactive electronic turning pages. These may not be the real thing, but as a means to appreciate the detail, artistry and consummate craftsmanship, they are even better.

The *Lindisfarne Gospels* – both the artwork and the lettering – are presumed to be the work of Eadfrith, a Bishop of Lindisfarne who died in 721. Writing and painting sacred texts was seen as a divine calling by Celtic monks. Each of the four Gospels opens with a decorative 'carpet page' (because they look like finely woven Persian rugs) and portrait of the Evangelist; these alone are considered to be among the greatest masterpieces of Anglo-Saxon and Celtic art.

Lindisfarne Castle

TD15 2SH ☎ 01289 389244 ⧉ www.nationaltrust.org.uk/main/w-lindisfarnecastle. The presence of a military fort on this sacred island where Celtic saints preached peace and pacifism as the essence of the Christian message, is an anomaly. Nevertheless, the rugged castle clinging to the summit of a sharp, cone-shaped rock thrusting up at the southeastern tip half-a-mile from Lindisfarne village, is the dominant feature on the Lindisfarne skyline.

The castle's very being speaks of the abandonment of peaceful monasticism in favour of war. The stones used in its construction were taken from the Benedictine priory in the 1550s, a few years after the monks were sent packing at the Dissolution. Its purpose was as a border fortress in the ongoing wars with Scots fought by the English Tudors. However, after the union of the two countries with the accession of James VI of Scotland to the English throne in 1603, its military usefulness declined.

Although the castle remained a garrison until the mid-18th century, it was eventually abandoned and remained uncared for until 1901 when it was bought by Edward Hudson, the magazine magnate and founder of *Country Life*. Hudson commissioned architect Edwin Lutyens to refurbish it in the then voguish Arts and Crafts style and turn it into a private, holiday residence. Since 1944 the castle has been in the care of The National Trust, along with the walled Gertrude Jekyll Garden and some 19th-century lime kilns in the grounds.

Lindisfarne National Nature Reserve

Free access.
As well as being a place of profound spiritual and historical significance, Lindisfarne and the connecting causeway, plus a stretch of adjoining Northumberland coast, are a designated National Nature Reserve. This is an area of ecologically important dunes, salt marshes and tidal mudflats; it teems with bird life, and is a habitat for common and grey seals.

To walk around the island's perimeter, or climb to the high ground and listen in solitude to the wind, the gulls and the waves breaking on the rocks, is to appreciate Lindisfarne's nature and sacredness as one. A highlight is the shore opposite the tiny St Cuthbert's Isle, where the saint used to retreat to meditate and commune with seals and seabirds.

Getting there

Lindisfarne is off the A1 between Berwick-upon-Tweed and Alnwick. There are car parks on the mainland, and on the island at the edge of the village. Check tide times for crossing on 🔗 www.lindisfarne.org.uk. The nearest **railway station** is Berwick-upon-Tweed, 10 miles north of the causeway. From here, Perryman's **buses** (*01289 308719; www.perrymansbuses.co.uk*) run south along the A1.

Where to stay and eat

Manor House Hotel TD15 2RX ☎ 01289 389207
🔗 www.manorhouselindisfarne.com. At the heart of Lindisfarne village, next to the priory ruins and with views of the castle. There are 10 double rooms, a bar, dining room and a garden where snacks are served.
Rose Villa TD15 2RZ ☎ 01289 389268. A simple, friendly, family B&B with 3 rooms; excellent value.
The Lindisfarne TD15 2SQ ☎ 01289 389273. Also has 10 rooms, with discounts for 3 nights or more.
The Pilgrims Coffee House Falkland House, TD15 2SJ ☎ 01289 389109
🔗 www.pilgrimscoffee.com. The unbeatable place for a light lunch – especially the garden on a sunny afternoon. Delicious homemade breads and cakes; young and trendy atmosphere. Aidan would approve.
The Ship Inn Marygate, TD15 2SJ ☎ 01289 389311

🍺 www.theshipinn-holyisland.co.uk. An 18th-century pub where islanders drink, with 4 guest bedrooms. Good bar food including locally caught fish.

Tourist information

There is no tourist information office on the island. For comprehensive information and listings, visit 🍺 www.lindisfarne.org.uk.

② The Farne Islands – Inner Farne

To follow the footsteps of St Cuthbert from Lindisfarne to Inner Farne, travel ten miles south down the coast to the fishing port and holiday village of Seahouses. In fine weather, boats leave daily to tour the Farne Islands, which lie between 1½ and five miles out into the North Sea.

The name Farne comes either from the Celtic *Fahren* meaning 'place of retreat', or from the Anglo-Saxon *Farena Ealande* meaning 'island of the pilgrims' depending on which scholarly authority you choose to believe. Both derivations, however, seem to augur a touch of sanctity.

There are between 15 and 28 Farnes, some sinking and re-emerging with the tide. The highest of these rise 100ft above sea level, their characteristic fluted stacks with angular corners looking as if they have been sliced off a bigger chunk of land. The archipelago is managed by the National Trust and inhabited by a few lighthouse keepers and wildlife wardens, who share the islands with hundreds of thousands of seabirds and several herds of grey seals.

Landing is permitted on only two of islands: **Staple**, a bird sanctuary where thousands of guillemots nest in the cliffs; and ten-acre **Inner Farne**, the largest, where St Cuthbert meditated alone in a cell for nine years.

Most tours from Seahouses allow about an hour on one of these islands, and a couple more weaving among the others. My boat, *Glad Tidings*, rounded the lighthouse on Longstone, one of the outermost islands, from where the young heroine Grace Darling, the lighthouse keeper's daughter famous throughout northeast England, rowed courageously to rescue the shipwrecked crew of the *Forfarshire* in 1838.

The birds are superabundant. Inner Farne, where we finally landed, has one of the largest colonies of puffins in the British Isles. There was no need for binoculars to watch the comical puffins, sleek razorbills, ugly herring gulls and crooning eider ducks still known in Northumbrian dialect as 'cuddy ducks' (Cuthbert's ducks) since the saint offered them sanctuary on his island, in what is sometimes taken as the world's first example of wildlife conservation.

The menacing, red-beaked Arctic terns appeared less welcoming. I saw one dive on an innocent visitor, a middle-aged woman who was clearly regarded as an intruder as she stepped ashore. Blood was drawn and the attack was successful in that she retreated angrily into St Cuthbert's Chapel to re-emerge, clutching a book to the top of her head, only when it was time to leave.

The chapel was built in the 14th century on the site where the saint meditated alone in his cell. However, amid a cacophony of seabirds and day trippers, it is hard to take oneself back to that age. It would be different, I felt, if you could spend a night alone there. A holy place it may be, on account of its sainted resident all those centuries ago, and the pilgrims that he drew.

But nevertheless, a later hermit on Inner Farne wrote about some of the malign spirits he had encountered, with which Cuthbert had also done battle, '*demons clad in cowls, and riding upon goats, black in complexion, short in stature, their countenances most hideous, their heads long*'.

'Living here is not like being a monk, let alone a hermit. For a start there are anything up to ten of us, including a lady or two quite often', Dave Steel, the head warden on Inner Farne, told me. 'We are all ornithologists, but seriously, this island certainly is a sacred place. From time to time I feel a presence … we all do, and it is a friendly presence. You'd have to spend a season here to understand, but anybody who does gets to know Cuthbert in a strange way, whatever their beliefs are.'

St Cuthbert and Inner Farne

St Aidan used to spend days meditating on Inner Farne, though the first recorded permanent resident in the Farne Islands was Cuthbert. He was the Prior (second in the monastic hierarchy) of Lindisfarne, with a reputation for devotion and sanctity, who longed for solitude and in AD676 was granted leave by the abbot to become a hermit.

At the age of 16, while he was a shepherd near Melrose (see page 202) in the Scottish Borders, Cuthbert had had a vision of St Aidan being carried to heaven. Nevertheless, he seems to have spent several years as a soldier before joining the monastic communities first of Melrose, then Ripon, before moving to Lindisfarne from where the austere rock of Inner Farne was visible on the horizon.

Cuthbert settled on Inner Farne, where he spent nine years living in a cell of wattle and thatch, sunken into the turf, with only the birds and seals for company. Here he listened to God and the sea and wrestled with demons. But in AD685 he was made Bishop of Lindisfarne, to where he reluctantly returned for a brief tenure. The following year he felt his death approaching, resigned his exalted position and returned to Inner Farne where he duly died.

After his burial on Lindisfarne, Cuthbert's tomb rapidly became a target for pilgrims as word of his miracle-working spread throughout Europe. Retreating from the invading Danes, his remains (miraculously uncorrupted) were carted off by monks first to Chester-le-Street, then to his old haunt, Ripon. On his final journey, his coffin grew unaccountably heavy as the monks rounded a rock on a bend in the River Wear as if to tell them that this place, Dunholme, was where he should rest. The place was, of course, Durham (see page 119).

Meanwhile, back on Inner Farne a succession of hermits took Cuthbert's lonesome place, before a community of ascetic monks built a monastery here which remained until the Dissolution in 1538. Pilgrims from around England and increasingly further afield made the voyage to seek his intercession. Parts of the monastery and its Pele tower survive today and are used as sleeping quarters for the National Trust wardens who now look after the place. St Cuthbert's chapel, on the site of his cell, was built by monks in the 14th century and restored in 1850 using – aptly – materials brought from Durham.

Getting there

Seahouses is on the coastal B1340, 6 miles from the parallel A1, about 10 miles south of the causeway to Lindisfarne. The nearest **railway station** is Chathill, 4 miles away, between Newcastle upon Tyne and Berwick-upon-Tweed. There are trains from Newcastle and Alnmouth. From Chathill there are **taxis**. Alternatively take the **bus** from Alnmouth station, operated by Arriva (*0871 200 22 33; www.arrivabus.co.uk*).

Farne Islands boat trips

There are several companies operating a variety of boat trips, among them:

Glad Tidings ☎ 01665 720308 🔗 www.farne-islands.com.
Golden Gate ☎ 01665 721210 🔗 www.farneislandsboattrips.co.uk.
St Cuthbert's Farne Island Boat Trips ☎ 01665 720388 🔗 www.farneislands.co.uk.

Where to stay and eat

Blacketts Restaurant 2–3 Lucker Rd, Bamburgh NE69 7BS ☎ 01668 214714 🔗 www.blackettsofbamburgh.co.uk. A popular little restaurant in Bamburgh village, specialising in simple dishes prepared with the freshest local produce.
Kingsway Guest House 19 King St, Seahouses NE68 7WX ☎ 01665 720621 🔗 www.kingsway-guesthouse.co.uk. A good value little guesthouse a few minutes' walk from the harbour.
Neptune Restaurant 3 Seafield Rd, Seahouses NE68 7SJ ☎ 01665 721310. Fabulous fresh fish and seafood, near the harbour where they are landed.
St Cuthbert's Hotel 192 Main St, Seahouses NE68 7UB ☎ 01665 720456 🔗 www.stcuthbertshouse.com. 6 beautifully renovated bedrooms in an 1810 former Presbyterian church, now a B&B.
Waren House Waren Mill, Bamburgh NE70 7EE ☎ 01668 214581 🔗 www.warenhousehotel.co.uk. A delightful, small hotel and restaurant in beautiful gardens at Belford just off the A1 about 3 miles from Seahouses.

Tourist information

Seahouses Tourist Information Centre Road Car Park, NE68 7SW
☎ 01665 720884 🖰 www.visitnorthumberland.com/site/seahouses.

③ Jarrow

Working-class heroics during the 1930s; and the life, some 13 centuries earlier, of a truly great Englishman. Here is a pair of unconnected motivations for modern pilgrimages to an industrial town on the River Tyne, I mused, while waiting for a South Shields-bound Tyne Metro train in Newcastle.

'No matter where I go in the world, pretty much everybody has heard of Jarrow, which is an amazing thing for a small town on Tyneside. It's either that genius Bede, or it's the marchers', said a fellow passenger, on her way home. Alighting at Bede station in Jarrow, I was confronted with redolences of both. Oil and gas storage tanks provided a backdrop of heavy industry on the short walk towards St Paul's Church, the adjoining ruined monastery, and Bede's World museum.

However, while Bede is celebrated at a museum founded in his name and at the ruins of the Jarrow monastery, I found that the town has pitifully little in the way of memorials to its 20th-century champions. These are restricted to a life-sized bronze sculpture immortalising the marchers, known as the 'Spirit of Jarrow' in the town's Viking Shopping Centre; and a plaque on the Town Hall commemorating the march.

Kate Sussams, Director of Bede's World museum told me: 'It is certainly true that the Jarrow marchers, as well as Bede, are an inspiration for people to visit. In fact, we are giving serious consideration to creating a permanent **Jarrow Crusade** exhibition within the museum. There are memorabilia such as banners and packets of cigarettes in storage somewhere in the Town Hall. These really ought to be accessible, because they are tangible links with the historic events.'

In Jarrow I met the locally born and bred historian Ged Lynn who recently walked from Jarrow to Westminster following the marchers' route, in an effort to raise awareness of the Wearmouth-Jarrow UNESCO World Heritage bid (see box, page 118). Said Ged: 'Bede and the March are two sides of a coin called Jarrow, separated by 13 centuries. On one side, we have the birth of scholasticism, the English language and high culture. On the other, the Industrial Revolution – and the consequences of placing mass production above nature. When you see it that way, most of English history is influenced by one side or other of the Jarrow coin.'

The Venerable Bede

So, what was so 'venerable' about The Venerable Bede?

To him we owe the idea of recording human memory in the form of written history. And because of him, we have eye-witness accounts from the age of Northumbrian monasticism. Among the 68 books which he scratched on parchment with his goose-quill pens, is *Historia Ecclesiastica Gentis Anglorum* (*'Ecclesiastical History of the English People'*) completed in 731 and covering the arrival of the Romans, through to his own time. The tome's title defies the wit, wisdom and impish humour, which went hand in hand with this man's deep piety and astonishing scholarship. Well, he was a Geordie boy through and through, so what else would you expect?

Bede's narrative is lively, and packed to the gunnels with human touches. He tells of monks winding each other up with barbed insults, adding an all-too-credible dimension to all the earnest holiness enshrined in the myth and legend of his era. He himself has a sceptical laugh at the expense of his Irish brethren, for their belief that St Patrick banished snakes from Ireland. Call him a nationalist, if you like: Bede was a proud Angle, also prone to a spot of Scots- and Welsh-baiting. Venerable no doubt, though not generally referred to as 'saint' despite having been canonised.

Bede was born in nearby **Monkwearmouth** (now a suburb of Sunderland) in, or around, AD672 and at the age of seven was placed by his family in Wearmouth monastery, later moving to the monastery's twin foundation at Jarrow where the Don tributary flows into the River Tyne.

One of the most gifted authors ever, Bede's books span subjects such as art, science, cookery, philosophy, carpentry, astronomy and theology as well as history. He surprised people with his belief in curious theories, such as the world being a sphere, rather than flat. (Never mind that the ancient Greeks had understood this, Bede had looked out at the North Sea horizon, so it was blindingly obvious to him.)

Bede's writing allows us to picture him in an uncannily personal way. For example, he tells of his walks along the Northumbria coastline, which allowed him to study and speculate on the phenomenon of tides. He worked out that the moon had something to do with these centuries before Newton discovered gravity. He tells of his boredom with the blandness of monastery food, leading him to introduce peppercorns and other spices to the monastic kitchen.

Such human touches add a quite extraordinary dimension to Bede's original theological commentaries, and his allegorical interpretations of the scriptures. Bede argued not only that life had a divine purpose, but that this purpose could be discovered through faith, labour and self-giving. He viewed Christ as simply 'love in action'.

However, as a theologian he was prone to getting himself into hot water (the vulnerable Bede?) by his unwillingness to hold back his own original takes on various orthodoxies and dogmas. Bede wrote about one occasion when, at a feast at Hexham monastery, a group of drunken monks accused him of heresy over his challenging of the chronology of the Six Ages theory of human history.

Nevertheless, Bede's scholarship became renowned across the Christian world, where his works were widely circulated. As well as inventing the concept of history (or at least the recording of it), it was Bede's idea to measure time from the birth of Christ. And as well as in Latin, he was the first to write an early version of English – the Anglo-Saxon of his day, into which he translated the gospels. He even wrote guides to grammar and spelling in the language he termed 'Englisc'. So in a sense, we also owe to him the small matter of the English language itself. Some linguists reckon that there are direct links between Bede's 'Englisc' and the modern 'Geordie' dialect of northeast England.

Bede lived to be 62 (a ripe old age for the 8th century) soon after which the veneration he attracted earned him the title to which his name has been attached ever since. Rumours spread of miraculous healings at his shrine in the monastery church. (It is not hard to imagine Bede himself asking a few pointed questions about his devotees' credulity on this matter.)

In about 1022 some Durham monks helped themselves to his remains from the monastery which had been laid waste by Vikings, and placed them alongside St Cuthbert's in their cathedral nave. They were later moved to the Galilee Chapel (see page 122). One paragraph from Bede's *History of the English People*, sums up his take on the mystery of human existence:

It seems to me that the life of man on earth is like the swift flight of a single sparrow through the banqueting hall where you are sitting at dinner on a winter's day with your captains and counsellors. In the midst there is a comforting fire to warm the hall. Outside, the storms of winter rain and snow are raging. This sparrow flies swiftly in through one window of the hall and out through another. While he is inside, the bird is safe from the winter storms, but after a few moments of comfort, he vanishes from sight into the wintry world from which he came. So man appears on earth for a little while – but of what went before this life, or what follows, we know nothing.

The Jarrow Crusade

What about those who venerate the Jarrow Crusaders of 1936? That was the year in which some 200 marchers walked 300 miles from the town to Westminster in London, to lobby parliament and protest about unemployment and poverty in northeast England.

The background was the global **Great Depression**, leading to the ravaging of the coalmining and steel industries, and especially the decimation of shipbuilding on Tyneside. Palmer's Shipyard, established in 1852, had made Jarrow world famous as a shipbuilding town and at one time employed 80% of the town's population. However, in the early 1930s it was forced to close. This resulted in mass unemployment and extreme poverty – even real hunger – among the working men of Jarrow and their families.

Specifically, the 200 marchers set off carrying a petition to parliament in the form of an oak box containing the signatures of 11,000 Jarrow people demanding government aid in their hour of need. After 15 days they reached London, and their petition was delivered to Prime Minister Stanley Baldwin by Jarrow MP **Ellen Wilkinson**. Baldwin declined to meet any of the marchers personally, though they were sympathetically received across the political spectrum. But they were given just £1 each for their return train journeys.

Much more significantly, however, the marchers had achieved hero status. They were billeted on the way by sympathetic trade unionist comrades or in church halls, and hailed as champions of the working class. The image of these men, in cloth caps and hobnailed boots, marching the length of the country, remains deeply ingrained in the national psyche. Singer Alan Price's 1974 hit 'Jarrow Song' – popular still and a YouTube favourite – is testimony to the enduring power of this image.

So too are the comments made to me by Reverend Daniel Davies, a lilting Welsh clergyman I fell into conversation with while wandering among the ruins of St Paul's Monastery: 'Through his writing, Bede brought the gospel message of social justice and Christ's preference for the poor to the masses. The Jarrow Crusaders simply took the same message down to Westminster. My belief is … when new spirits walk, older spirits are awakened and become their companions.'

It was intriguing to find the Rev Davies treating the ruins of St Paul's Monastery as much as a destination to pay his respects to the marchers, as to the Venerable Bede. Perhaps the two motivations for a Jarrow pilgrimage really are as connected as Ged Lynn suggests.

Bede's World

Church Bank, NE32 3DY ☎ 0191 489 2106 🖥 www.bedesworld.co.uk.

The purpose of this fascinating museum is to bring to life the extraordinary story of Bede, and the early medieval Northumbrian people of his time. The museum does its subject credit by appealing in different ways to all visitors, from school groups to academics.

The main museum building is the 18th-century Jarrow Hall. Soft Gregorian plainchant enhances the monastic mood at the 'Age of Bede' exhibition which includes archaeological finds from St Paul's Monastery, life-sized models and computerised interactive displays. You can dress up in a monastic habit, if the mood takes you, and sit in an alcove listening to the recorded voice of 'Bede' reading from *Historia Ecclesiastica Gentis Anglorum*.

The museum encompasses ten acres of grounds on the site of an Anglo-Saxon farm known in Bede's time as Gyrwe (from which the name 'Jarrow' derives). The farm has been recreated with farm buildings based on Anglo-Saxon 'pit-type' houses excavated in the area. There are enclosures of oxen, pigs and small sheep which we are told are '*more like those which Bede might have seen on the monastery farms.*' Costumed characters re-enact 7th- and 8th-century village life, making pottery and using farming implements and tools of the time.

St Paul's Church and monastery ruins
Church Bank, NE32 3DZ ℃ 0191 489 7052 ✆ www.stpaulschurchjarrow.com. Free access.

St Paul's Church and the ruins of Jarrow Monastery are next to Bede's World, across a small grassy park with a picnic area.

The ruins outside the church were Bede's stomping ground. Here the monk lived, worked, prayed and laughed for most of his life. The monastery was founded in 681 by Abbot Benedict Biscop a few years after its twin foundation at Monkwearmouth. Both thrived till they were sacked by Vikings in 794 and again in 860. Most of the remains that stand today are from the monastery re-founded on the site by Abbot Alwin in the 11th century, this time as a daughter house of the Benedictine community at Durham (where the Wearmouth monks had gone). At the Reformation the monastery was abandoned and began its slow decline into ruin.

St Paul's Church, however, survived as a working Church of England parish church and so has been a place of Christian prayer for 13 centuries. The original chapel from the earliest days of the monastery forms the chancel of today's St Paul's. While Bede gave the world memory in the form of written history, he also left a powerful atmosphere in this place.

'**Bede's Chair**', a low, ancient seat made of blackened, fragile-looking wood stands next to the altar. There have been legends about the chair for centuries. According to an ancient tradition whose origins are lost, a splinter of its wood simmered in boiling water, produces a liquid with great healing powers. For some reason such holy water became particularly associated with childbirth, and in time women began to make pilgrimages to St Paul's where they would sit in the chair praying for fertility, deliverance from miscarrying, or simply for easy childbirth.

No doubt the monk in whose venerable memory the chair is named, would be highly entertained at the idea of his having gynaecological powers – 'You havin' a laff? Me, I'm a celibate monk!' I can hear him protesting in his broadest Geordie Englisc. And modern dating techniques have poured cold (rather than simmering) water on the idea of Bede's venerable backside having been anywhere near it. Nothing wooden is believed to have survived the Vikings' burning of the monastery anyway, and the chair probably dates from the 11th century.

However Jimmy Guy, the verger, is not convinced. 'Bits of the chair date from different times, you can see that', he insisted, pointing out some charred bits to me. 'See these, they could have been burned in the Viking raids. But it is best not to get too scientific about these things. Better to remember what faith can do for people.'

Getting there

Jarrow is 5 miles from the centre of Newcastle upon Tyne, near the A19 Tyne Tunnel south entrance. From the A1(M) it is reached from junction 65, the motorway's northern terminus, via the A194. Bede **railway station** is on the South Shields (yellow) line of Tyne and Wear Metro. St Paul's Church and the monastery ruins are signposted, and are about 15 minutes' walk away.

Where to stay and eat

Hadrian Lodge Hotel Hadrian Rd, Wallsend, Tyne and Wear NE28 6HH

World Heritage Site?

The twin Anglo-Saxon monastery of Wearmouth-Jarrow – 'one monastery in two places' – was the UK's 2010 nomination for UNESCO World Heritage Site status. They were the creation of one man, Benedict Biscop, who returned from a pilgrimage to Rome in the 650s determined to build a monastery 'in the Roman manner' which frequently involved twin foundations.

The pair he chose were at Monkwearmouth in Sunderland and Jarrow on Tyneside, following the gift of land at these places by King Ecgfrith of Northumbria. While the latter receives large numbers of visitors on account of Bede's World and the monastery ruins, the bleak industrial landscape of Monkwearmouth attracts few. Nonetheless, Wearmouth and its church, St Peter's, is older by a few years, having been founded in 674. The monastery was sacked by Vikings in 870, after which most of the monks moved to Durham.

There are no monastic ruins to see at Wearmouth, but St Peter's Church survives, adjacent to the St Peter's Campus of the University of Sunderland. It is one of the oldest churches in England, with much of the original structure including the west wall (begun in 674), and the tower which still stands.

According to the World Heritage Convention, '*World Heritage Sites are places or buildings of outstanding universal value recognised as constituting a "World Heritage" for whose protection it is the duty of the International Community as a whole to co-operate*.' At the time of going to press the nomination remains under consideration by the UNESCO World Heritage Committee.

St Peter's Church St Peter's Way, Sunderland SR6 0DY ☏ 0191 5160 135
🖥 www.wearmouth-jarrow.org.uk.

📞 0191 262 7733 🖥 www.hadrianlodgehotel.co.uk. Smallish, excellent value hotel in the Wallsend suburb. Just opposite Hadrian Road Metro station about 2 miles from Jarrow.

Jarrow Hall Café Bede's World. Serves pretty good hot and cold meals at reasonable prices. Open to all, with or without a museum entrance ticket.

Malmaison Newcastle Quayside, Newcastle upon Tyne NE1 3DX

📞 0191 245 5000 🖥 www.malmaison-newcastle.com. Swish, very fashionable, contemporary-style hotel on the Tyne quayside. Easy access to Jarrow by Metro.

The Sir William Fox Hotel 5 Westoe Village, South Shields NE33 3DZ

📞 0191 456 4554 🖥 www.sirwilliamfoxhotel.com. A small historic South Tyneside hotel, and birthplace of the three-time prime minister of New Zealand.

Tourist information

Newcastle upon Tyne's Tourist Information Centre Central Arcade, NE1 5AF

📞 0191 2778000 🖥 www.newcastlegateshead.com. There is no tourist information centre in Jarrow.

④ Durham

When – as happens from time to time – a Bishop of Durham sparks an unholy storm by straying off the prevailing theological or political message, he does so within quite a tradition of boat rocking.

My first sight of the cathedral nave produced a powerful aesthetic jolt. It was not so much the sheer dimensions of the columns, piers and vaults as the shocking giant chevrons, lozenges and spirals carved deep into the stone, each one different. Nothing could be less traditional. In fact, I learnt that 11th- and 12th-century Norman architects had treated Durham as a sort of guinea pig for some of the outrageous creations which they could not have got away with back home across the Channel.

Bill Bryson claims to have barely heard of Durham, when he caught sight of the vast, reddish-brown triplet towers, while travelling on a train to Newcastle. '*I unhesitatingly gave Durham Cathedral my vote for the best cathedral on planet Earth*', he wrote in his 1995 *Notes from a Small Island*, explaining how he stopped off on a whim, walked down the hill from the station and unexpectedly fell in love with Durham. Requitedly so, apparently, since a decade later Durham University proposed to him in the form of an invitation to replace Sir Peter Ustinov as its Chancellor.

Bryson was titillated by the cathedral's stained-glass windows '*spattering the floors with motes of colour*'; enraptured by the '*unutterable soaring majesty*' of the nave; and later allured by the '*no less ancient and beguiling*' old quarter of Durham city. '*It's wonderful*', he concluded.

Any visitor to Durham should be prepared to be similarly seduced. Without a doubt, the cathedral and city are blessed with natural and artistic astonishments to set the heart aflutter. But would Durham have the same capacity to bewitch body and soul, were it not for centuries of sacredness? Bryson didn't mention them, but were St Cuthbert and The Venerable Bede his secret matchmakers?

Or, to put it another way, can a place attribute its special atmosphere to a saint lying entombed at a shrine? And to the artists and architects who created that shrine to celebrate his sacredness? And to the millions who followed in faith and expectation?

These questions broke the stillness in my head, as I climbed the narrow stone staircase worn smooth by numberless pilgrim feet. I stopped before the plain marble slab where St Cuthbert lies. Alone and in virtual silence, I felt my boat well and truly rocked.

History and legend

The story of Durham starts with St Cuthbert and remains intimately entwined with him. Cuthbert died and was buried at Lindisfarne in AD687 where his tomb attracted pilgrims from across Europe. In 875 the Lindisfarne monks fled from the marauding Danes, carrying with them Cuthbert's body which they discovered to be miraculously uncorrupted. After seven years' wandering they arrived at Chester-le-Street, where Cuthbert remained till about 995 when another Viking invasion threatened and he was removed temporarily to Ripon.

Returning Cuthbert's coffin to Chester-le-Street a few months later the monks found that it suddenly became unaccountably and unmoveably heavy. Enter a forlorn milkmaid, plaintively pleading with them to help her find her mislaid cow, last seen on a nearby rocky outcrop almost entirely encircled by a meandering gorge of the River Wear. At which point the coffin's weight relented, allowing them to follow the distressed damsel to the hill which forms the peninsula of 'Dun Holm'. A sign! This is where Cuthbert intended to spend eternity.

Accordingly, they settled here and built first the White Church to house Cuthbert's remains. This was soon superseded by one of the finest cathedrals in Christendom, with most of the present structure completed by the mid-12th century. Cuthbert lay in a glorious, gilded shrine behind the high altar, which became one of the most revered sites in England. Kings, queens, nobles and commoners in huge numbers from across Europe sought his intercession. His fabled sanctity grew exponentially as tales of miraculous healings mushroomed. The arrival (some say theft by Durham monks) in 1022 of The Venerable Bede's remains from Jarrow further strengthened Durham's power as a puller-in of pilgrims.

Durham's geographic position also gave it strategic importance. After 1066 the Normans built a great castle next to the cathedral, from where they projected their power across northern England. The castle became a bastion in the wars against the Scots. Durham Castle became the seat of the 'Prince

Bishops', who – such a long way from Westminster and Canterbury – enjoyed unfettered ecclesiastical, political and even military power over swathes of northeast England. Their reign survived the Reformation, when the Durham theocrats accepted the break with Rome and were incorporated into the Church of England. The monks either became lay workers in the new church order, or were sent packing.

The last Prince Bishop, William Van Mildert, was one of the great boat rockers. Affronted by the wealth and worldliness of the institution, he abolished the Prince Bishop title (becoming plain old Bishop of Durham) in 1836, and transferred his non-church powers to the Crown. He moved the Episcopal seat to nearby Bishop Auckland, and used the castle to found Durham University – England's third oldest, after Oxford and Cambridge.

Cuthbert, meanwhile, had had rather a rough ride. In 1540, during the Reformation, his shrine was vandalised by Henry's henchmen and his remains buried under a great flagstone. In 1827 he was disturbed again; this time his skeleton was found wrapped in silk stoles and still wearing his pectoral cross. He was reburied in the tomb where he lies today, and the stoles and cross are on display in the cathedral's Treasury Museum.

And what of Bede? For some three centuries his venerable bones lay next to Cuthbert's. Then in 1370 he got his own magnificent shrine, in the Galilee Chapel at the western end of the cathedral. But this too was destroyed in the Reformation and, like Cuthbert's, his remains were buried under a flagstone on the site of the shrine. His present simpler altar tomb, of polished black marble, stands on the same spot.

Durham Cathedral

Palace Green, DH1 3RW ☎ 0191 386 4266
🌐 www.durhamcathedral.co.uk. Free access (donation expected).

From whatever direction you approach the city, the cathedral is the dominant feature – vast in scale, beautiful in proportion, and awe-inspiring in sheer presence. Just imagine the effect it must have had on the local population when it rose above huddles of medieval hovels. The soaring walls, the high windows, the huge rise of the central tower must have been overwhelming.

Nowadays it is the university colleges along the Bailey that squat at the feet of this greatest of all Europe's Romanesque architectural achievements. At the main entrance, on Palace Green, there is a sacred symbol to pause at before you even go in: the famous **Sanctuary Knocker**, a bronze lion's head holding a huge ring in its jaws. In the Middle Ages any fugitives from the law who could reach the doors and grasp hold of the ring, were guaranteed 37 days 'sanctuary' within the cathedral. Sanctuary meant entitlement to protection by the Church from any other authority and remained law until 1623.

Once inside, it is probably best not to make a beeline for Cuthbert's tomb. Rather, pause first in the **nave**. If the gigantic, 900-year-old pillars with their astonishing carvings knock the metaphorical (or even literal) stuffing out of you, try and picture the sheer energy they must have conveyed in the Middle Ages when they were painted black and scarlet. In those days there would have been no seating, just an expanse of stone beneath the rib vaulting.

With luck there will be some music to enhance the atmosphere – perhaps a choir practice or piano recital – the cathedral is a venue for numerous events as well as being a place of worship.

Next, move to the far west end of the nave (the back), to visit Bede at his raised tomb in the **Galilee Chapel**. A modern wooden sculpture depicting Bede with a quill in his hand stands next to the shrine, looking on. His expression is benign and compassionate, tinged with wry amusement that he should be observing the slab inscribed with the words *Hac sunt in fossa Baedae Venerabilis Ossa*. In other words, the resting place of his own relics.

St Cuthbert's shrine lies at the other end of the cathedral, beyond the high altar in the **Chapel of the Nine Altars**. The staircase leading up to the chapel, rising several feet above the Cathedral floor, is narrow and dark. However, at the top you spill into an area startlingly large, constructed so in the 13th century to accommodate the throngs of pilgrims who used to congregate here. Until the Reformation, of course, the shrine would have been a riot of gold and jewels, and heaped with bountiful offerings from royalty, nobles and wealthy pilgrims.

Look around the chapel and you will still see treasures such as the stunning **Rose window**, 30ft in diameter, depicting Christ surrounded by his apostles; and some beautiful black marble piers. There is also a rather striking white statue of Bishop William Van Mildert.

But you might not notice any of these at first, because St Cuthbert's powerful and magnetic presence washes over the senses of those receptive to his aura. However, his tombstone today is of simple grey stone, lying on the ground. Modern visitors can pay their respects, meditate in his sacred presence, pray or simply contemplate his life, legend and legacy, in whatever way works for them. Few will leave the chapel unmoved.

Huge wooden doors lead from the cathedral nave into the adjoining monastic **cloisters**, where rewinding through the centuries to pre-Reformation times feels effortless. Then, the covered, carved stone quadrangle around a small green was the habitat of cowled monks. Today, sightings of robed choristers – a similar species, in appearance at least – are common.

Among the surviving monastic buildings is the 14th-century oak-beamed **Monks Dormitory** above the western walkway, which houses a collection of Anglo-Saxon stone crosses. The small **Treasures of Cuthbert** museum is rather unmemorable. It does contain the saint's cross and coffin among various paraphernalia, but not his spirit; that is to be found in the Nine Altars Chapel.

Finally, climb the 325 steep steps spiralling the top of the 217ft **Central Tower** for views over the winding River Wear and the expanses of County Durham, across which the monks carried Cuthbert and met a milkmaid (see page 120).

Durham Castle

Palace Green, DH1 3RW ☏ 0191 334 4119 🖰 www.dur.ac.uk/university.college.
Across Palace Green from the cathedral entrance is the gateway to the city's other great monument, Durham Castle. The pair are jointly recognised as a UNESCO World Heritage Site.

Your experience of the castle will be coloured somewhat by whether you visit during university term time, or holidays. This is because Durham Castle, formerly the seat of the Prince Bishops, became the University of Durham in 1837 and is today University College, affectionately known simply as 'Castle' among its students and those at the 15 other colleges which also now comprise the university.

About 100 students live within the castle, in rooms built during the reign of William the Conqueror who founded the fortress in 1072. Outside term time, the rooms are used for conference accommodation, or can be booked by the public (see below). Rumours also abound of resident ghosts, who are unconcerned by such changes in the corporeal world. Visits are guided tours lasting a little less than an hour, by appointment and beginning at the Porters' Lodge. You visit the medieval kitchens and Great Hall, now the college dining room, various chapels and the forbidding 17th-century Black Staircase.

Getting there

Durham is 14 miles south of Newcastle upon Tyne, reached from junction 62 of the A1(M) via the A690. Durham **railway station** is between Darlington and Newcastle upon Tyne on the East Coast Main Line. The station is about 15 minutes' walk or 5 minutes by **taxi**, from the city centre.

Where to stay and eat

Castle View Guest House Crossgate, DH1 4PS ☏ 0191 386 8852 🖰 www.guest housesdurham.co.uk. Lovely old house, with views of the cathedral as well as the castle. Excellent central location near Framwellgate Bridge. To finish one of landlady Mrs William's mountainous full English breakfasts, is a feat.

Durham Castle ☏ 0191 334 4106 🖰 www.dur.ac.uk/university.college. Stay in student accommodation out of term time. A variety of rooms, some with bathrooms, others not. Rooms are also available at the other Durham colleges through 🖰 www.durhamrooms.co.uk.

Farnley Tower Hotel The Avenue, DH1 4DX ☏ 0191 375 0011 🖰 www.farnley-tower.co.uk. Warm and friendly Victorian hotel, old-fashioned and unflashy, up a steep hill from the city centre.

Oldfields Restaurant 18 Claypath, DH1 1RH ✆ 0191 370 9595
☜ www.oldfieldsrealfood.co.uk. Restore your faith in 'classic British food', as this relaxed, two-storey restaurant describes its fare. Seasonal dishes made with local, organic ingredients.
Radisson Blu Hotel Framwellgate Waterside, DH1 5TL ✆ 0191 372 7200
☜ www.radissonblu.co.uk. Plush, contemporary-style 4-star which sometimes offers alluring weekend deals. On the river, a short walk from the centre.
The Undercroft Restaurant The College, DH1 3EQ ✆ 0191 386 3721. Serves OK snacks and simple meals at reasonable prices. Ideal location – on the monastic cloister in the cathedral complex. Habits and cowls optional.
Zen Restaurant Court Lane, DH1 3JS ✆ 0191 384 9588 ☜ www.zendurham. co.uk. Excellent, if rather pricey Thai and oriental food. Great for sharing dishes.

Tourist information
Durham Tourist Information Centre 2 Millennium Pl, DH1 1WA
✆ 0191 384 3720 ☜ www.thisisdurham.com.

⑤ Cumbria's stone circles

Did the Neolithic people who met amid the Cumbrian fells marvel at the magnificence of their surroundings? Did they come here to worship, to celebrate, give thanks, to mourn or to warn off malign forces? The answers are beyond the realms of archaeology, but the circles of stone where they gathered in ritual retain a mysterious power.

Castlerigg
Free access.
The stones of Castlerigg appeared out of the mist like a ring of wraiths enacting a solemn ritual. About 40 of them – some dwarfs, others 10ft giants – formed a silent circle amid the bare Lakeland fells. Were they a herd of enchanted, eternally milk-giving cows tricked by a jealous witch?

It was 05.30 on a summer morning and I was trudging across a wet field in search of this ancient monument, my head full of legends and whimsical nonsense I'd read about the origins of stone circles in Britain. Except that none of it felt so nonsensical then. The eastern horizon above the humps of Clough Head and Great Mell Fell was thick with inky rain clouds streaked with shafts of light. The stones stood their ground, defiantly erect, with faces of mottled grey hung with sinister lichen beards.

I had come alone at this unearthly hour hoping to have the place and its atmosphere to myself. But a flock of hooded crows had beaten me to it. Some were foraging in the middle of the circle while others perched on top of the stones. They made a hell of a fuss, cawing loudly into the damp air as they flapped off to sulk in a chestnut tree.

But I also stood my ground. I was soon seduced by this magic-tinged spot, surrounded by a 360° panorama of green fields and blue fells. I could only disagree with Keats, who once dismissed Castlerigg as 'a dismal cirque of Druid stones upon a forlorn moor.'

Later that day I returned to Castlerigg with a head full of questions: who really built the stone circle? When? How . . . and why? With me was Robert Maxwell, an archaeologist working for the National Trust, which owns and looks after the site. I wanted the professional's view. While we sheltered from a

heavy shower in the lee of one of the largest stones, Robert told me, 'The first thing to understand about stone circles is that there are far more enigmas than "right" answers.'

However, there is general agreement that it was Neolithic, or late Stone Age, farming communities in Britain that first started erecting slabs of rock into circles from around 3000BC. The practice appears to have lasted a couple of thousand years into the Bronze Age. There are several hundred of these circles in Britain, along with 'henges' – circular earthwork banks and ditches – built in the same period.

Some, such as Stonehenge (see page 34), are national monuments with ticket booths and turnstiles. Others are barely recognisable ruins, plundered over the centuries to build churches, houses or walls, and marked on maps simply as 'Stone Circle'. Castlerigg seems to be one of the earliest but has survived pretty much unscathed, perhaps because it is so isolated. 'So, what was the purpose of this place?' I pressed. 'Are the stones really astronomically aligned, as claimed?'

'The trouble with looking at a place like this through 21st-century eyes is that we demand specific answers to specific questions', said Robert. 'Just imagine that you are a farmer a few thousand years ago, and that f rom time to time you and your fellow villagers get together in a common place with farmers from other settlements. You have had a good harvest, for which you give thanks to the sun. You swap your grain for a few tools and you have a chat about how to get things right. When the best time to plant is, for instance.'

Robert pointed to two different places high on the fells. 'Up there is High Rigg where, from here, the sun rises on this point at Candlemas. Over there is Skiddaw, where the sun sets on the winter solstice. If I want to be sure to plant, or plough or whatever on a particular day of the year, how do I remember? How about lining up a stone, so that on the day the sunrise hits it ...' I was beginning to get the message – stone circles might have been 'religious', 'social' and 'economic'. 'But we don't know, we don't know.'

The modern-day functions of the circles also vary greatly. There are all those New Age powers that the stone circles are said to bestow upon believers. From time to time, for instance, Castlerigg hosts a Druid wedding. On the wet summer's day of my visit, most of the visitors I spoke to were more down to earth. Hikers stopping at a point of interest on their route across the fells, or tourists with a guidebook entry to tick off. But there was also a sylph-like girl called Eustacia dressed in black with white hair right down her back, flitting from stone to stone. She offered this theory:

'Ancient societies in Britain were matriarchal, and the earth was worshipped as a mother. Ceremonies were conducted by priestesses. By the Middle Ages, only traces of this religion remained in folklore, but those women who inherited them were the ones branded as witches.'

Then she pointed to a chestnut tree, where the crows I had banished that morning were still in raucous residence. 'Those birds could be the reincarnated souls of those witches burnt at the stake or drowned', she said in deadly earnest.

Getting there
Castlerigg is about 1½ miles east of Keswick, signposted from the A591 and A66. The stones are about 100yds from a road and lay-by.

Where to stay and eat
Lyzzick Hall ☎ 01768 772277 🖰 www.lyzzickhall.co.uk. A small country house hotel on Skiddaw Fell above Castlerigg.

Tourist information
Keswick Tourist Information Centre Moot Hall, Keswick CA12 5JS ☎ 01768 772645 🖰 www.visitcumbria.com/kes/keswick-tourist-information-centre.htm.

Long Meg and Her Daughters
Free access.

Were it not for her gender, Long Meg would certainly have to answer charges of being gratuitously phallic. She is a former witch, now an 11ft standing stone about 27yds from her similarly petrified coven of offspring (or lovers, according to some), who form one of the largest stone circles in Britain.

One legend tells how all of them were turned to stone by a Scottish wizard called Michael Scott. A twist in this story is that it is unaccountably hard to count them. Impossible even. If anybody can reach the same figure in two attempts, then Scott the Scot's spell will be broken and the stones will revert to being witches.

Quite a challenge, I told myself, as I followed the lane towards Long Meg, bringing with me some words of William Wordsworth's. The Lakeland poet's imagination was clearly stirred more by ancient monoliths, than that of Keats.

He wrote to Long Meg after a visit in 1833:

Speak Thou, whose massy strength and stature scorn
The power of years pre-eminent, and placed
Apart, to overlook the circle vast –
Speak, Giant-mother! Tell it to the Morn
While she dispels the cumbrous shades of Night;

Long Meg, I found, is a pink-tinged outlier standing erect about 12ft high, pointing a few degrees from the perpendicular; one side is engraved with some mystifying spirals and concentric circles. Her daughters are grey bulky boulders forming a huge oval, more than 100yds in diameter at its widest. Some are upright, others flattened.

I attempted, of course, to count them and reached 51 in total. But that didn't include the pair of large boulders just outside the circle but clearly part of the complex. That's a pack of cards plus a joker I told myself as a mnemonic, as I began counting again just to check. But had I included Long Meg herself? God knows. Because the next count made 54 (a pack plus two jokers).

At which point I took the hint and wandered over to a copse of trees near the site, where strips of rotting cloth and tiny bundles dangled from branches. There was no clue as to who had tied them there, or why. Their presence did, however, make me a little uneasy about what powers there are, that this place retains from its sacred past.

Getting there
Long Meg is 6 miles northeast of Penrith, just off a lane beyond Little Salkeld. Signposted from the village.

Where to stay and eat
The George ☎ 01768 862696 🖰 www.georgehotelpenrith.co.uk. A traditional, 300-year-old coaching inn in the centre of Penrith.

Tourist information
Penrith Tourist Information Centre Middlegate, CA11 7PT ☎ 01768 867466
🖰 www.northpennines.org.uk/index.cfm?articleid=4444.

Swinside
Free access.
Swinside is magnificently set in a field surrounded by Lakeland fells. Although it is one of the most complete stone circles in Britain, it is still little visited, mainly because it is on private land about 1½ miles on foot from the road, along a stony track. Walking this track, I first glimpsed Swinside from above,

an enchanting picture as I approached the plateau on which the circle stands. The stones are so close together, that it looked like a complete round wall.

Swinside consists of 55 stones forming a circle about 30yds across, with the tallest stone standing due north. A pair of portal stones at the circle entrance is aligned precisely with the mid-winter sunrise when viewed from the centre, according to some very precise studies.

Less scientific is the legend surrounding Swinside, which seems to have arisen in the Middle Ages. It exists in various forms, one of which is that the stones are blocks from a church which Satan pulled apart with his bare hands. Despite this feat, however, their great weight defeated his plans to fly away with them, and they fell to the ground – curiously into a perfect circle. Beneath them are said to lie the remains of the church, which accounts for Swinside's alternative name of 'Sunkenkirk'.

Getting there
5 miles north of Millom. The track to the stones is signposted from the A595.

Where to stay and eat
Swinside Lodge Hotel Newlands, Keswick CA12 5UE ☎ 01768 772948
🖰 www.swinsidelodge-hotel.co.uk. A charming and romantic country house hotel surrounded by fells.

Tourist information
Millom Tourist Information Centre Millom Council Centre, St Georges Rd, LA18 4DD ☎ 01946 598914 🖰 www.visitcumbria.com/wc/millom.htm.

⑥ The medieval monasteries of North Yorkshire

The era of the medieval monastic orders may have lasted only 300 years or so, but they had a profound impact on the landscape and the spiritual life of Britain. Their demise was sudden and violent, but the ruins of the great abbeys they left behind have an enduring magnetism as we imagine the lives of the monks who worked, prayed and sang in them.

Fountains Abbey and Studley Royal

The abbey
Ripon HG4 3DY ☎ 01765 608888 🖰 www.fountainsabbey.org.uk.
Picture this: it is the year 1132 and a band of 13 tattered monks are making their weary way, on foot, through a far-flung valley in North Yorkshire.

Unencumbered by personal possessions and united in their longing for a life of frugality and harsh discipline, they are in search of a setting that will mirror these needs.

The brethren have purposefully left behind the wealthy St Mary's Benedictine abbey at York (see page 136), where they had become disturbed by the laxity and luxury of the lifestyle. In particular, they found the lavish meals a constant reproof to their weakness of soul and flesh. St Mary's elderly *bon viveur* Abbot Geoffrey was a kindly man, but he simply did not 'get it'.

So instead these monks seek the patronage of Archbishop Thurstan of York. He understands their concerns and grants them some uncultivated land in a valley which, he promises, is '*a place uninhabited for all the centuries back, thick set with thorns, lying between the slopes of mountains and among rocks jutting out on both sides; fit, rather, it seems, to be the lair of wild beasts than the home of human beings.*'

Perfect. Here they would find spiritual nourishment. Using the trunk of an elm for a roof pole, they erect a simple thatched hut where they live in suitably harsh conditions, particularly over the ferocious first winter. The following year their rudimentary monastery is admitted to the stricter Cistercian branch of Benedictine monasticism.

Strolling down a steep, tree-lined path from the Fountains Abbey Visitor Centre to the ruins, which are now a UNESCO World Heritage Site, I found all this rather hard to imagine. Because, the sight before me was bewitchingly lovely: a sweeping green vista leading to the pink-gold abbey ruins, vast in scale and glowing serenely next to the winding River Skell. Most of the buildings, including the abbey church, are roofless. The remains of Romanesque arches around the cloisters, and sublimely symmetrical vaulting arching over carpets of green turf, are not only beautiful but suggest staggering wealth. And the huge perpendicular tower speaks of raw power.

So much remains of the monastic complex that it is one of the finest sites anywhere in which to appreciate some of the realities of Cistercian life. For example, wandering among the ruins I was able to gain a feeling of some of the more workaday remnants of the community's day-to-day existence. The remains of a 12th-century watermill for grinding corn survive, for instance; so does the communal reredorter (latrine), cleverly built over the river. In fact, so much of the monastery is intact, that images of the bustling enterprise that the abbey must have been in its heyday came easily to mind.

How did all this come about, I mused, after such beggarly origins?

The first point is that, despite Archbishop Thurstan's unprepossessing description of this place, there was an abundance of streams and springs in the vicinity. The founders originally named their little monastery *De Fontibus* – 'Of Springs' – and successive generations of monks became adept at harnessing water power. There was also plentiful wood in the surrounding forests, and stone for building in nearby quarries.

Still, the early years were severe enough to test the most resilient faith. One legend tells of the day a starving man arrived, asking for food and shelter. There were just two loaves of bread left for the entire community, but nevertheless one was given to him. And behold, within half an hour two men appeared from Knaresborough Castle with a plentiful supply of bread, over which the monks recited the, '*inasmuch as ye have done it of the gospel*'.

The circumstances under which Fountains was founded so clearly revealed the inner spirit of Cistercian asceticism, that noblemen endowed the monastery with money and land, in penance for their sins. The Dean of York resigned his position to join the monastery, bringing with him more money, land and a valuable library. The monastery attracted so many vocations that, within 15 years, Fountains was able to send out 90 monks to found six new monasteries. The thriving community was made up of monks, lay brothers and pilgrims; and of the sick and the poor who came here for help. Large numbers of the lay brothers were illiterate peasants who were permitted to substitute the reading of prayers with their labour, which helps explains how the abbey grew so prosperous.

Also important to the monastery's success, was the centralised farming organisation. Over the years Fountains and its numerous daughter houses acquired vast swathes of grazing pastures in Yorkshire and Lincolnshire. They owned mills and ironworks, and sold wool to Flemish traders. At one time the Abbot of Fountains held a seat in parliament, where he wore his mitre.

The Reformation came at a time when Fountains was near the apex of its power and influence. According to some estimates, the abbey may have owned as much as a million acres of land, and 20,000 sheep. Rich pickings, then, for Henry VIII's commissioners. In 1539 the abbey and monastery were plundered and set fire to. The monks were disbanded and this place – whose sacredness is illuminated by the story of its origin – was left to ruin in the valley.

Studley Royal

The land on which the ruins of Fountains stand was sold by the crown and passed through various hands. A grand country house, Studley Hall, was built on the estate which became known as Studley Royal, before it was acquired by wealthy politician John Aislabie in 1699. Aislabie then lost his money, position and reputation in the 'South Sea Bubble' debacle and returned to Studley. Here he devoted his energies to the landscaping of what is now recognised as of one of the most lavish and imaginative examples of a Georgian water garden, using the neglected ruins of Fountains Abbey as the focal point.

A path along the Skell riverside from the abbey ruins meanders down to a stone archway and a long avenue of limes, to approach a series of ponds, classical statues, pavilions, bridges and temples embowered in plantations of trees. There are surprises at every turn. Reaching the **Serpentine Tunnel**, for example, you plunge through a dark passage that seems to go on endlessly, before it bends very suddenly to spill out into daylight on a high path surrounded by the gnarled roots of immense trees.

Fountains Abbey tells a curious tale of power and wealth rising from pious and ascetic roots. The presence of Studley Royal on the same site adds an even stranger dimension to this place.

Getting there

Fountains is 4 miles southwest of Ripon, from where it is signposted all the way. Ripon is signposted from the A1. The nearest **railway station** is Harrogate, from where there are regular **buses** to Ripon (*www.the36.co.uk; www.dalesbus.org*) and connecting services on to Fountains Abbey.

Where to stay and eat

The Old Deanery Minster Rd, Ripon HG4 1QS ✆ 01765 600003 www.theolddeanery.co.uk. A small, charming old hotel, with an up-market and very popular restaurant in the centre of Ripon.

Tourist information

Ripon Tourist Information Centre Minster Rd, HG4 1QT ✆ 01765 604625 www.ripon.org.

Rievaulx Abbey

The abbey

Rievaulx, Helmsley YO62 5LB ✆ 01439 798228 www.english-heritage.org.uk/daysout/properties/rievaulx-abbey/

Everywhere peace, everywhere serenity, and a marvellous freedom from the tumult of the world.

This was the first impression made by Rievaulx Abbey upon Aelred, a young man from an influential Scottish family, employed as a steward to King David I of Scotland.

Aelred was sent, on the king's behalf, to pay a visit to Archbishop Thurstan of York in 1134. However, calling at Rievaulx Abbey on the way he spontaneously requested and was granted admission as a novice. By 1147 he was abbot, a position he held until his death. These were Rievaulx's greatest years, with the monastery blossoming under his influence while monks and lay brothers joined in their hundreds. Through his preaching and writing, word spread of Aelred's wisdom, compassion and dynamism.

A modern working monastery

The revival of Catholicism in the 19th century led to the re-establishment of monasticism in Britain. Several of the new monasteries founded by the Benedictines, particularly Downside and Ampleforth, became best known for the private boarding schools to which the Catholic elite sent their sons to be educated. The latter also came to particular prominence when its abbot, Basil Hume, became the Cardinal Archbishop of Westminster in 1976, remaining in post till his death in 1999. Ampleforth, the largest active monastery in Britain is, as it happens, just a few miles from Rievaulx. Visitors are welcome to visit the grounds, and the abbey church where mass is celebrated and the divine office is sung five times daily. You can also make an appointment with Fr Rainer (on the number below) to visit the monastery's apple orchard and cider mill. Refreshments are served in the Ampleforth Tea Room.

Ampleforth Abbey Ampleforth YO62 4EN ✆ 01439 766000
🖰 www.ampleforth.org.uk.

Arriving at this hauntingly beautiful place on a bend in the River Rye, it is almost impossible not to share those initial, 900-year-old impressions of Aelred's. The abbey is, of course, a ruin and is now in the care of English Heritage. It is also an archaeological site where digs and studies continue to throw light on the astonishing extent and industry of Rievaulx.

Having previously revelled in some of the writings of Walter Daniel, Aelred's pupil and biographer to whom we owe so much of what is known about the place and the man, I experienced the rather dreamlike sensation of everything being simultaneously recognisable but nevertheless unfamiliar. As at Fountains, the main abbey walls are surprisingly intact; I found this sense of surprise enhanced when I craned my neck up to the shafts where the ribs of vaulting once sprung, to see a wheeling buzzard silhouetted against the clouds as I rewound through the ages.

Rievaulx was founded in 1132 when St Bernard of Clairvaux sent a dozen monks from France to found the first Cistercian outpost in northern England. The monks were granted the present site and a substantial holding of land by the pious Walter Lese, Lord of Helmsley. However, it was the elevation of Aelred to the abbotship that transformed the fortunes of the monastery.

Walter Daniel records that Aelred:

doubled all things in it – monks, conversi (lay brothers), laymen, farms, land and every kind of equipment; indeed, he trebled the intensity of the monastic life and its charity. On feast days you might see the church crowded with the brethren like bees in a hive, unable to move forward because of the multitude, clustered together, rather, and compacted into one angelical body.

Among several daughter houses founded from Rievaulx was the greatest of the Scottish border abbeys, Melrose (see page 202).

Aelred became recognised as England's pre-eminent theologian and even travelled to Westminster Abbey in 1163 to preach in the presence of King Henry II. He was famed as an arbitrator and negotiator of peace. However, despite hobnobbing with royalty his holiness was evident in his extreme personal austerity, as related by Walter Daniel:

> he had built a small chamber of brick under the floor of the novice house, like a little tank, into which water flowed like hidden rills...Aelred would enter this contrivance when he was alone and undisturbed, and immerse his whole body in the icy cold water and so quench the heat in himself of every vice.

Brrrrrrr ... I was there on a reasonably warm summer's day. But on a winter's day he must have been well and truly nithered (as they say in Yorkshire dialect).

Unlike Fountains, come the Dissolution of the Monasteries Rievaulx's best days were already long behind it. After Aelred's time the community faced terrible difficulties, including financial problems, famine and disease. Worst was the Black Death in 1348–49. When Henry VIII's commissioners turned up in 1538, there were just 24 poverty-stricken monks remaining.

Rievaulx Terrace and Temples

Rievaulx, Helmsley YO62 5LJ ℭ 01439 798340 ⊕ www.nationaltrust.org.uk/main/ w-rievaulx-terrace.

While the ruins of Rievaulx are constant evokers of the imagination as you wander among them, there is no disputing that the best views of the abbey are from the spectacularly landscaped Rievaulx Terrace and Temples on the steep hillside above.

The terraces were laid out in 1758 by Thomas Duncombe, who owned the land and the adjoining Helmsley Estate, at the height of the landscaping craze. There are two 'temples' – follies, really – on the site: the domed, pink-stone 'Doric Tuscan' temple at one end and the 'Ionic' temple at the other. Both were constructed above Rievaulx so that the abbey ruins could be viewed through gaps in the trees on the slopes below.

The site was taken over by the National Trust in 1972. With Rievaulx Abbey in the hands of English Heritage, there is no access between the two and separate entrance charges are levied, to the frustration of some.

Getting there

Rievaulx is on the B1257, 2 miles northwest of Helmsley, reached via the A170 between Thirsk and Pickering.

Where to stay and eat

Feversham Arms 1 High St, Helmsley YO62 5AG ☎ 01439 770766
☎ www.fevershamarmshotel.com. Delightful country house-style hotel with a
spa and gourmet restaurant. Nothing like it for miles around.

Tourist information

Helmsley Tourist Information Centre The Town Hall, Market Pl, YO62 5BL
☎ 01439 770173 ☎ www.ukinformationcentre.com/yorkshire/helmsley-tourist-
information-centre.htm.

Whitby Abbey

Whitby YO22 4DR ☎ 01947 603568 ☎ www.english-heritage.org.uk/daysout/proper-
ties/whitby-abbey/.

On a windswept headland high above a harbour and seaside town, Whitby
has an unbelievable setting! But what a daft place to build an abbey in the
first place, you might conclude with the benefit of hindsight. Because, like
other sacred sites (such as Lindisfarne, see page 105, and Jarrow, see page 113)
vulnerable to attack from the North Sea, Whitby came under the Viking cosh
to bloody and devastating effect.

I panted breathlessly up the 199 steps cut into the cliff side, towards high
Gothic arches that looked like scissored cardboard against the sky and seascape.

This is a place sanctified by saints
and enlivened by legend, I
reminded myself. But it was here,
too, that a nail was driven into
the coffin of perhaps the purest,
most beautiful and spiritually
rich Christian tradition ever to
have emerged in Britain.

Whitby is of an age and origin
quite different from those of
Yorkshire's great Cistercian abbeys. It dates back to the era of Northumbrian
monasticism, having been founded in 657 by the Anglo-Saxon Christian King
Oswy, and led by the formidable St Hild.

We know what we know about Hild because of the accounts of her in Bede's
The Ecclesiastical History of the English. Of noble birth, she was a pupil of St
Aidan's and became Abbess of the Hartlepool Monastery (of which nothing
survives). She was sent by Aidan to found a new monastery at Streoneshalh
(the name Whitby, meaning 'white town', was later introduced by the Danes).
Initially, it was a 'double monastery' including communities of both monks
and nuns, over whom, Bede insists, she ruled wisely, humbly and prayerfully.

To Bede we also owe the story of Caedmon, the illiterate lay brother
who worked as a cowherd at Whitby. One feast day while the monks
were singing and reciting poetry, Caedmon left the gathering to prepare the

The Synod of Whitby

Christian Britain in the 7th century had two parallel traditions, the 'Celtic' and the 'Roman'. There is plenty of evidence that St Augustine, leader of the latter, had attempted reconciliation with Celtic bishops of the West. However, some accounts suggest that he was arrogant, and that his goodwill was questioned when he rudely refused to rise from his chair when they met him.

Whatever the truth, there were sharp divisions between the two branches of Christianity. Many of these ostensibly boiled down to trivial matters: the different methods of calculating the date of Easter was one; the manner of administering a monastic 'tonsure' haircut was another. The Synod of Whitby was convened in 664 to bridge the divide between the Northumbrian and the Roman Christianity.

Wilfrid, who had studied in Canterbury and Rome although originally a Northumbrian, was chief advocate for the Romans and seems to have used his well-honed rhetorical skills to run rings round the Northumbrian opposition in debate. So the outcome was that the Northumbrian church was brought into the mainstream Roman culture. The Bishopric of Northumbria was transferred from Lindisfarne to York. Wilfrid himself later became the bishop (and later still, a saint).

cattle for the night, because he knew nothing of music and verse. Later, he had a dream in which he heard, and remembered word and note perfect on waking, a song entitled *principium crematorium* – 'the beginning of created things'. Abbess Hild knew a gift from God when she heard one, and ordered Caedmon to take monastic vows. The gift was to last for the duration of Caedmon's long life, over which he produced an extensive oeuvre of songs and poems.

Despite such wonders it was here that, in 664 and almost by accident, the Northumbrian Christian tradition was dealt a slow, but ultimately fatal, wound at the Synod of Whitby (see box, above).

More literal, and dramatic, violence was inflicted on the abbey when it was sacked and burned in successive raids by Danes between 867 and 870. However, as at Lindisfarne (see page 105) the monastery rose again. Reinfrid, a Norman soldier under William the Conqueror who had turned his back on warfare to become a monk, was granted the remains of Whitby to found a new Benedictine monastery at the end of the 11th century.

It is the ghostly and emotion-saturated ruins of this second monastery which I wandered through, day dreaming of Hild and Caedmon, and of all the violence visited on this place sanctified by prayer and learning. After the reconstruction, next to put the boot in were Henry VIII's henchmen at the Dissolution in 1536, after which stone was carted off to build the mansion next door. This building now houses an intriguing visitor centre and museum. All sorts of Anglo-Saxon and medieval finds are on display, while computer-generated images and touch-screens make a reasonable fist of introducing us to characters who have shaped Whitby over the ages – including, of course, Hild.

In one final (we hope) act of violence against Whitby, a stray German naval shell hit the abbey in 1914.

Getting there
Whitby is on the A171, 16 miles northwest of Scarborough and 24 miles southeast of Middlesborough. By **train**, the town is reached on the Esk Valley Railway from Middlesborough.

Where to stay and eat
The Black Horse Inn 91 Church St, YO22 4BH ☎ 01947 602906
🌐 www.the-black-horse.com. A 16th-century pub with rooms. A fine array of beers, traditional Yorkshire food and delicious tapas. Nor is the selection of snuffs to be sniffed at.

Tourist information
Whitby Tourist Information Centre Langbourne Rd, YO21 1YN ☎ 01723 383637
🌐 www.whitby.co.uk.com/yorkshire/helmsley-tourist-information-centre.htm.

⑦ York

The old cliché that the history of York is the history of England is not much of an exaggeration. There is a medieval mien about the warren-like streets enclosed within the 13th-century city walls, and ruins to be explored taking you back through Anglo-Saxon to Viking times when Jorvik (from which the name York is derived) was for nearly a 100 years (866–954) the Norse capital under Danelaw. But, as a visit to the York Minster Undercroft will testify, York had been founded (as Eboracum) by the Romans in the 1st century AD.

York Minster
YO1 7HH ☎ 01904 611118 🌐 www.yorkminster.org.
In the early hours of 9 July 1984, York's beautiful and imposing Gothic cathedral was struck by lightning. The resulting fire caused massive damage, destroying much of the roof and south transept. It took four years of meticulous restoration to repair them. At the time, however, much of the media coverage focused on the vocal minority who suspected that the strike was divine retribution for the consecration as bishop of the ultra-liberal Dr David Jenkins two days before. His perceived heresies included the likening of the Resurrection to '*a conjuring trick with bones*'. Reading about this episode,

including the full quotation, it is perfectly clear that Jenkins's meaning was exactly the opposite of what his critics suggested. But no matter: a thunderbolt flew and York Minster burned.

Interestingly, York Minster's history is punctuated with conflagrations. The first wooden church on the site was built in 627 as a place to baptise Edwin, the Anglo-Saxon King of Northumbria. The church gained a school and a library, but in 741 the whole lot was destroyed by fire. It was rebuilt in stone after the Norman invasion. Fire struck again in 1137, after which construction in the Gothic style began, lasting until 1472 when the cathedral was finally declared complete.

While the Reformation took the neighbouring St Mary's Abbey (see page 139) as its bounty, York Minster became a Protestant archbishopric, second only to Canterbury in the pecking order as it remains today. Blaze number three was an act of arson in 1829, when one Jonathan Martin started a fire in the quire which destroyed the roofing and internal timbers. Eleven years later another fire (accidental, this time) burnt the roof and vaulting in the nave.

The minster today

The cathedral exerts an almighty presence, not only over the city but from further afield with the colossal tower coming into view from miles outside the centre. York Minster is the largest medieval cathedral in northern Europe. However, to feel it as a sacred place of exceptional richness does sometimes involve seeing beyond the throngs of visitors. For many, the starting point is the **Great East Window** above the Lady Chapel,

Yes, minster

The word 'minster', is a rather imprecise honorific title which has been given to certain churches in Britain over the centuries. It shares, with 'monastery', a common derivation from the Latin *monasterium*. In Old English a mynster refers variously to a monastery, nunnery, church or cathedral. At one time there were two minsters in London. Eastminster was the abbey church of the Cistercian St Mary de Graces on Tower Hill which was dissolved in 1538 and the site now occupied by the Royal Mint. Its counterpart to the west of the city, on the other hand, became known as Westminster Abbey (see page 2).

Today, the title attaches itself to a motley collection of parish churches (such as St Andrews Minster at Ashingdon in Essex or Dewsbury Minster in Yorkshire); a City Church (Stoke Minster, Doncaster Minster); or a ruin (South Elmham Minster, Suffolk). A handful of other cathedrals are minsters (Lincoln, Southwell), but York Minster is the only one invariably referred to in this way.

the world's largest medieval stained-glass window. It is hard to argue with those who see in this, and in the glinting magnificence of the cathedral's other windows, artwork of peerless beauty illuminating the expanses of the nave and transepts, the pillars and the vaulting. Architecturally, the greatest treasure is the octagonal **Chapterhouse** which, on the day of my visit, was hosting a meeting of the cathedral's Dean and Chapter as it has done regularly (allowing for a few interruptions) since the 13th century.

The **Undercroft**, **Treasury** and **Crypt** offer a glimpse of Roman York, dating from centuries before the first church existed on the site. This space underneath the minster was excavated in the 1960s, and now houses finds from both the Roman Principia building and the Norman cathedral. The treasury has a motley collection of sacred objects, including chalices and plates from around the diocese which survived the Reformation. In the crypt are more Norman remains. The 275 steps up to the summit of the **tower** take you past medieval pinnacles and gargoyles, and you are rewarded by commanding views over the city and dales beyond.

The Shrine of St Margaret Clitherow

35 Shambles, YO1 7LX ⌖ www.insideyork.co.uk/margaretclitherowshrine.html. Free access.

Of York's sacred sites, this is the easiest to miss despite being about half way along The Shambles, York's quaintest, most famous and best preserved medieval alley. I did not find it hard to imagine the blood and offal, the squelch underfoot and stench which carried the street's name into the English lexicon to mean a 'mess' or 'muddle', after the butchers' shops that once concentrated here. It was to such a background that Margaret Clitherow was sent to her own gruesome death and became a Catholic martyr in the newly Protestant England of 1584.

Margaret (*née* Middleton) was the daughter of a wax merchant who in 1571 married John Clitherow, a butcher on The Shambles, and had three sons. Three years later she converted to Catholicism, an action for which her Protestant husband had to pay her fines for not attending Protestant services as the law required. However, Margaret's devotion to her Church went much further than most recusants. She secretly instructed her children in the Catholic faith; she had a concealed cupboard in which clerical vestments, bread and chalice wine for mass were stored; and – most dangerously and illegally – she gave sanctuary to Catholic clergy on the run and had built a secret 'priest's hole' cut from her attic to the house next door, through which fugitives could flee if there was a raid.

In 1586 there came a crackdown. Margaret was arrested, charged with harbouring papist priests and imprisoned. Her children were taken to live with a Protestant family; she never saw them again. Her husband was permitted to visit her just once, in the presence of a jailer. And when her case came to court a large crowd gathered to hear her plea,

But Margaret said only, '*I know of no offence whereof I should confess myself guilty. Having made no offence, I need no trial.*'

Pronouncing the penalty for refusing to plea, the judge told her that she should be, '*stripped naked, laid down, your back on the ground, and as much weight laid upon you as you were able to bear, and so to continue for three days without meat or drink, and for the third day to be pressed to death, your hands and feet tied to posts, and a sharp stone under your back.*' Ten days later, on Good Friday 1586, the sentence was carried out.

All this is recounted in the 'Margaret Clitheroe Story', a leaflet on sale for £1 in the little former butcher's shop on The Shambles where the Clitheroes lived and suffered. There is now a discreet little chapel and shrine to the martyr who was finally canonised by Pope Paul VI in 1970. My first impression of the shrine was the moment of calm it offered in the busy tourist vein that The Shambles is today. It consists of just a single, small downstairs room, a plaque on the wall telling her story, and a simple statue of the saint behind a low altar where pilgrims offer prayers.

At the time of my visit I was joined by a lady from New Zealand who whispered to me, '*One thing nobody knew is that Margaret was pregnant again at the time of her martyrdom.*' Well I never.

St Mary's Abbey

YO1 7FR ☎ 01904 687687 🏛 www.yorkshiremuseum.org.uk/page/gardens.aspx.
Free access.

I reckon the best views of St Mary's Abbey are from the top of York Minster's tower. From here, the ruined arches and columns look like broken playthings, scattered amid the lawns, shrubberies and trees in the grounds of the Museum Gardens. From this perspective at least, first impressions are very unlike those created by, say, the breathtaking abbeys of Fountains (see page 128) or Rievaulx (see page 131).

However, St Mary's was once the most important Benedictine monastery in the whole of northern England. The original abbey on the site was founded in 1055 while York was still strongly Viking in character. It was dedicated to St Olav, whose shrine at Trondheim in Norway remains the most significant place of pilgrimage in Scandinavia. After the Norman Conquest – quite a long time after – it was re-established by William II who is said to have personally laid the foundation stone of the monastery which rapidly grew into a bastion of power and wealth.

The fact that the abbot of St Mary's features variously as a glutton and a general baddy in the early medieval ballads of Robin Hood, is telling. For in 1132, St Mary's true gift to the sacredness of Britain was given in the form of the band of 13 monks who, yearning for the spiritual rewards of asceticism which were not on offer here, left St Mary's and founded Fountains Abbey (see page 128) which was admitted to the stricter Cistercian monastic regime.

With these recalcitrants out of the way the monastery continued to prosper, becoming one of the largest landholders in the York area. But come the Reformation, boy did the mighty fall! Lands and riches were plundered and stones taken for new building projects.

Back down at eye level with the ruins, I found that the surrounding gardens and lawns made a perfect picnic spot for office workers over a sun-drenched lunchtime. The surviving ruins include a large hunk of the north transept and the west end of the nave, plus a few other bits and bobs of stone which were once parts of a cloister or warming house. Yet even these are the result of excavation and restoration after 1878 by the York Philosophical Society who remain the guardians of the site.

A certain serene temper does, for all St Mary's inglorious history, attach itself to the place. Perhaps the wraiths of the 13 holy monks linger while those of their bloated brethren have fled in shame?

Clifford's Tower
Tower St, YO1 9SA ☎ 01904 653611 🖰 www.cliffordstower.com.
Precious little remains of York Castle, the city fortification established by William the Conqueror, other than the sturdy stone keep known as Clifford's Tower. This is the site of an infamous massacre of Jews which has caused the tower to loom large in Anglo-Jewish history. Some Jewish pilgrims compare the heroic happenings at Clifford Tower, to the mass suicide at Masada in the 1st century AD.

By the early 12th century York had a large, wealthy and well-established Jewish community. However, the accession of crusading King Richard (The Lionheart) to the throne of England in 1189 heralded an era of burgeoning anti-Jewish sentiment throughout the country. Jews had been banned from Richard's coronation in Westminster Abbey, and there had been isolated attacks on Jews and their property in London and other towns.

Then, on the night of 16 March 1190 (the Jewish feast of Shabbat Ha-Gadol) about 150 Jews fled York's Jewish quarter as it came under attack. They took refuge in the castle keep (then known as the King's Tower). The tower was besieged all night by a frenzied mob brandishing torches and calling for their slaughter. The rabbi, Yom Tom of Joigny, called on the Jews to take their own lives rather than fall into the hands of their persecutors. Some did, with men killing their wives and children first.

As flames engulfed the tower, the survivors who emerged were massacred.

Before making my way to the tower, however, I had already found that Jewish history is something York's tourism authorities are keen to highlight. There is a walking map of the city's medieval Jewish quarter, for example, along streets with names such as Jewbury and Jubbergate. Nowadays Clifford's Tower is in the care of English Heritage, which treats it as a place of poignant memorial to victims of racial and religious intolerance. The tower's present name, incidentally, is in memory of Sir Roger Clifford, the defeated leader of a rebellion against King Edward III, who was executed here in 1322.

Once inside the empty tower there is little to actually see, though much to think about. A Hebrew plaque unveiled in 1978 remembers the massacred Jews on the spot where some remains from a Jewish cemetery unearthed during an archaeological dig in the 1970s, were reinterred in the presence of the British Chief Rabbi. Daffodils, their six petals and yellow colour symbolising the Star of David, are in flower on the anniversary of the massacre. And every 27 January, Holocaust Memorial Day, a vigil is held here remembering the victims of 1190 along with their millions of 20th-century counterparts.

Getting there
York is 204 miles north of London and 56 miles east of Manchester. By **train** it can be reached directly from both these cities and many others.

Where to stay and eat
Dean Court Duncombe Pl, YO1 7EF ℂ 01904 625082 ☏ www.deancourt-york. co.uk. Bang next to the minster (so 'bong!' next to the bells!). Curious mixture of old and new. The Court bistro is good value.
Golden Fleece 16 Pavement, YO1 9UP ℂ 01904 625171 ☏ www.goldenfleece. yorkwebsites.co.uk. One of the oldest pubs in York right in the city centre. Just 4 rooms. Possibly haunted.
Hotel du Vin 88 The Mount, YO24 1AX ℂ 01904 557350 ☏ www.hotelduvin. com/hotels/york/york.aspx. Swish, contemporary-style hotel and restaurant just outside town.
The Blue Bicycle 34 Fossgate, YO1 9TA ℂ 01904 673990 ☏ www.thebluebicycle. com. A fun and relaxed restaurant specialising in fish and seafood.
Yorkshire Terrier 10 Stonegate, YO1 8AS ℂ 01904 676722 ☏ www.york-brewery.co.uk. Beautiful old pub, and flagship of the famous York Brewery.

Tourist information
York Tourist Information Centre 1 Museum St, YO1 7DT ℂ 01904 550099 ☏ www.visityork.org.

⑧ Chester

Three orgiastically entwined figures make up a modern sculpture outside Chester's imperious town hall. The somewhat controversial work, by sculptor

Stephen Broadbent, is entitled *A Celebration of Chester* and was unveiled in 1992 to mark the 900th anniversary of the foundation of St Werburga's Abbey, now known as Chester Cathedral.

Closer inspection reveals that the trio represent Industry, Protection and Thanksgiving, referring to commerce, the city walls and Chester's sacred traditions.

Chester is one of those small tourism-driven English cities which, like Bath or York, is both fun and fascinating without resorting to theme-park style 'attractions'. Large numbers visit Chester for some of the most extensive and accessible Roman remains in Britain. Chester was the fortress city of Deva, founded by the Romans in the 1st century AD to subdue the troublesome Celtic north Welsh tribes. It was the base for 200 years of the 20th Valeria Victrix Legion. A further 2,000 years of action-packed history featured Vikings, Normans, civil warriors, medieval monks and industrial revolutionaries.

Chester Cathedral is, to put it kindly, not one of Britain's top ten cathedrals. It does, however, have an unusual history and an aura to match, which is why I chose it as the starting point in my exploration of the city.

Chester Cathedral, St Werburga and her shrine

The seat of the Bishopric of Chester is also known as St Werburga's after the saint whose cult drew medieval pilgrims in their thousands to the great Benedictine monastery. St Werburga's Abbey was eventually to become the cathedral where today occasional devotees still supplicate themselves at her shrine.

Looking at the pinkish, Victorian-style façade, I could only wonder how the cathedral could possibly be 900 years old. The answer is that it is a hotchpotch of different styles, with different sections having been added over the ages since it first housed the remains of Chester's patron saint. The oldest sections were part of the Benedictine monastery and incorporate several of the monastic buildings, including the refectory which now functions as a café.

St Werburga was the daughter of Anglo-Saxon King Wulfhere of Mercia. Her mother was St Erminilda and her grandmother the alluringly named St Sexburga. As if that was not enough royalty and saintliness for one family, her great-aunt was Etheldreda (see page 94), the first Abbess of Ely and former Queen of Northumbria.

Werburga was born at Stone in what is now Staffordshire around AD640 (there is no record of exactly when) and duly became a nun at Ely under the tutelage of her great-aunt who she eventually succeeded as abbess.

Her father's brother and successor, Aethelred, also invited her to take charge of various monasteries in his kingdom, include Hanbury, Trentham and Weedon. Although not a vast amount is known about her life, St Werburga is credited with numerous miracles, the latter monastery being the scene of the most famous. Weedon's lands were being devastated by a gaggle of wild geese which were ravishing the crops and causing untold damage. One day when the birds were being particularly obstreperous the saint drove them into a pen and ordered them to leave, sternly lecturing them on the iniquities of greed. They agreed. However, before they could depart a monastery employee killed and plucked one of the penitent geese. Hearing of the injustice, Werburga restored it to life and plumage, whereupon the flock kept their side of the bargain and flew away forever. To this day St Werburga's symbol is a pair of geese, as evidenced by a wood carving in Chester's cathedral choir.

St Werburga died at Trentham Monastery in AD699. Her first shrine was at Hanbury where she was interred and remained until the Viking raids of the mid-9th century. In 875 her relics were carried out of harm's way to the church of saints Peter and Paul within the protection of Chester's city walls, on the site of which a new church to house her was built in 907.

In 1092, after the Norman Conquest, Henry Lupus, Earl of Chester and nephew of William the Conqueror, founded the great Benedictine Abbey of St Werburga whose centrepiece was an elaborate and bejewelled shrine to the city's new patron saint. When the monastery was dissolved at the Reformation the shrine was broken up and its pieces scattered, along with the remains of St Werburga. Rather than being destroyed by Henry's henchman, however, the abbey became the cathedral of the newly created Diocese of Chester. In 1876 surviving fragments of the shrine and of St Werburga's remains were pieced together and a new, simpler pink stone shrine was built in the Lady Chapel behind the High Altar, to accommodate them.

I had expected to have this peaceful place to myself, and so was surprised to find four women and a man kneeling in prayer before a row of candles they had lit at the shrine, where a wooden sculpture of the serene-looking saint in a cloak gazes into the middle distance. The group, it turned out, was composed of both members of the Church of England and Roman Catholics. They were on an ecumenical pilgrimage and had been drawn here by their common belief that women should play more central roles in the leadership of both churches.

I had to remind myself that, like other powerful Anglo-Saxon abbesses such as St Hild (see page 134), St Werburga held a position of huge authority within the Church establishment of her day. If she could have only imagined proponents of sexual equality praying at her shrine more than 1,200 years later.

A walk around Chester

From *A Celebration of Chester*, I followed the incline of 'Industry' towards the main shopping streets. First I passed the **Forum**, a shopping precinct suggestive of Chester's eminence as the Roman fortress town of Deva. This is a 21st-century shopping arcade, although the Roman marketplace probably lies below. Like so much of Chester, most of which is built on Roman foundations, nobody really knows what is underneath.

What is truly bizarre, however, is the way you can find unexpected fragments of the Roman era in the unlikeliest of places. For example, on my way down Eastgate, a street lined with black and white 'magpie' timber-framed houses, I stopped at 'Spudulike', a fast-food joint specialising in baked potatoes. In the basement, behind a glass panel, is a perfectly excavated section of a hypocaust which once warmed a Roman bigwig's residence, probably as efficiently as the ovens upstairs bake potatoes today. Similarly, in the basement Miss Selfridge on Northgate Street I had to fight my way through a delivery of lingerie to explore the foundations of the Praetorium; and at Castle Galleries on St Michael's Row, I admired a section of mosaic flooring that once decorated a bathhouse.

I stopped for a beer at the **Marlbororough** to clear my senses. This is a fairly ordinary pub whose notoriety has been spreading ever since a sign painter returned somewhat over-refreshed from his lunch break and completed his work with an 'O' and an 'R' beyond the call of duty. The barman told me he is still waiting for a visit by the Duke of Wellingington – a line I suspect he has used before.

A few paces away on a footbridge spanning the road was the splendidly ornate **Eastgate Clock**, reputedly Britain's most photographed timepiece after Big Ben. From here I climbed an old, worn stone staircase to walk round the two mile-long, virtually unbroken **defensive walls** which enclose Chester's heart. Originally Roman ramparts, they were extended and so strongly reinforced by Saxons and again during the Middle Ages, that during the Civil War they withstood Cromwell's cannon.

Passing the semi-excavated **Roman amphitheatre**, the largest in Britain, I made my way to the River Dee. The Romans founded Deva to subdue the Celtic north Welsh tribes and the Old Dee Bridge is still a main gateway to Wales, about $1^1/_2$ miles away. Over centuries of cross-border lawlessness, Chester remained a frontline fortress with powerful anti-Welsh traditions. A 1402 bylaw, said to be still on the statute book, entitles any citizen who catches a Welshman within the city walls between dusk and dawn, to shoot him with a crossbow.

I followed the wall alongside the Dee, past the bridge and weir on the left. Atop a mound to the right are the battlements of **Chester Castle**, originally build by William the Conqueror and now a Crown Court. Just beyond, the wide green plain of Roodee Racecourse opens out with the river looping round its far boundary several hundred yards from the remains of the quay where Roman galleys once docked. The Dee subsequently silted up and changed course, so the quay has been high and dry for more than 500 years.

It was a stiff climb to Morgan's Mount, the highest point, from where there are views across to Moel Fammu ('Mother Mountain') in Wales. Last stop on the walls was at **King Charles Tower** where, according to an inscription, '*King*

Charles stood on September 24th 1645 and saw his army defeated on Rowton Moor.' The king had come to Royalist Chester, but had been unexpectedly besieged by Roundhead forces. The moor is obscured by buildings, but there are still views over into north Wales, where the king escaped to the following day.

Back on Town Hall Square next to the cathedral, I felt able to assess *A Celebration of Chester* with perhaps a little more sympathy.

Getting there

Chester is 15 miles south of Liverpool, reached via the M53 motorway. Chester is on a **rail** intersection, reached directly from London, Birmingham and Liverpool.

Where to stay and eat

ABode Chester Grosvenor Rd, CH1 2DJ ☎ 01244 347000 🖰 www.abodehotels. co.uk/chester. Large, modern, boutique 4-star hotel near the walls with sweeping views over the city or Roodee Racecourse – especially from the 5th floor Champagne Bar.

Joseph Benjamin 134–140 North Gate St, CH1 2HT ☎ 01244 344295 🖰 www.josephbenjamin.co.uk. An alluring mid-market restaurant brimming with the enthusiasm of the owners, brothers Joe and Ben. Fresh ingredients, unstuffy presentation.

Mitchell's of Chester Guest House 28 Hough Green, CH4 8JQ ☎ 01244 679004 🖰 www.mitchellsofchester.com. Comfortable, small, family-run guesthouse less than a mile from the city centre. Excellent value.

The Chester Grosvenor and Spa Eastgate, CH1 1LT ☎ 01244 324024 ☎ 01244 895600 🖰 www.chestergrosvenor.com. The place to stay and dine if you can afford it. Top-notch for location in the heart of Chester, luxurious rooms, impeccable service and Michelin-starred dining in Simon Radley at the Chester Grosvenor. Parisian-style La Brasserie serves more affordable, excellent food.

The Marlbororough Arms 3 St John St, CH1 1DA ☎ 01244 323543. Good choice of local beers, and wholesome pub food served with anecdotes about the spelling.

Tourist information

Chester Visitor Information Town Hall, Northgate St, CH1 2HJ ☎ 0845 647 7868 🖰 www.visitchester.com.

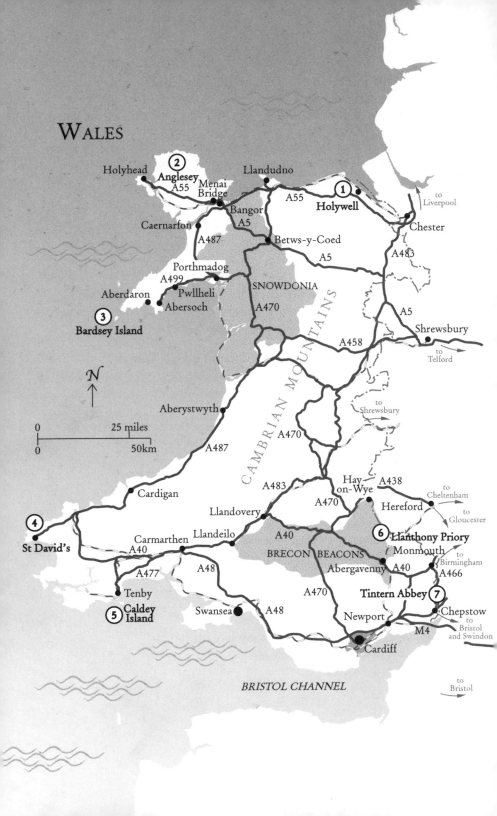

6. WALES

S acred sites in Wales vary as much as the cultures that have revered them over the ages. However, from eerie burial chambers and 'henges' on islands where Druids met in their hallowed oak groves, via shrines to which relays of pilgrims once journeyed over the mountains, to the scenes of extraordinary miracles which were to become havens for persecuted Catholics, a common factor stands out: an affirmation of the identity and spiritual values of Wales.

Nowhere in Wales is more sacred than St David's. Here – in a venture unparalleled in Britain for centuries – modern pilgrims will soon venerate Dewi Sant at a new shrine being created in the cathedral. This project reawakens an ancient tradition which has been dormant (not dead, as some had thought) since the Reformation.

① Holywell

CH8 7PN ☎ 01352 713054 ⚲ www.saintwinefrideswell.com.

'Holywell – The Lourdes of Wales', declared a large road sign as I turned off the main A55 along the north coast between Chester and Anglesey, to find this village by the Dee estuary. Fair enough, I thought; after all, I was not far from Snowdon – 'The Everest of Wales', or Rhyl – 'The St Tropez of Wales'.

Mick-taking aside, the rather startling parallel with Europe's biggest and most vibrant pilgrim shrine does rather distil the essence of what makes this infinitely more discreet little holy place tick. No doubt many visitors are surprised to discover that Holywell has been a place of pilgrimage continuously for some 1,300 years.

My arrival received an unexpected twist of exoticism by coinciding with a bus load of exuberantly high-spirited Christians of south Asian origin from Birmingham. We all paid the nugatory entrance fee and traipsed first through a visitor centre starting with a series of rather gaudy life-sized tableaux of figures depicting scenes from St Winefride's colourful life. They reminded me of the statues paraded through streets during holy week in Latin countries. The museum ended with a huge pile of crutches discarded by cured pilgrims over the years, rather as one sees in Lourdes ('The Holywell of France').

Then we all wandered across the hedge-fringed lawns of the shrine precincts, past an outdoor rectangular bathing pool of green-tinged, clear water. Beyond was the chapel built of dusty-pinkish sandstone over the original well-head in 1490, by Lady Margaret Beaufort (see below). It is an odd architectural arrangement, with the chapel balancing stilt-like on stone pillars above the large, open octagonal well.

Inside, under a fan-vaulted ceiling, we processed round the pilgrims' walkway which encircles the deep, dark well. It was here that, until the 19th century, the faithful would plunge themselves into the icy water – usually three times, in deference to St Bueno's prayer (see below). A mass of ancient graffiti and secret Catholic symbols and messages are scratched into the walls.

Nowadays the bathing takes place at appointed times of day only, in the shallower, rectangular pool outside. Next to it there are four yellow canvas changing huts with spiked blue roofs, which looked as if they would be happier at a fairground. Alas, there were no takers on the wind-whipped day I was there, though some of the brummies and I sat on the steps and tipped our toes in. About 54°F, perhaps? A single full immersion would have been some penance, never mind three.

Suddenly, we were saved by the bell. It was rung by Father Anil Akkara, a Catholic priest from Kerala in India who is one of the Vocationalist Fathers to whom St Winefride's parish, and hence the shrine, is entrusted by the Diocese of Wrexham. Father Akkara had arrived, in full ceremonial vestments, for the daily service. We returned to the chapel and gathered around the well, as the priest carefully opened a battered old leather case out of which he took, with great reverence, the gilt monstrance containing a tiny relic of St Winefride. This fragment of her finger nail became our focus during 15 minutes of prayers and adoration.

History and legend

The story of Holywell starts in the 7th century, in a north Wales valley known as Sechnant or 'dry valley' because it was barren for lack of a natural water supply. Winefride, a chaste young maiden and daughter of a Welsh nobleman, was the object of unwanted sexual advances by the boorish Caradoc, son of a local priest. One day, while her family were in church, the brute arrived drunk at her home and tried first to seduce, then to rape her. She slipped his clutches and ran towards the church. Enraged, he pursued her, caught up and hacked off her head in righteous indignation at being rejected.

At which point Bueno, one of her uncles, came running out of the church and cast curses on Caradoc, causing the earth to open up and swallow his body whole. Then, turning to the butchered victim, he prayed that she be restored to life. Bueno placed Winefride's head back on her shoulders, and she stood up alive and kicking. Furthermore, a well had burst forth on the very spot where his niece's head had fallen moments earlier, with her blood turned to cool, fresh water.

St (as he would become) Bueno later took St (as she would become) Winefride to the well and declared that, '*Whoever shall at any time in whatever sorrow or suffering implore your aid for deliverance from sickness or misfortune, shall at the first or the second or certainly the third petition obtain his wish and rejoice at the obtainment of what was asked for*'.

St Winefride lived out her days as a nun at nearby Gwytherin convent, eventually becoming abbess. Her remains were taken to Shrewsbury Abbey, where they stayed until its destruction at the Reformation. Uncle Bueno, meanwhile, built a chapel on the site of the miracle and so began the tradition of pilgrimage to this sacred healing well, with many faithful praying to the saint both here and at Shrewsbury.

We do, however, have to advance a few hundred years for recorded accounts of miraculous healings such as the 12th-century penitent whose wrists had been shackled for years in punishment for some awful misdeed. As he prayed for forgiveness at St Winefride's shrine, a pair of hands appeared shimmering in the well water and untied the chains in answer to the prayer.

This rather curious legend apart, Winefide's saintly specialism appears to have been in the gynaecological department, with numberless women making the pilgrimage to north Wales to pray for her intercession in all matters relating to reproduction. It was in response to this that, in 1490, the formidable Lady Margaret Beaufort, an ardent devotee of Holywell, enlarged and rebuilt the shrine. Most significantly she added the chapel that survives today with the well in its undercoft.

Lady Margaret Beaufort was the mother of Henry Tudor, who had become Henry VII of England in 1485 after defeating Richard III at the Battle of Bosworth Field. She was, therefore, the grandmother of Henry VIII on who she had had a powerful influence. His reign began in 1509, the year she died, which may be one reason why, uniquely within the realm, the shrine survived the Reformation.

Nevertheless, the fact that Holywell is the only shrine in Britain with a continuous history of pilgrimage from the early Middle Ages to the present is at least as miraculous as any healing (or even re-attachment of a severed head). The high regard in which Henry held his granny might have inhibited any initial destruction, but this alone cannot explain why St Winefride and her shrine have proved so astonishingly resilient.

So it is also worth remembering that there was widespread resentment at Henry's incorporation of Wales into his kingdom. Loyalty to the forbidden faith and visiting the shrine, therefore, very likely became symbols of Welsh identity and defiance. Certainly, Catholic recusants from further afield continued to regard Holywell as a focus for their religion, since the faith was still practised in this tiny pocket of north Wales.

Queen Elizabeth I actually tried to have the waters poisoned – unsuccessfully, it seems, since James II visited in 1686 without ill effect, during his short reign when Catholicism was briefly back in the open.

The pioneering travel writer Celia Fiennes was horrified to see Catholics openly bathing in the holy well. In her 1685 memoir *The Journeys of Celia Fiennes* she noted:

> *I saw abundance of ye devout papists on their Knees all round a well. Poor people are deluded into an ignorant blind zeale and to be pity'd by us that have the advantage of knowing better and ought to be better. There is some stones of a Reddish Colour in ye well said to be some of St Winifred's blood also, which ye poore people take out and bring to ye strangers for Curiosity and Relicts.*

Daniel Defoe was another amazed witness to the undisguised popery at Holywell, writing in his 1727, *A Tour Through The Whole Island of Great Britai':*

> *The stories of this Well of St Winifrid are, that the pious virgin, being ravished and murdered, this healing water sprung out of her body when buried; but this smells too much of the legend, to take up any of my time; the Romanists indeed believe it, as is evident, from their thronging hither to receive the healing sanative virtue of the water, which they do not hope for as it is a medicinal water, but as it is a miraculous water, and heals them by virtue of the intercession and influence of this famous virgin, St Winifrid; of which I believe as much as comes to my share.*

In the 1890s the Catholic Church felt free enough to start organising processions through the village every 22 June, St Winefride's feast day. Custodianship of the shrine was handed to the Jesuit order who proclaimed the sacredness of Holywell throughout Britain. The faithful came in ever-increasing numbers, as stories of miraculous healings were reported in the press and on the radio. Hostels opened to accommodate up to 100,000 pilgrims a year and in 1913 a branch line to Saint Winefride's Halt station was constructed from the Chester to Holyhead railway, in response to this huge and unexpected resurgence of Catholic pilgrimage, matched only by Walsingham (see page 96).

Numbers declined after World War II and the branch line was pruned by the 'Beeching Axe' in the 1960s. These days about 35,000 pilgrims a year – of various faiths, not just Catholics – come to Holywell.

Getting there
Holywell is reached on the A5026, via the A55, 9 miles west of Chester. The nearest

train station is Flint on the north Wales Coast Line, from where there are Arriva Wales buses to Holywell on Arriva Wales (*0871 2002 233; www.arrivabus.co.uk*).

Where to stay and eat

Celyn Villa Carmel, near Holywell CH8 8QP ☏ 01352 710853 ✆ www.celynvilla. co.uk. A delightfully located B&B with a view over the Dee Estuary, just 2 miles from Holywell. Set dinners served.

Greenhill Farm Guest House Bryn Celyn, Holywell CH8 7QF ☏ 01352 713270 ✆ www.greenhillfarm.co.uk. An old stone and timber farmhouse and family-run B&B on the edge of Holywell.

Tourist information

Tourist Information Point Holywell Library, North Rd, CH8 7TQ ☏ 01352 713157 ✆ www.holywell-town.co.uk.

② Anglesey (Ynys Môn)

The 'Sacred Isle' label effortlessly attaches itself to Ynys Môn or Anglesey, to use the Norse-derived Anglicised name. I noticed the term used on a road sign welcoming me to the island as I crossed the Menai Strait on the A55. This is where I had paused to admire the unexpected sight of a pirate ship flying the Jolly Roger, sailing under Thomas Telford's extraordinarily beautiful 1826 iron suspension bridge.

The reference to Anglesey's sacredness sometimes lacks focus, but the notion of the island having been a last refuge of the mysterious and magical Druids, is deeply ingrained in the north Welsh consciousness. It was to this remote island, divided from mainland northwest Wales by a narrow stretch of water, that the Celtic civilisation, identity and religion retreated as the Roman armies overran Britain.

This was why, on the bridge over the Menai Strait, I tried to imagine the sight that met the Roman forces under Agricola when, after several failed attempts, they finally launched their successful AD78 assault on 'Mona' as they called the island. To the southeast are the mountains of Snowdonia, which would have been the most dramatic that any Roman soldier had seen since they left the Alps. Across the strait, by contrast, was a green, flatter island on whose shores were ranged the woad-painted Druid warriors riding in their chariots with their swords, shields and crested helmets.

'*At this sight our soldiers were gripped with fear*', wrote the Roman historian (and son-in-law of Agricola) Gaius Cornelius Tacitus. According to Tacitus, the Druid warriors, both men and women, '*howled blood-curdling curses in the style of Furies. In robes of deathly black and with dishevelled hair, they brandished their torches*'. Nevertheless, the Roman soldiers and their horses crossed the Menai Strait on rafts and set about slaughtering the Druids. They made it their business to attempt to obliterate every trace of the degenerate and savage religion whose adherents drenched their holy altars with the blood of sacrificed humans.

Well, as an apologist for the civilising Romans, Tacitus would paint that sort of a picture of Druids and Druidism, wouldn't he? The trouble is that unlike the Romans who had writers to record their versions of history for posterity, the Druids wrote nothing about their beliefs. Druidism relied on oral traditions, and lore inherited and transmitted through the generations by memory. Distilled and concentrated as it now was on Anglesey, the Romans were able to all but annihilate this magical Celtic culture in a single, bloody invasion.

All the same, through a combination of archaeology, folklore and a variety of accounts including Roman (albeit seen through the victors' prism), it is possible to put together a rather more complex picture of this ancient civilisation. It is now understood, for example, that the Druids worshipped at least 400 gods and believed, in a way similar to Buddhism or Hinduism, in reincarnation. Ceremonies were led by priests and priestesses who were also healers and teachers, and underwent years of training.

There was a revival of interest in Druidism during the 18th and 19th centuries in which poets and romantics tried to revive Druid ceremonies, and unearth traces of their Celtic traditions which had been absorbed into indigenous cultures. One of the more plausible of these is that our Christmas custom of kissing under the mistletoe has its ancestry in the Druidic belief that mistletoe had the power to ease childbirth.

We know that Druid religion focused on the sacredness of natural phenomena such as woodlands, lakes and streams. Oak groves in particular were important as centres of ritual and ceremony. Tacitus wrote about the destruction of the sacred oak groves on Anglesey, which suggests that the Romans understood how significant these were.

Of course, almost by definition natural phenomena such as the groves have left no mark on Anglesey. In fact, I had joined a group of amateur archaeologists on a tour of the island of which the main features were the remains of Neolithic, Bronze and Iron Age civilisations dating back to long before the invasion by warrior Celts. It was to this facet of the 'Sacred Isle' that we were being welcomed as we drove from the Menai Bridge, out across the wind-flattened grass and pitted rocks of Môn.

Bryn Celli Ddu

There is a small parking area on the A4080, 2 miles west of Llanfair PG. The site is reached on foot, about half-a-mile from the road. Free access.

A rusty signpost points the way across some fields towards one of the less pronounceable of Anglesey's ancient monuments (and that really is saying something). Bryn Celli Ddu translates as 'the mound in the dark grove', and is actually pronounced (even more roughly) 'Bryn-keh-hlee-thee'. I found that

the low-key approach does not even hint at the scale, much less the mystery and aura, of this Stone Age burial chamber inside a grassy mound within an earth embankment and ditch. The 'henge' is thought to be the oldest part of the monument and was constructed about 4,000 years ago, along with a stone circle of which little survives.

Fortunately I had a torch to help me creep along a dark passage under two huge capstones into the chamber where, when it was excavated in 1928, fragments of Neolithic human bone were found. A standing stone carved with spirals outside the entrance is a copy of the original which has (unfortunately in my view), been removed to the National Museum and Galley in Cardiff. It is aligned with the summer solstice.

Barclodiad Y Gawes

The site is just of the A4080 a mile south of Llanfaelog village. Free access, though there is a door to the burial chamber which is sometimes locked. If it is, ask for the key at the Wayside village shop in Llanfaelog (*01407 810153*).

Another Neolithic burial chamber, this one spectacularly set on a windy sea cliff amid a cacophony of screeching seabirds, overlooking the Irish Sea. Waves pound on to Porth Trecastell cove. The site's name translates (roughly) as 'apronful of the giantess'. It consists of a long passage leading to a central chamber which is decorated with spirals and zigzags, lozenges and chevron designs. It was excavated in 1952–53, when the remains of a stew which might have been palatable to the witches of Macbeth was analysed. The meal was found to have consisted of, amongst other ingredients, frog, toad, grass-snake, mouse and shrew.

Getting there

Bangor on the north Wales mainland is the gateway to Anglesey. Two bridges near the town span the Menai Strait: the old A5 crosses via Telford's famous 1826 iron bridge; a modern one a little way south carries the A55 main road to Holyhead.

Where to stay and eat

Neuadd Lwyd Penmynydd, Llanfair Pwllgwyngyll LL61 5BX ☎ 01248 715005 www.neuaddlwyd.co.uk. This hotel is a beautiful Victorian former rectory in open countryside, with spectacular views across the Menai Strait to Snowdonia. 4-course dinners with local ingredients.

Ucheldre Kitchen Millbank, Holyhead LL65 1TE ☎ 01407 763361 www.ucheldre.org. A great place for a glass of wine and tasty snack for lunch. The café, in a converted chapel, is attached to the town's arts centre.

Ye Olde Bulls Head Inn and Townhouse Castle St, Beaumaris LL58 8AP

☎ 01248 810329 🌐 www.bullsheadinn.co.uk. A 15th-century posting inn where Charles Dickens once stayed, with the more expensive boutique Townhouse hotel across the road. Rooms named after Dickens characters, but don't be afraid to ask for more in either the Brasserie or the fancier Loft Restaurant.

Tourist information
Llanfair Pwllgwyngyll Tourist Information Centre Station Site LL61 5UJ
☎ 01248 713177 🌐 www.walestouristguide.com.

③ Bardsey Island (Ynys Enlli)

A salty zephyr wafted across Bardsey Sound as about a dozen of us clambered from motor launch to put-putting rubber landing craft. First ashore as we grated into the shingle, was a tall man with an elongated grey beard, clasping a wooden staff. Prostrating himself to kiss the Bardsey beach, he was followed by a woman in a voluminous black habit. Spot-the-pilgrim was proving an easier sport than I had expected.

'There is quiet revival in pilgrimage going on, if by that we mean making a journey to search for something beyond the material', poet Christine Evans told me. Christine has published a collection of verse, *Island of Dark Horses*, inspired by her life on Bardsey (or Ynys Enlli, meaning 'Island in the Current' in Welsh). She is one of just a handful of residents on this far-flung scrap of green, two miles off the tip of north Wales's Llyn peninsula. Christine explained further what she meant, 'Bardsey satisfies a hunger for nature and simplicity … for somewhere to unwind, where distinctions between the physical and spiritual are less pronounced.'

History and legend
On Bardsey you not only unwind, but also rewind through the ages. Traces of Stone Age huts provide the earliest evidence of human settlement. However, the island appears to have been uninhabited when, in the 5th century AD, monks of the early Celtic churches arrived in search of wild and remote refuges from the temptations of the world. They settled here and established St Mary's Abbey, the first monastery.

Over the next thousand years, the isle became one of the holiest places in the British Isles. In the 13th century the Augustinian order took over the abbey and expanded it as pilgrims arrived to pray at the graves of the Celtic saints Deniol, Cadfan and Dyfrig who had all died here. Meanwhile, Bardsey's mythical status grew further, when some versions of Arthurian legend put it about that Merlin the Magician – Myrddin Emyrs, in Welsh – had died and was buried on Bardsey. Other accounts even suggested that Bardsey might be the real Isle of Avalon and final resting place of Arthur himself, despite the far more widely accepted claims of Glastonbury (see page 55).

Throughout the Middle Ages untold numbers of pilgrims made the torturous journey, sometimes several weeks long, across the Welsh mountains. When the Pope inflated Bardsey's spiritual stock by pronouncing that three journeys to Bardsey were worth one to Rome, the numbers burgeoned still further. Many pilgrims were old or in an advanced state of illness, because it was believed that to die on Bardsey bought a fast ticket to heaven. There are stories of coffins being carried in relays to Bardsey because, short of dying there and reaching paradise, at least being buried on the island might be a way of avoiding hell. The popular claim that the bones of 20,000 'saints' lie in the island's soil, is probably a reference to the number of pilgrims who succeeded in these endeavours.

Like monasteries everywhere, St Mary's Abbey was destroyed at the Dissolution and the island was given over to farming. Records show that in 1881 there were 132 islanders. There was a grocery store, and a school which remained open till 1953 – the same year that the island was first designated a bird sanctuary. In 1961 numbers were down to 19, and today are in single figures.

Visiting the island

These days the Rome=3xBardsey equation seems to have reversed; even on a budget airline, reaching Rome is at least three times quicker and more comfortable than trying to reach Bardsey from many parts of Britain. An expedition from London or even Cardiff to the end of the Llyn peninsula takes most of a day by car, or train and bus. Then there is the crossing which may be only 15 minutes, but is always dependent on the weather, with times changing according to the currents, winds and sluicing tides.

Boatman Tony Bruce told me, 'Casual day-trippers are deterred by the inaccessibility, and the fact that the return crossings can never be guaranteed – you never know when you might be stranded … Bardsey is probably more remote now than it was a thousand years ago.'

Owing to a tidal whim, our boat had to leave from nearby Porth Meudyn, or Hermit's Cove, where I met Howard Hughes of the beard and staff who (despite his name) described himself as 'a penniless pilgrim through a barren land'. The nun was Russian Orthodox Mother Nektaria McLees, originally Californian, who had travelled from Moscow on a quest for 'the spiritual purity of a place that has been holy since Celtic times, before the schisms that divided Christians'. The motives of my other fellow passengers for visiting Bardsey were less obvious: pilgrims of sorts perhaps, solitude seekers or nature lovers lured by the abundant bird life. The island is on important migratory routes and a nesting place for choughs and Manx shearwaters.

I wandered towards the ruins of St Mary's Abbey where, standing round a stone altar in a roofless chapel, a group was reading aloud from the Collected Work of R S Thomas, the poet who was once Vicar of St Hywyn's in Aberdaron. I made a point of later looking up his poem 'Pilgrimages' which is about Bardsey and begins:

There is an island there is no going
to but in a small boat, the way
the saints went, travelling the gallery
of the frightened faces of
the long-drowned, munching the gravel
of its beaches.

Sheep grazed lazily amid the crumbling abbey walls and tower, and on the steep gradients of Mynydd Enlli (known as 'the mountain'), which rises 548ft out of the sea dividing the island into heather-strewn highlands and flat, low-lying pasture fenced and walled into neat shapes. To the background chee-ow of choughs, I scrambled up a steep track to the peak, from where Ireland's Wicklow Hills were visible as a smudge on the horizon. I could just make out colonies of grey seals slobbing on the skerries which necklace the island. Palls of white smoke rose peacefully from Bardsey's scattering of farmhouses and cottages, then disappeared in violent gusts.

From my vantage point I followed tiny figures roaming the Bardsey byways, and reflected on the spiritual pull that has drawn them here. Reverand Evelyn Davies, the current Vicar of St Hywyn's, had suggested to me that, 'When hundreds of thousands have made a journey with spiritual motives, that place will have a timeless call to people in search of the spiritual.' I certainly agree with her that the island has a calming, shoulder-relaxing aura.

Back on the mainland, I still had a little miracle to investigate. Out on the forbidding grey headland of Mynydd Mawr facing the island, I found the remains of St Mary's Church where pilgrims would have stopped to pray at the end of their walk along the Llyn peninsula. Then, as they waited for their boats at the end of the land journey, they would kneel at a seaweedy rock pool and slake their thirst on running water miraculously turned pure and sweet.

Sceptics should do as I did, and scramble down over rocks worn smooth by innumerable pilgrim feet, into a salty, spume-flecked cleft in the forbidding grey headland facing Bardsey, and drink a fulsome draft of fresh water from this pool, the so-called St Mary's Well. I was astonished, almost bewitched.

Freshwater springs below the high tide mark are a rare, if not unheard of geographic phenomenon. Nevertheless, this was a moment that felt truly blessed by miracle.

Getting there
Boats to Bardsey leave from Aberdaron, or occasionally Porth Meudyn, at times variable with the tide. Call ☎ 07971 769 895 for times and bookings or check on ⊕ www.bardseyboattrips.com. Aberdaron is on the westernmost tip of the Llyn peninsula, reached via the A499 and the B4413. The nearest **train** station is Pwllheli from where there are Arriva Wales **buses** to Aberdaron (*0871 2002 233; www.arrivabus.co.uk*).

Where to stay and eat
Self-catering cottages on Bardsey without electricity are rented on a weekly basis, between March and September. Contact the **Bardsey Island Trust** (*Plas Glyn-y-Weddw, Llanbedrog, Pwllheli LL53 7TT; 08458 112233; www.enlli.org*).

The Ship Hotel Aberdaron, Pwllheli LL53 8BE ☎ 01758 760204 ⊕ www.theship hotelaberdaron.co.uk. This small, friendly hotel with a good restaurant by the beach is an excellent place to overnight before crossing to Bardsey.

Tourist information
Abersoch and Llyn Tourist Information Centre The Vestry, High St, Abersoch LL53 7DS ☎ 01758 712929 ⊕ www.abersochandllyn.co.uk.

④ St David's

If size mattered, Britain's smallest city would count for little. With a population of barely 1,700, the fact that St David's is a city at all seems rather peculiar, but it has a cathedral and that is what counts. I approached from the Pembrokeshire Coast Path, walking for ten minutes inland through the rugged wilds of this westernmost tip of Wales. My destination felt like little more than a village, with a few shops, pubs and small hotels. Even strolling down the main street I could only just see the cathedral, sunken as it is into a natural dip.

The city dedicated to Saint David (or Dewi Sant, in Welsh) is the most sacred place in Wales. Celtic missionaries came and went from this coast; the cathedral, founded by and named after the nation's patron saint, is the mother church of Wales.

History and legend
So who was Saint David? He was born somewhere near the place that now bears his name in, give or take a decade or so, AD520. Dewi was the son of a local nobleman, the Prince of Ceredigion, or just possibly, as some traditions have it, a chieftain called Xantus who seduced his mother, St Non. Either way, Dewi's birth on a Pembrokeshire clifftop was marked by a violent storm. During the paroxysms of childbirth Non clung to a boulder which was then

struck by lightning, splitting it in two. The pair of riven rocks eventually became the foundation stones of St David's Cathedral and St Non's Well. (The philosophy of 'non'-violence, by the way, has nothing to do with this tale.)

David was prepared for his saintly life at Llanilltud Fawr monastery in Glamorgan. The first signs of his miraculous powers became apparent when, as a young monk, he attended a synod at Llanddewi Brefi in Cardiganshire which descended into an unruly squabble. Suddenly, the ground he was standing on rose of its own accord placing David in the commanding position from which he calmed the crowd and preached with great wisdom.

Next David retreated to the wild and remote Ewyas Valley (see page 164) in the Black Mountains where he lived in austerity as a hermit, preparing himself for his ministry. After this he travelled widely throughout Wales and further afield in Britain, preaching the gospel. There are tales of him having visited the chapel founded by St Joseph of Arimathea at Glastonbury (see page 57). He was cured of an illness by taking the waters at Bath (see page 49) and had churches named after him in Devon, Cornwall, Lincolnshire and Herefordshire. He also made the 'Great Pilgrimage' to Jerusalem, the most demanding journey that could be made at the time from western Europe. He travelled overland to Italy, then by sea to Egypt and across the Sinai Desert first to the monastery of St Catherine, then on to the holy city where he visited the sites associated with Christ and the Passion.

With this adventure under his belt, he returned to the rocky, barren region of his birth, far from the worldly temptations he had encountered on his travels. Here he founded a monastery beside a little river, the Alun, in whose waters he was to baptise numerous converts.

Dewi's death on 1 March (still celebrated as St David's Day in Wales) in around AD580 was as serene as his birth had been dramatic: choirs of singing angels filled the monastery as his soul was carried up to heaven.

His body, meanwhile, was placed in a tomb within the cathedral. It soon became a shrine for local people awed by his renowned kindness and sanctity, and by degrees a place of pilgrimage attracting the faithful from around Wales, then Ireland, England, Scotland and eventually continental Europe. Despite being out of sight from the sea, the cathedral was repeatedly raided by Vikings in the 10th and 11th centuries. The shrine was desecrated and its gold and silver looted, but this sacrilege appears only to have increased the allure of David.

A new shrine was build, with the saint's relics kept in a portable casket at the base. (A second reliquary held the bones of St Justinian, a contemporary of St David who had lived as a hermit on Ramsey Island just off the tip of Pembrokeshire.) New pilgrim routes threaded their way across Europe, leading the faithful to west Wales. Kings and queens came, including Henry II, and by the 12th century the shrine was so famous that Pope Calixtus II decreed that two pilgrimages 'in search of St David' were the equal of one 'in search of the Apostles' – meaning to Rome. Three were on a par with a journey to

Jerusalem, though it is hard to find records of any penitents clocking up such a hat-trick.

For centuries the little Welsh town played in the premier league of European pilgrimage destinations, up there with the likes of Santiago de Compostela. To many in the Welsh Church, the Bishopric of St David's was considered equal to its counterpart at Canterbury.

At the Reformation, Bishop Barlow of St David's became a firebrand Protestant and stripped the shrine of its treasures and adornments. The relics of saints David and Justinian were somehow spirited away and hidden. The cathedral became Protestant and remains today the see of the Church in Wales (ie: Anglican) diocese of St David's.

Exactly what happened to David's casket remains a mystery, but out on the extremity of Wales the traditions of venerating the saint never quite died out. At some stage, so the trustful believe, the casket was returned in secret to the cathedral. If this is true, then the reliquary lying in the tiny Trinity Chapel behind the altar could indeed contain the bones of Dewi Sant himself.

Meanwhile, in a move unmatched anywhere in Britain, the cathedral has launched an appeal to restore the original shrine. The idea is that it will resemble as closely as is possible its pre-Reformation appearance, with an oak canopy and rows of pilgrim shelves. The background is to be painted blue, with icons of saints Patrick, Andrew and David next to the main feature, the reliquary reputedly containing the bones of Dewi Sant himself (see below). The back of the shrine will be simpler, with icons of St Non and St Justinian.

St David's Cathedral

The Close, SA62 6RH ☎ 01437 720202 🖥 www.stdavidscathedral.org.uk. Free access (but donation expected).

Approaching from the Pembrokeshire Coast Path, my first glimpse of the cathedral was of some crowning crenellations poking above the tiny city. In the Celtic tradition, St David's huddles in its hollow, out of sight from the sea and protected from storms. The contrast with the proud and commanding eminences of your average cathedral, is striking.

Closer up, there was not even anything particularly prepossessing about the exterior. I entered the precincts through a towered gateway and down a flight of steps with old buildings of the ruined Bishop's Palace (see page 160) all around. Then, reaching the main, west end portal I was confronted by one extraordinary feature: the long nave sloping up towards the high altar, so that by the time I had reached the east end my head was below the level of the main entrance. In a ski resort the central aisle might count as a mere nursery slope, but in a cathedral the effect is dramatic. Did the 12th-century architects do this deliberately, I wondered? On reflection, it was more likely it was imposed by the lay of the land.

The other arresting thing is the purplish-grey hue of the sandstone walls, whose colour seemed to wave and shimmer in the watery light. Nothing, however, remains of St David's original 6th-century church. There have been four cathedrals on the site, with the present building being mainly Norman and strongly Romanesque in character. However, many other styles have been added since, such as the late 14th-century nave ceiling which is elaborately carved with Irish oak.

Beyond the nave's crossing with the transepts I paused before the high altar at the tomb of Edmund Tudor, grandfather of the king who unleashed the horrifying violence which led to the destruction of so many sacred sites in Britain. Close by, on the north side, are the bare, stripped arches of St David's medieval shrine. I noticed the openings at the base into which pilgrims could thrust their afflicted limbs, and leave offerings.

But St David is no longer there. His bones, along with those of St Justinian, lie in a small chapel behind the altar. At least, they do for those who have filled the historical gaps about their destiny after the Reformation, with leaps of faith. I peered through a gilded grille at the studded oak reliquary resting in a niche, and wondered ...

The Bishop's Palace

The Close SA62 6PE ☎ 01437 720517 🖰 www.cadw.wales.gov.uk.

On the other side of the little Alun River, where St David used to stand barefoot in baptismal ritual, filling and tipping cups of water over converts, are the astonishingly extensive ruins of the palace presided over by the bishops of St David's during the medieval era of power and influence. Parts of the palace date to the 12th century when construction started on the present cathedral, though some of the most prominent buildings were added later.

The 14th-century *bon-viveur* Bishop Gower added the vast Great Hall with a rose window at one end, and an entrance porch reached by a flight of steps at the other. Gower imported masons from Florence, adding Italianate flourishes such as the arcaded parapet that circled the building.

Then came the Reformation, with the palace not being spared as the cathedral was. But even in its ruined state, there is a clear impression of greater affluence having been lavished on the bishop's own home, than on the cathedral raised to the glory of God. I imagined Dewi turning in his reliquary at such manifestations of wealth and power.

Getting there

St David's is at the westernmost tip of south Wales, reached via the A487 from Haverfordwest. The nearest **train** station is at Haverfordwest, from where there are **buses** run by Summerdale Coaches (*01348 840270*).

St Non's Chapel and Well

At the moment and very place of St David's tempestuous clifftop entry into the world, a spring gushed forth to mark the sacred spot for eternity. From the city, a clearly marked and well-trodden footpath of a little under a mile leads to this spectacular location overlooking a rocky bay named after Dewi's mum. A stone arch covers the holy well where a white statue of St Non gazes out at the pilgrims and visitors, many of whom still throw coins into the water. For centuries the spring has been held to have healing properties.

The ruins of a 13th-century chapel next to the well is believed by some to have been built on the site of St Non's 5th-century home, which would make it one of the oldest Christian sites in Wales. In one corner is part of the stone which was struck by lightning as Non gripped it, in the moment of her son's birth. The nearby tiny modern chapel dates from 1934.

Where to stay and eat

Old Cross Hotel Cross Sq, SA62 6SP ✆ 01437 720387 🖰 www.oldcrosshotel. co.uk. A delightful, creeper-clad old stone hotel in the centre of St David's, with a garden where meals are served when it is warm enough.

The Farmer's Arms 14–16 Goat St, Haverfordwest SA62 6RF ✆ 01437 720328 🖰 www.farmersstdavids.co.uk. A legendary pub with good food and wide choice of local beers.

Y Glennydd Hotel and Restaurant 51 Nun St, SA62 6NU ✆ 01437 720576 🖰 www.yglennydd.co.uk. A small, budget hotel in a quiet location a few minutes' walk from the centre.

Tourist information

St David's Tourist Information Centre Orie Y Parc, SA62 6NW ✆ 01437 720392 🖰 www.visitsouthwales.com.

⑤ Caldey Island

Contemplative religious communities are frequently to be found on small, relatively inaccessible islands. They can tuck themselves away from the world in places of limited and very obviously defined horizons, where atmosphere is concentrated and can become exaggerated. Caldey, three miles off the coast of Pembrokeshire, has been home to monks of various descriptions since before St Columba arrived on Iona.

History and legend

There is evidence of Neolithic people and Romano-Celtic tribes having lived here, though the first recorded settler was the Celtic hermit St Pyr, who legend credits with having had a bit of a drink problem. He met his end when, inebriated, he fell into a pond and drowned.

Later, between 1136 and its destruction in 1536 after the Dissolution, there was a small Benedictine monastery on Caldey. Whether the spirit of St Pyr had any bearing on this is moot, but in around 1890 the now uninhabited island was acquired by temperance activists as a drying-out retreat for alcoholics. However, monks returned in 1906, this time Anglican Benedictines who in 1913 converted en masse to Roman Catholicism but left in 1925 to found a new monastery at Prinknash in Gloucestershire. They sold the island to the more austere Reformed Cistercian order (also known as Trappists) who took up residence the following year and have been there, living, working and praying, ever since.

Visiting the island

Throughout the summer, day trips to the island are among the attractions offered in the resort town of Tenby, just 20 minutes away by boat. A prominent notice displayed on the quayside pointedly reminds visitors that it is only through the kindness of the abbot that they are allowed on Caldey at all.

What a change from the 'welcome and have a nice day!' approach to tourism that we have become used to. It seems to work, though; there was a sense that we were going somewhere rather special when I climbed into a small boat with a handful of fellow passengers. After a choppy crossing we scrambled on to Caldey's concrete slipway where the first person I met was a black-and-white habited monk who I tried to engage in conversation. 'We come here for a life of seclusion, in search of God', pronounced a laconic Brother Gildas, smiling behind his grey beard. His tone seemed to suggest that, while I was very welcome, our discourse was at an end.

The monks of Caldey do not, as is often believed of Trappists, take vows of silence. They simply refrain from 'unnecessary' talk. In this spirit, I found it was better to gain an explanation of the geography of the island, the monastery and work of the 13 resident monks, by watching *The Monks of Caldey Island* video in the small museum which shares a cottage with the post office.

According to the Rule of St Benedict by which they live, Cistercian monks have to support themselves by their own labour as far as possible. Traditionally, this has been done on Caldey by farming. Three hundred acres – more than half the island – is given over to the monastery farm where a herd of beef cattle, mainly Herefords, wander around fairly unrestrained.

A less likely venture is the perfumery, run by Father Cenan who I glimpsed at work over his bubbling apparatus. Caldey's indigenous gorse is the key ingredient in the distinctive fragrances, which are exported worldwide and include Caldey Perfume, Caldey Cologne, Caldey Skin Fragrance, Caldey Bath Essence, Caldey Hand Lotion, Caldey for Men, you name it.

Whether by luck or divine providence, having the thriving holiday town of Tenby on its doorstep has provided the monks of Caldey with a captive market for their products. The island shop (which also retails its products at the online Caldey Island Products Webshop, ✆ www.caldey-island.co.uk), seemed to do swift business in the perfumes along with Caldey Chocolate and Caldey Shortbread made by the monks, and Caldey-branded sweatshirts.

But if you are trying to live a life of spiritual contemplation, commercial success of this kind, particularly participation in the tourist industry, clearly has its dangers. An example of the balance struck between commercial activity and solitary prayer is that no tourists may come on Sundays or certain religious holidays such as Good Friday, which would otherwise be some of the island's busiest days. And from the end of September until the Spring Bank Holiday there are no visitors to Caldey at all, save the odd lost soul in need of help who may arrive and be taken in by the charitable monks.

Trying to form a picture of what life on the island might be like, I wandered around the 'village' buildings clustered about the red-tiled, whitewashed monastery, while keeping my distance from the monks who were concentrating on their solitary tasks. In a workshop next to the perfumery, an elderly monk was working away on a wood-turning machine; another was supervising the hand-making of Caldey chocolates for sale in the shop.

Strong winds and rain had nearly cancelled crossings to Caldey on the day I visited. Nevertheless, having explored the village and left most of the other visitors sheltering in The Tea Gardens, I headed down a lane to the lighthouse at the highest point of the island near Chapel Point, the southernmost tip. With squalls buffeting in from the sea, I gazed out over Caldey's cliffs and the splintered south Pembrokeshire coast and began for the first time to feel the isolation that is the heart of the island's rich atmosphere.

Returning to the village, I joined the daily mass just starting in St David's Church, which stands on the site of a pre-Christian Celtic burial ground. Archaeologists believe that bigwig pagan mainlanders may have been laid to rest here, because of the Celtic belief that islands represented a bridge between Earth and the afterlife. The Christian Celtic monks built their first church on the site which had been sacred to pagans; it was rebuilt by the Norman Benedictines and eventually restored by their 20th-century brethren, having fallen into disrepair after the Dissolution. It is probably the oldest British church now in Roman Catholic hands.

The monks' life is extraordinarily austere; they rise at 03.15 every morning for the first of the seven prayer sessions that punctuate the day's work and study. Listening to the plainsong chanted with a haunting serenity, I think I tasted just a suspicion of a glimpse into what motivates these men to live such extraordinary lives. It made me feel, on the boat back to Tenby, that I had travelled infinitely further than across a three-mile stretch of water.

Getting there

Boats to Caldey leave from Tenby harbour and run Monday to Friday from Easter till the end of October, and on Saturdays from May till September. Details on ⬧ www.caldey-island.co.uk.

Where to stay and eat

Caldey Island SA70 7UJ ☎ 01834 844453 ⬧ www.caldey-island.co.uk. Stays on Caldey are reserved for people on spiritual retreat. There is a choice of the full-board St Philomena's Guest House, or a few self-catering cottages. For day visitors, snacks and drinks are available in The Tea Gardens.
Fourcroft Hotel North Beach, Tenby SA70 8AP ☎ 01834 842886 ⬧ www.fourcroft-hotel.co.uk. This hotel on a Georgian terrace, with a reasonably priced restaurant, is a safe bet.

Tourist information

Tenby Information Centre Unit 2, Upper Park Rd, SA70 7LT
☎ 01834 842402 ⬧ www.pembrokeshire.gov.uk.

⑥ Llanthony Priory

Llanthony NP7 7NN
⬧ www.breconbeacons.org.
Free access.
My first glimpse of Llanthony was from the windblown cairn at Cwm Bwchel ridge on a stretch of the Offa's Dyke footpath, where I had stopped to catch my breath. From this distance, the 11th-century priory ruins looked like a broken toy among scattered blue-grey houses on the deep green valley floor. Through binoculars I could see the surrounding meadows speckled with chestnut horses, and a threadlike plume of white smoke rising above the ruins.

The Black Mountains scenery all around me was wild and dramatic, and the faraway solitude of the priory very evident. However, as the smoke suggested, Llanthony Priory is not deserted; rather, there is a hotel, no less, constructed among the very ruins. And, snuggled around the priory is a little hamlet of farming cottages, and a pub where I had been warned that the local brew is called Bullmastiff's Son of a Bitch and has a bite like a rottweiler.

Time to check out the sights of Llanthony, in all their rich diversity.

History and legend

The story of Llanthony goes back hundreds of years before 11th-century Augustinians made their way up the wild Vale of Ewyas. The name Llanthony is a contraction of 'Llan-ddewi-nant-honddu' which translates, roughly, as 'The place of St David's on the Honddu stream'. According to legend, this is where Dewi Sant – St David – retreated in the 6th century before setting off on his travels around Britain, and to Rome and eventually Jerusalem. Here in the Black Mountains he built a simple chapel and single-cell hermitage, and lived alone in conditions of the utmost frugality, drinking only water from the stream and eating wild leeks. This is why a leek, as the national emblem of Wales, adorns lapels on 1 March, St David's day; and why giant plastic leeks are waved in the air at international rugby matches.

In around AD1100 Sir William de Lacey, a knight in the service of his wealthy land-owning relative Hugh de Lacey, Lord of Ewyas, was out hunting when a storm struck and he took refuge in the ruins of the chapel. There had long been folk-tales that Dewi Sant had once been a hermit in these deserted mountains, but Sir William was moved beyond measure by the aura of this blessed place. He promptly renounced the life of courtly glamour and chivalry, and dedicated himself to prayer and study.

De Lacey was joined by other holy men including Erinius, chaplain to Queen Matilda, and together they built, on the chapel ruins, a small church which they dedicated to St David. Remarkably, they orientated the altar so that it faced the first rays rising above the eastern ridge on 1 March. I cannot think of any comparable case of solar alignment in Britain after the Stone Age. Although it has been rebuilt several times, today's small, squat St David's Church next to the priory is on foundations dating right back to the original hermitage.

About a decade after William and his pals arrived, they were joined by a group of Augustinian canons from England. Together they founded Llanthony Priory under the patronage of Hugh de Lacey who endowed the foundation with extensive land. The priory church (dedicated to St John the Baptist and separate from neighbouring St David's Church) was finished in 1230, with cloisters and outbuildings – today's ruins – added to at various times through an era of great prosperity lasting into the 15th century. Although Llanthony became famous throughout Britain, the priory's remoteness in the Welsh border country also made it vulnerable to attack from rebels, and as early as the 12th century the clergyman chronicler Gerald of Wales noted that Llanthony was '*fixed among a barbarous people*'.

By the mid-15th century Llanthony had declined as a monastic centre, and certainly lagged behind the Cistercian Abbey of Tintern (see page 167) in the Wye Valley. In 1481 the struggling priory merged with its daughter house Llanthony Secunda in Gloucester, with both foundations being disbanded in 1538 after the Dissolution of the Monasteries.

While St David's remained a working parish church after the Reformation, the priory decayed, crumbled and was neglected until the 18th century when, like Tintern, it came to be viewed as beautiful and romantic by poets, and artists such as J M W Turner. In the 19th century it was bought by Colonel

Sir Mark Wood who rebuilt some of the outbuildings as a domestic house and shooting lodge, later selling the estate to the English poet and author William Savage Landor. It is these buildings that eventually became Llanthony Prior Hotel (see below).

The ruins

Beautiful and romantic though these ruins are, I unaccountably felt something hauntingly uneasy about this place. I roamed the grassy floor of the skeletal priory, trying to concentrate on the surviving fragments. Enough remains to give a sense of both the size and the sophisticated workmanship – particularly the large section of the north aisle which stands to pretty much full height. There are surviving pieces of both round-headed Norman windows and arches, and Gothic pointed ones demonstrating the era of architectural transition which the building of Llanthony spanned.

Amid the moody shadows, I read about how the early canons saw their main life's work as providing a continuous service of prayer for the dead, the purpose being to experience a foretaste of the communion of saints. But I was suddenly distracted when, in a moment of bathos, one of the hotel's tattooed chefs strode across the front lawn which morphs into the great medieval ruins. Created out of cloister buildings and one of the towers, the context of this hotel does feel very odd indeed. Moreover, the eerie atmosphere never seemed to subside, even when beautiful early evening light started to play on the fabulous mountain backdrop all around.

What I needed was to escape across a field to the Half Moon Hotel for a pint of Son of a Bitch. Then another.

Getting there
Llanthony is 10 miles north of Abergavenny, reached on the narrow, mostly single-track road through the Vale of Ewyas between Llanfihangel Crucorney and Hay-on-Wye.

Where to stay and eat
Half Moon Hotel NP7 7NN ℂ 01873 890611 ⌂ www.halfmoon-llanthony.co.uk. More of an inn, really, with a few good-value rooms, pub grub and that canine ale.

Llanthony Priory Hotel NP7 7NN ℂ 01873 890487 ⌂ www.llanthonyprioryhotel.co.uk. An opportunity, unmatched anywhere in the UK, to drink, dine and sleep among the ruins of a medieval priory in the company of spectres.

Tourist information
Abergavenny Tourist Information Centre Swan Meadow, Monmouth Rd, NP7 5HL ℂ 01873 853254 ⌂ www.visitabergavenny.co.uk.

⑦ Tintern Abbey

In the first stanza of his famous poem 'Tintern Abbey', William Wordsworth wrote:

– Once again
Do I behold these steep and lofty cliffs,
That on a wild secluded scene impress
Thoughts of more deep seclusion; and connect
The landscape with the quiet of the sky.

It is true that the first and most famous Cistercian monastery in Wales has an incomparably beautiful setting in the Wye Valley. This, and the fact the towering walls of the abbey church are exceptionally complete, were my first impressions when I rounded a sharp bend on the A466. Wordsworth actually viewed the abbey from further away; the full (uncommonly prolix) title of the poem is 'Lines Composed A Few Miles Above Tintern Abbey, On Revisiting The Banks Of The Wye During A Tour. July 13, 1798'. He then went on to revel in the abbey's architectural splendour and intensely romantic associations.

At the time of Wordsworth's writing, artists had already become captivated by the ruins of Tintern. In 1794, J M W Turner painted several landscapes of the abbey, the most famous being his *Chancel and Crossing of Tintern Abbey, Looking towards the East Window* showing the ruins overgrown with twining creepers.

However, it was William Gilpin and the publication of his illustrated *Observations on the River Wye* in 1782 which had caught the public's imagination. This book was probably responsible for attracting the first tourists to Tintern including, undoubtedly, Turner and Wordsworth.

Tintern village has grown up entirely around the ruins.

History and legend

More than at any of the other great medieval monastic remains – even Fountains Abbey (see page 128), and that really its saying something – the staggering beauty of the scenery is at the heart of Tintern's allure. The irony being, of course, that in an age before the Romantics and the splendour they saw in lofty cliffs and overgrown ruins, the rocky Wye Valley was chosen by 12th-century Cistercians as the site of the order's first monastery in Wales, because of the sheer inhospitability and austerity of the location.

The Cistercian order had been founded at Citeaux in France in the previous century by St Bernard of Clairvaux whose purpose was to revive the order's lost purity and simplicity. St Bernard's call to monks was that they renounce wealth and luxury, and seek wilderness and make it flourish while their souls experienced the heights of spiritual enlightenment.

The call was heard by Walter de Clare, a nobleman who had renounced his wealth and become a monk at Waverley in Surrey. He arrived in the Wye Valley in 1131 to establish a monastery in the Cistercian tradition which, over the following 200 years, would rise to become Wales's greatest. The 13th century saw work begin on the cloisters, and on the vast abbey church of which such a surprising amount survives. Meanwhile, Tintern prospered both through cultivating land as the founder had ordered, and under the patronage of successive Lords of Chepstow who endowed the monastery with tracts of land in Monmouthshire and Gloucestershire.

King Edward II visited for two days in 1326, but barely 20 years later the monastery was decimated as the Black Death swept through Britain. This, compounded by attacks on abbey property by Welsh rebels in cross-border skirmishes with English armies, marked the beginning of a gradual but steady decline.

By the time of the Reformation, Tintern's best days were already behind it. Nevertheless, the monastery which had been founded on principles of simplicity and poverty still had considerable wealth to be plundered for the King's treasury. Richard Wiche, the last abbot, and 12 remaining monks were dispersed and the building granted to the incumbent Lord of Chepstow who had conveniently come over to Henry's cause.

Over the ensuing centuries, stone from the encircling walls and buildings within the monastery domain were used for the construction of tiny Tintern village.

The abbey

Approaching the abbey I passed numerous crumbled fragments of the masonry left behind, making the vast, largely intact shell of the abbey seem even more astounding. These are the ruins (tangled with creepers in those days), which moved and inspired the 18th-century Romantics.

The roof and most of the internal division in the abbey church have collapsed and decayed, so I sauntered over the smooth, grass-carpeted nave darkened by the soaring abbey walls. The arches of the south aisle are scarred and eroded by weather, while there is little left of the north aisle arches. But the cross-shaped outline is perfectly preserved with the nave, transepts and chancel complete, as is a spiral staircase leading up to a gallery. I paused at the foot of an enormous, vaulted arch, evidently the remains of a fine Gothic window; the shafts and tracery have crumbled away, so instead of stained glass I could see white clouds scudding across a blue sky.

It was all enough for me to picture what the abbey might have been like in its glory days. Instead of the exclamations of tourists with cameras and daypacks, I imagined the abbey echoing to incantations chanted by cowled monks.

Getting there

Tintern is on the A466 which runs through the Wye Valley between Chepstow and Monmouth, 10 miles north of the former and 11 miles south of the latter.

Where to stay and eat

Abbey Hotel Monmouth Rd, NP16 6SF ℃ 01291 680020 ⌂ www.tinternabbeyhotel.co.uk. With unrivalled views over the Wye Valley and abbey ruins, this hotel has been hosting romantic visitors since the early 1800s. The restaurant serves probably the finest food in the valley.

The Anchor Inn Chapel Hill, NP16 6TE ℃ 01291 689582 ⌂ www.anchortintern.co.uk. A lovely riverside pub with homely food and local beers, and an adjacent café.

Wye Valley Hotel and Restaurant NP16 6SQ ℃ 01291 689441 ⌂ www.wyevalleyhotel.co.uk. A small, comfortable. family-run hotel near the river and abbey, with a good restaurant.

Tourist information

Chepstow Tourist Information Centre Castle car park, Bridge St, NP16 5EY ℃ 01291 623772 ⌂ www.visitwyevalley.com.

170

7. Scotland

It is no coincidence that many of Scotland's most sacred sites are at the furthest-flung and least accessible extremities. We know enough about the early Celtic Christians to understand that their mysticism was distilled and intensified by the isolation of settings such as Iona and Whithorn. And in recent times, similar yearnings have enticed Tibetan Buddhists to the Scottish Borders and to remote Holy Island.

It takes a greater leap of imagination to picture the people of Stone Age Orkney Islands and the Outer Hebrides raising their mysterious megaliths in ritual zeal. However, the locations they chose for their great circles were surely as eerily beautiful 4,000 years ago as they are now.

For people sensitive to atmosphere etched into landscapes over aeons, there are powerful moods attached to all of these places.

① Orkney Islands

From the window of my Orkney farmhouse bed and breakfast, I gazed across a sea of molten mercury rippled by wind. It was the Pentland Firth, lit up by the sinking sun. Soon, the lights of Caithness, Scotland's northernmost tip, began to twinkle on the horizon. 'That there's doon sooth', said Louise Budge, my hostess. 'Doon sooth' to Orcadians is Scotland, England, the rest of the world. 'We are the odd islands out. We're not Celts, English or Scots. In some ways we feel closer to Norway.'

Orkney (never 'The Orkneys' here) is a scattering of bottle-green islands, 18 of them inhabited, strewn helter-skelter across a wind-harassed stretch of cold grey water, where the North Sea meets the Atlantic. There are hardly any trees, bushes or scrub. Place names alone are enough to transport you back to an age of myth and legend – Dwarfie Stane, Loch of Doomy, Twelve Hours Tower.

Orkney's largest island, on the other hand, is rather unimaginatively known simply as Mainland. However, driving through the flat pastures speckled with brown cows and crumbling croft houses, I was to find that the landscape is pocked with an utterly astounding collection of connected sacred prehistoric sites. In scale and extent, they are comparable with Avebury, Silbury, West Kennet and Windmill Hill in Wiltshire; and they are far more approachable than Stonehenge, Woodhenge, Durrington Walls and Bluehenge.

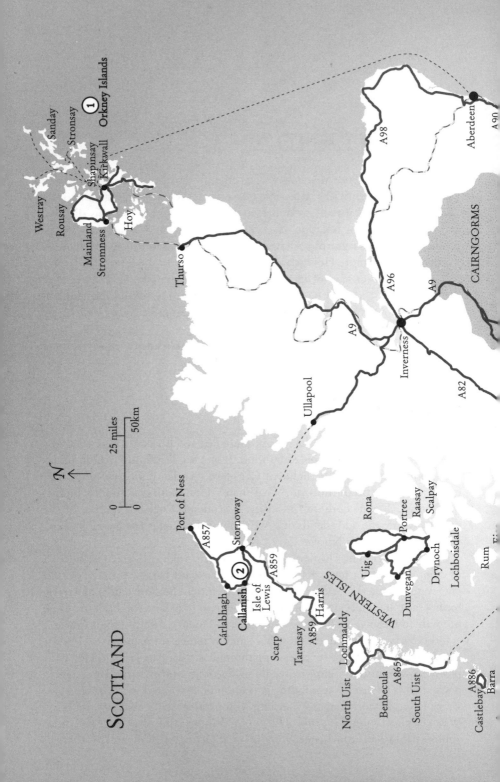

SCOTLAND

N

0   25 miles

0   50km

Port of Ness

A857

Stornoway

Càrlabhagh

Callanish (2)

A859

Isle of Lewis

A859

Scarp

Taransay

Harris

A859

Lochmaddy

North Uist

Benbecula

A865

South Uist

Castlebay A886

Barra

Rum

Uig

Rona

Portree

Raasay

Scalpay

Dunvegan

Drynoch

Lochboisdale

WESTERN ISLES

Ullapool

Thurso

Westray

Sanday

Stronsay

Rousay

Shapinsay

Kirkwall

Orkney Islands (1)

Mainland

Stromness

Hoy

Inverness

A9

A96

A98

Aberdeen

A90

A9

A82

CAIRNGORMS

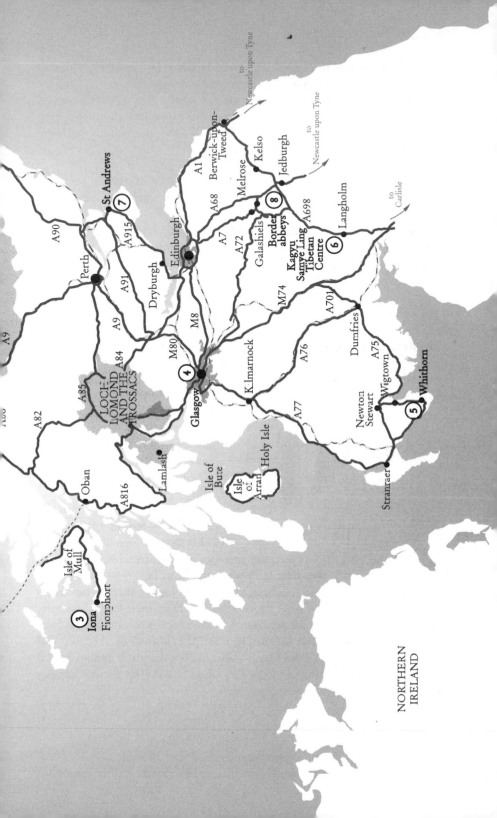

UNESCO proclaimed the complex a World Heritage Site in 1999, adopting on its behalf the rather precious tag 'Heart of Neolithic Orkney'.

Despite this, nothing had prepared me for what I was to encounter on Orkney Islands, because one thing that Orcanians never do is shout about the beauty, mystery and sacredness of their islands. We folk from 'doon sooth' are expected to discover these things for ourselves.

The Ring of Brodgar and Stones of Stenness
The B9055, 10 miles west of Kirkwall, crosses the isthmus on which the circles stand. Free access.

This ring of tall, angular-sided slabs within, and slightly raised above, a shallow 'henge' ditch have stood on a low-lying isthmus cutting through the dreamily beautiful lochs of Harray and Stenness, for perhaps 4,000 years. It is a magical and strangely haunting place. As I strode along the isthmus watching flights of eider duck sweep across the sky, the ancient megaliths appeared uncannily to grow and shrink as they rose out of the heather to the watery backdrop of the lochs.

The **Ring of Brodgar** is actually a little over 100yds across with 29 stones remaining of about 60 megaliths which originally comprised the circle. Nobody knows what happened to the others, though empty spaces and indentations

in the ground show where they once were. A little less than a mile away, and linked by an avenue on the isthmus, are four more monoliths. These ones are strikingly different. Exceptionally tall and vaguely threatening in their bearing, they are like blades aimed at the heavens. The **Stones of Stenness** are believed to be even older than the Ring of Brodgar, and the fact that they present different attitudes suggests that the purposes for which they were built were not the same.

Frustratingly, very little has been discovered about either circle. Their ages are only guesswork as are various theories about their lunar and solar alignments, none of which are persuasive. These theories rest mainly on local lore, of obscure origin, that has Brodgar as 'The Temple of the Sun' and Stenness as 'The Temple of the Moon'. With such a dearth of archaeological fact, I was left only with the certainty that whoever did erect these structures must have had some overpowering purpose.

Maeshowe
Maeshowe is beside the A965 between Stomness and Finstown.

Whatever the purposes may have been for building Brodgar and Stenness, it seems fair to assume that death and rites of burial were highly important to the prehistoric people who once lived in this area. Because, less than a mile beyond the Stones of Stenness is the most enthralling chambered tomb anywhere in northern Europe.

From the outside, all you see is a hump about 25ft high standing in a flat field of lumpy clods. A passage about 4ft above the ground bores through to the interior. Bent double, I followed my guide Tommy Bale through. Fear welled in my viscera. A demon disguised as claustrophobia reminded me that above was an immense weight crushing the stone slabs which line this hellish, dimly lit, tunnel.

After getting the better of the demon (just), I emerged from the passage to stand upright in a roughly square chamber walled with stone slabs so finely joined that you'd be hard pressed to slip a playing card between them. I was, unexpectedly, reminded of the trapezoidal Inca walls at Sacsayhuaman outside Cusco in Peru. As my eyes adjusted to the low light, I could see that there were openings in three of the four walls leading to recessed cells, and that the walls corbel out to make a pyramidal ceiling.

Tommy, meanwhile, was pointing out some 12th-century graffiti. This was the handiwork of Vikings who broke in through the ceiling looking for treasure, and while they were about it etched rune marks on the walls. These are, Tommy insisted, 'one of the largest collections of runic inscriptions in the world.'

To the uninitiated it is hard to make head or tail of these squiggly shapes. They look rather like limestone marine fossils. But one rough grouping of runes is apparently authored by 'Hakon' who claims to have found treasure here. 'Hakon woz ere n got lucky' is the gist of it. 'These runes are by number one rune maker', brags another. But my favourite was the set of scratchings which has been interpreted as meaning, 'Ingeborg is the most beautiful'. Never before had I any inkling that while centuries come and go, the fundamentals of graffiti remain a constant across the ages.

Rewind back to Neolithic times, however, and the purpose of Maeshowe becomes more of an enigma. There is general agreement that its purpose was predominantly funerary; the main chamber and the recessed cells are consistent with this, as is the burying of treasure with deceased bigwigs. However, as I re-emerged, blinking, into daylight I found it hard to believe that this intricately built chamber had been constructed simply to be sealed for eternity. Those corbelled walls and beautiful ceiling were finished to an incredible architectural standard. So my personal reading of the runes is that this mausoleum was intended to be viewed, and must also have been a place of some kind of ritual and ceremony.

Skara Brae
Skara Brae is 7 miles north of Stromness, at the end of the B9056.
Skara Brae is Orkney's Pompeii, except that the natural disaster that buried this Stone Age settlement occurred about 2,500 years before Vesuvius blew its

top covering the Roman town with ash. And Skara Brae was not discovered until 250 years after the accidental unearthing of Pompeii.

During the winter of 1851 a ferocious Atlantic storm tore into the Bay of Skaill, ripping the grassy scalp off a high dune known as Skara Brae. After the tempest subsided, local villagers were amazed to discover a cluster of ten stone houses, roofless but otherwise remarkably intact. Admittedly, the scale of this exposure comes nowhere near that of Pompeii. However, so perfectly preserved was this Neolithic village that it has probably revealed more about the people who lived in these times that any other site in Europe.

Arriving here from Maeshowe, my attention was distracted by a bob of seals quizzically poking their heads out of the sea just a few metres from the beach. Were the 5,000-year-old ancestors of these marine mammals similarly curious about human goings on in the dunes of Skara Brae, I wondered? For that is the approximate age of the settlement which came to a sudden end in about 2500BC. That the event was sudden is a fair guess, because the skeletons of two women were excavated lying huddled together on a stone bed, with artefacts such as necklaces, pendants and pins scattered around the floor. These details suggest some catastrophic interruption to what they were doing.

Nobody knows what: some mega-sandstorm is as good as any guess gets. What we do now understand is that this civilisation by the beach subsisted on farming and fishing. Their houses were set into mounds of midden (household waste yielding vast amounts of archaeological information). Each dwelling was about 40m², and furnished with stone tables and double beds à la Flintstones. There were stone shelves and cupboards where tools and ornaments were kept.

The Skara Brae people seem to have been in communication with civilisations on mainland Britain. They used the same grooved-style pottery engraved with spirals and chevrons, for instance, and stone axes which may have had ritual purposes. All of this adds a stirringly human dimension to a civilisation more often imagined in the mysterious light of megaliths and stone circles.

Getting there
Ferries from Aberdeen to Kirkwall; Gills to St Margaret's Hope; and Scrabster to Stromness. Contact Northlink Ferries (*0845 6000 449; www.northlinkferries.co.uk*) for further information. **Flights** operate from Glasgow, Edinburgh, Aberdeen and Inverness to Kirkwall; see Flybe (*www.flybe.com*) for up-to-date timetables.

Where to stay and eat
The Ayre Hotel Ayre Rd, Kirkwall KW15 1QX ✆ 01856 873001
✆ www.ayrehotel.co.uk. Of the limited accommodation in Kirkwall, this harbourfront hotel is the pick of the bunch. Probably the best place to eat as well.
The Creel Front Rd, St Margaret's Hope KW17 2SL ✆ 01865 831311
✆ www.thecreel.co.uk. A superb restaurant with 3 bedrooms overlooking

St Margaret's Hope Bay on South Ronaldsay, linked to Mainland by a bridge.
Woodwick House Evie KW17 2PQ ☎ 01856 751330 🖰 www.woodwickhouse.
co.uk. A charming, 8-bedroomed house with an excellent restaurant on the
beautiful and tranquil coast of west Mainland.

Tourist information
Kirkwall Visitor Information Centre West Castle St, KW15 1GU
☎ 01856 872856 🖰 www.visitorkney.com.

② Callanish and the Western Isles

My journey to the Outer Hebrides, the far-flung archipelago more commonly
referred to locally as the 'Western Isles', started with a propeller-plane flight
from Glasgow to the toy-sized airport serving trim, busy little Stornoway on
the Isle of Lewis, where two thirds of the islands' 20,000 souls live.

Only minutes out of the town, I was among rolling 'machair' grassland,
scatterings of brown-fleeced Soay sheep and scribbly patterns of peaty-black
little 'lochans', pocked with lumpy islands. My target was the standing stones
of Callanish, or 'Calanais' in Gaelic (pronounced 'gallic'), the Celtic language
still spoken by some islanders. Everything and everywhere has two names in
the Western Isles.

Callanish (Calanais)
Isle of Lewis HS2 9DY ☎ 01851 621422 🖰 www.callanishvisitorcentre.co.uk.
Nothing could have prepared me for the haunting first impressions of this
cluster of tall, gleaming stone blades pointing skywards from a whaleback
ridge overlooking an inlet of a sea loch.

The 'Stonehenge of the North' is a label that has sometimes been attached to
Callanish by observers down south in England. In terms of the magnificence
and mystery of the megaliths, they have a point. But the remote location and
the fact that relatively few people visit them make these megaliths, to my
mind, the most moving and magical in Britain.

If Callanish was on Salisbury Plain, no doubt there would be a ticket booth
and turnstile. Here I just strolled along the jutting headland where these stones
have stood for at least 3,800 years, possibly longer; archaeologists agree that
the site was created in various phases over a long period. There is a Callanish
Visitor Centre with a café and small museum which is worth a quick visit to
see a model of the site, demonstrating how the complex is arranged in a cross
shape with the four avenues radiating out. Other than seeing it from the air, it
would be hard to appreciate this any other way.

The core of the monument is a lone monolith, surrounded by a ring of
slender white – or silvery in some light – stones arranged elliptically. What was
the significance of an ellipse to the people who created Callanish? Nobody has

The road through the Isles

From a small lighthouse on the edge of an immense cliff, I watched waves surge over the jagged stacks below as the screeches of skuas and kittiwakes filled the air. This was the Butt of Lewis, a name immortalised in the poetry of the BBC shipping forecast, on the northernmost tip of the Outer Hebrides. My plan was to drive, head to toe, the 130-mile skein of five main islands that make up the Western Isles. First, however, I revelled in the elemental high drama and lonely, compelling beauty.

Scouring my map, I found places such as Gleann Bhruthadadail and Gob Rubha Bhalamuis Bhig, whose names seem to conjure up Tolkeinesque fantasies of ogres and dwarves. And who could resist the doomsaying 'Bridge to Nowhere'? I found myself irresistibly drawn to this stone arch spanning Ghearadha stream, where a metalled road along the northeast Lewis coast was planned in the 1920s. It never happened and there is only a track hugging the coastal cliffs with views across to the purple smudge of the Sutherland Hills on the Scottish mainland.

Although the Isle of Harris is, confusingly, on the same landmass as Lewis, it is strikingly different. The road south twists into crag-capped hills reminiscent of the Highlands, which themselves form a backbone dividing the two contrasting faces of south Harris. Westwards are huge, white sandy beaches – ones for walking rather than lying on – backed by dunes, while the east side crumples into a stark, lunar-like landscape of twisted rocks and jagged inlets, leading down to Leverburgh harbour.

On the choppy car ferry crossing to North Uist I met Neil Nicholson who introduced himself as, 'the only thatcher in the Western Isles', and later demonstrated his craft to me, as he worked on restoring the roof of an ancient croft house, using fish netting to secure the marram grass he had cut from the dunes.

Nicholson, who is in his thirties, told me that he is one of only two or three from his North Uist school still to live on the island. He pointed out the remains of 'shieling' shepherds' shacks, suggestive of abandoned ways of life. He mused, 'These islands are battered not just by the wind, but by contemporary economics, so depopulation is a major problem – the more remote the island, the more acute. Living here means giving up conveniences ... but also stress – I reckon that's a fair swap.'

Blink and you might miss pancake-flat Benbecula which, with the help of a few causeways and bridges, links North and South Uist. Arriving on the latter, however, I felt a palpable sense of having reached somewhere different. It is partly the landscape, which becomes softer, greener and hillier. But more significantly, the tall, willowy, white Our Lady of the Isles statue holding the infant Christ aloft, which marks a transition from the Calvinist northern Hebrides, to the more relaxed, jollier, Catholic south. Suddenly, you find modern murals on village walls, or a cottage with its roof tiles painted a vivid blue. And it took a pinch to remind me that I was not in Ireland as I drove past roadside shrines to various saints, and churches glittering with stained glass.

'Och, indeed we are a bit like the Irish, and not necessarily the best of them ... you are familiar with *Whisky Galore!*, I presume?', agreed a twinkling Father Callum McLennan, parish priest of St Michael's Church, near the Am Politician pub named after the ship whose famed cargo was 'rescued' by islanders, after it foundered on the rocks of Eriskay in 1941. The novel and film have fused fact with fiction, but the former home and simple grave of rambunctious writer Compton Mackenzie on neighbouring Barra are real enough, attracting 'more pilgrims than you might believe likely', according to Father Callum.

The ferry ride across Bharraigh Sound to Barra was millpond-calm. Spangles of sunlight were dancing on clear, emerald-green water fringing fingernails of brilliant-white sand, and I could sort of see how the only half-ironic epithet 'Barrabados' has come about. 'Ah, but wait till you experience the thrills of a raging Barra storm', tempted Guy Adams, owner of the Isle of Barra Beach Hotel which faces the elements over on the island's west side.

However, it was for the thrill of flying from the only airport in the world where the runway is a tidal beach, with flights scheduled accordingly, that I had resolved to end my journey on Barra. I waited with a handful of fellow passengers in a one-room terminal in the dunes, as the daily Twin Otter from Glasgow skimmed down on to Cockle Strand as gracefully as a greylag goose. Then it skittered across the wave-washed sand to collect us.

Getting there

There are **ferries** from Ullapool to Stornoway and from Oban to South Uist and Barra. Consult MacBrayne Ferries (*0800 066500; www.calmac.co.uk*) for the latest schedules. There are **flights** to Stornoway from Glasgow, Edinburgh and Inverness, and from Glasgow to Barra with Flybe (*www.flybe.com*). There are also services from Aberdeen with Eastern Airways (*01652 680600; www. easternairways.com*).

Where to stay and eat

Scarista House Sgarasta Bheag, Isle of Harris HS3 3HX ☎ 01859 550238 ⌂ www.scaristahouse.com. A former manse on a dreamily beautiful spot, serving, into the bargain, unbelievably fine food. Pricey but worth every penny.
The Isle of Barra Beach Hotel Tangasdale Beach, Tangasdale, Isle of Barra HS9 5XW ☎ 01871 810383 ⌂ www.isleofbarrahotel.co.uk. Fantastic location, excellent restaurant, meet the Adams family.
Tigh Dearg Hotel Lochmaddy, Isle of North Uist HS6 5AE ☎ 01876 500700 ⌂ www.tighdearghotel.co.uk. Best hotel for a stop between Harris and Barra.

any idea. It has been established, however, that the principal avenue – the one that leads north from the ellipse and is lined with elongated standing stones – is aligned with the setting of the moon.

In common with many other ancient sites I have visited, there are legends that the stones were once alive and kicking, but were petrified by some malign being. 'My granddad used to tell me that they were ogres turned to stone for getting drunk', a young mother called Alice told me in the sing-song local accent , hardened with a Nordic throatiness to sound more Irish than Scottish. We had fallen into conversation while her own children, the only other visitors, played hide and seek among the megaliths.

However, much more original and intriguing are the oral traditions recorded by Otta Swire in her 1966 book, *The Outer Hebrides and their Legends*. According to Swire, there have long been variations on a story told in the Isles that the stones were brought here by a king from far off who arrived in a fleet of ships with an entourage of Africans and priests. The Africans erected the stone circle, with some of them dying in the endeavour and being buried there. The king and Africans later left, leaving behind the priests who invited the local populous to rituals at Callanish. Swire recounts:

The priests wore robes made of skins and feathers of birds, that of the Chief Priest being white with a girdle made from the neck feathers of mallard drakes; the other priests wore feather cloaks of mixed colours. The Chief Priest never appeared without wrens (or a wren) flying near him.

Curiouser and curiouser, as another Alice once said.

Getting there

There are **ferries** from Ullapool to Stornoway with Caledonian MacBrayne Ferries (*0800 066500; www.calmac.co.uk*). Callanish is signposted just off the A858, 13 miles west of Stornoway.

Where to stay and eat

Broad Bay House Back HS2 0LQ ☎ 01851 820990
🌐 www.broadbayhouse.co.uk. A superb luxury guesthouse on the east coast of Lewis north of Stornoway, offering family hospitality and local delicacies for dinner such as 'hand-dived scallops' and venison.
Calanais Visitor Centre HS2 9DY ☎01851 621422
🌐 www.callanishvisitorcentre.co.uk. The visitor centre has a café serving snacks and main meals. Good, locally caught prawns.

Tourist information

Stornoway Tourist Information Centre 26 Cromwell St, Stornoway HS1 2DD
☎ 01851 703088 🌐 www.visithebrides.com.

③ Iona

Foam and spray whipped off the Sound of Iona as I stood unsteadily on the pitching ferry deck remembering the Rev George MacLeod's description of the approaching island as *'a thin place, with only a tissue separating the material from the spiritual'*. My own first impression of Iona was of a green place. A tiny, three-mile-long strip of land as beautiful as any in the Hebridean islands. A smooth lump like a polished Granny Smith's apple, strewn with grey rocks and girdled with silvery-white sand.

Most of my fellow passengers were day-trippers, holidaying on Mull just a mile across the water. However, a few carried suitcases or rucksacks, and wore 'Make Poverty History' ponchos or the distinctive 'flying goose' logo of the Iona Community.

People are drawn to Iona on a medley of spiritual quests. Many belong to the ecumenical Iona Community founded by MacLeod, a socialist Christian, in 1938. They come to pray; to commune with the Celtic saints; to enjoy fellowship with like-minded people; and to find a spiritual basis for a variety of political beliefs.

Maybe it's that 'thinness' they're after – something Iona appears to have had forever. In an uncanny way, the island eludes attempts to explain its powerful atmosphere. Even before St Columba landed here from Ireland in the 6th century AD, it was already a holy isle, known as the 'Island of Druids'. In the Middle Ages it became one of the most important places of pilgrimage in northern Europe.

After his 1773 visit, English author Dr Samuel Johnson famously remarked that, *'the man is little to be envied whose piety would not grow warmer among the ruins of Iona.'*

I found my imagination wandering easily over the centuries but was brought back to earth with a rather surprised bump to find so many people making a beeline for the grave of John Smith, the British Labour Party leader who died suddenly while in office and was buried here in 1994. What I found unlikely was not that Smith used to find spiritual sustenance on the island, but that anybody still remembers him. However, at this most recent of Iona's shrines, a Presbyterian minister told me, 'Iona is all about seeing God at work in the world, building communities – the things that Christian socialism has always stood for.'

Huh, I thought, aren't you profaning aeons of spiritual richness by stirring in contemporary politics? But later, over a cup of tea at a long trestle-table of pilgrims in the Iona Community MacLeod Centre, I could only feel humbled by the elderly, softly spoken couple who had been camping out on anti-nuclear or anti-war protests for nearly half a century. Each year they come to Iona 'to examine where we are and our belief in God.'

Iona, I was told, has declared itself a 'fair-trade island'. It also supports 'eco-tourism'. Across the table, somebody remarked that St Columba had inspired

Walks

Anyone who comes to Iona on a Tuesday between March and October, whether guest or day visitor, can join a 'pilgrimage' walk around the island, organised by the Iona Community. There are two options: the long walk lasting six hours, and a shorter two-hour version. The walks are punctuated with breaks for prayers, singing and silent reflection.

her to offset her carbon emissions – a practice she termed 'ecospirituality'. I took this as my cue for a bit of mischief-making. Columba, I had read, banished all frogs and snakes from Iona in his desire for purity – what sort of example was this for conservation? And how about the saint's well-known contention that, *'Where there is a cow there is a woman; and where there is a woman there is trouble.'*

A comfortably proportioned lady with raven hair (a dead ringer for Dawn French) put me back in my place with this, 'The point is, Martin, that at any place of pilgrimage it is the abstract fact that journeys are being made for sacred reasons that makes it holy, not any particular individual.'

Fair point Vicar of Dibley, I had to admit as I set off for a dusk climb up 332ft Dun-I, Iona's highest point, amid an unexpected calm after the morning's near gale. I paused at the Well of Youth spring below the summit, where a legend pre-dating Columba has it that everlasting youth will be granted to those who bathe in its waters. My mortality was confirmed by there being not enough water to contemplate a bath.

The hill was dotted with sheep, tiny wild flowers and the occasional ancient Celtic cross, while the light at the summit was startlingly clear and green. The contrast with Mull and the massive crags of its crowning brown mountain Ben More, was striking.

Behind Bail Mór (literally 'large village') which consists of a row of stone cottages by the port, I could make out the hummocks lining the Street of the Dead leading towards the abbey. It was also a good place to get some perspective on the pinkish ruins of the Augustinian nunnery which, like the Benedictine monastery, was abandoned at the Reformation. These ruins helped me imagine what the abbey might have been like before its restoration.

Tracks led through undulating pastures dotted with sheep, highland cattle and a few remote cottages. On Iona's west side I saw brilliant white fingernail coves and cliffs swirling with seabirds. Finding my way to a bluff at the most lonesome extremity, I followed lanes trodden by Celtic saints, pilgrims and shepherds.

My journey across the Highlands and islands had taken me through a panoply of kilts, bagpipes and tartan shortbread tins. Iona is different. Certainly, it seems to be a place where worldly temptations are replaced with enticements to interpret one's own ideology as the theology of the gospels.

The 1812 Alton Barnes Horse on Milk Hill (below: GD/D) is one of several in Wiltshire inspired by their Bronze Age counterpart at Uffington (right: P). The latter has been loping across the Berkshire Downs for 3,000 years.

Chalk hill figures

'There is a word for the art of cutting white horses into hillsides: leucippotomy. Myths and legends abound about the origins of these chalk figures.'

Nobody knows for sure who cut the Whiteleaf Cross into a Chiltern escarpment in Buckinghamshire. (RE/A)

A sign marks the way from Cerne Abbas village to the 'member's enclosure' on Giant Hill. (NH/A)

Northern England

'Landscapes and cities are sculpted in all kinds of ways by the radical new religion that arrived from Iona in the 7th century.'

BEDE LEVENERABLE

The Venerable Bede and the 1936 Crusade: two sides of a coin called Jarrow. (WC & K/F)

The *Lindisfarne Gospels* – the medieval masterpieces are presumed to be the work of Eadfrith, the Lindisfarne bishop who died in AD721. (P)

Whitby and Rievaulx, two of North Yorkshire's great medieval monasteries, now atmospheric ruins. (main image: P & above: MK/A)

Astonishing Swinside in Cumbria is one of the most complete stone circles in Britain, though its inaccessibility means that it receives few visitors. (P)

The entwined trio of *A Celebration of Chester* represent Industry, Protection and Thanksgiving. (P)

Durham Cathedral is vast in scale, beautiful in proportion and awe-inspiring in sheer presence. (GD/D)

York Minster exerts a mighty presence over the city, its colossal towers coming into view from far afield. (SS)

Work is underway to restore the original shrine to Wales's patron saint, at St David's Cathedral. (P)

Bryn Celli Ddu – 'the mound in the dark grove' – one of the mysterious ancient monuments of Anglesey. (MS)

The spring feeding St Non's well sprung forth at the moment of St David's birth. (P)

Once, a pilgrimage to St David's on the wild extremity of west Wales was considered the equal of a journey to Santiago de Compostela. (P)

Wales

'Here sacred sites vary as much as the cultures that have revered them, but a common factor stands out: an affirmation of the identity and spiritual values of Wales.'

Tintern Abbey in the Wye Valley inspired Wordsworth, Turner and other leading lights of the Romantic Movement. (P)

The ruins of Llanthony Priory are surrounded by the wild and dramatic Black Mountains. (P)

Viking youths scratched love messages and other graffiti on to the walls of the Maeshowe chambered tomb. (P)

Skara Brae is Orkney's Pompeii, albeit 2,500 years older. (P)

Scotland

'It is no coincidence that many of Scotland's sacred sites are at the furthest flung and least accessible extremities. For people sensitive to atmosphere etched into landscapes, there are powerful moods attached to these places.'

There are some who believe that St Mungo's remains still lie under this chapel in the crypt at Glasgow Cathedral. (WC)

Kagyu Samye Ling, with its temples and stupas, tempts 'Guests in Quest' to a piece of Tibet in the Scottish Borders. (SS)

The gleaming stone blades of Callanish point skywards from a whaleback ridge overlooking an inlet of a sea loch. (MS)

Beaches of brilliant white sand on the west side of Iona. (P)

The ruins of St Rule's Church where the saint's remains were housed before St Andrew's Cathedral was built. (P)

The extraordinary pink sandstone is as shocking as the scale and grace of Melrose Abbey. (C/D)

Hoy is one of the scattered green islands that make up the Orkney archipelago. (P)

Far-flung places

'Places of raw beauty and elemental high drama far removed from wordly temptation.'

Surrounded by dramatic seascapes, some of Britain's most intriguing sacred prehistory are on the Land's End Peninsula. (P)

But nevertheless, sacred associations are everywhere; people of conviction are pausing to pray. It is a thin place and the atmosphere is still Columba's.

History and legend

Iona was already a sacred place, known as an 'Island of the Druids' with wells and springs possessed of magical healing powers, when St Columba landed from Ireland in AD563. According to some theories, Druidic priests and their followers from southern Britain had fled here from the invading Roman armies in the early years of the millennium.

However, it is because of St Columba that this tiny speck of land in the Inner Hebrides, a mile off the southwest tip of much larger Mull, has been famed as a place of devoted Christian pilgrimage and prayer for more than 1,400 years.

Columba (also known variously as Columcille and Callum) came from Donegal in the north of Ireland and was a scion of the Irish nobility. He became a monk and founded monasteries at Derry and Durrow. Columba's holiness, however, was compromised by a hot-headed temper which on one infamous occasion resulted in his embroilment in a dispute with the abbot of another monastery about a manuscript said to have been copied without permission (perhaps the first recorded forerunner of copyright disputes). Accounts of what happened next vary in detail, but it seems as if the issue snowballed into what became known as 'The Battle of the Book' in which men were killed – as many as 3,000 of them, according to some historians.

Columba was blamed for the bloodshed and exiled from Ireland forever. Profoundly penitent for what he had done, he resolved to settle in Scotland and convert as many heathens to Christianity as had died in the battle he had caused. Little was he to know that more than 1,400 years later, his legacy would still be drawing pilgrims.

The disgraced Columba set sail from Ireland in a coracle with 12 followers, probably fellow monks, and came ashore at a rocky cove at the south end of Iona, still known in Gaelic as *Port na Curaich* ('Port of the Coracle'). After climbing Bail Mór to ensure that Ireland was out of sight, he resolved to stay. The monks built a simple church of wood, wattle and daub, and founded a monastery dedicated to the contemplation of God through prayer and learning, and as a base from which to set about evangelising the pagan Picts of western Scotland. Iona also became a great seat of learning, with the monks compiling illuminated manuscripts including the famed *Book of Kells* (which still survives and is on display at University College Dublin).

Columba died in 597, the year (and according to some accounts on the very day) Augustine arrived on the pagan shores of Kent (see page 23), with his legacy established as one of the leading figures in Celtic monasticism. Despite (or perhaps because of) his own violent history and the pride and foolishness that had led to it, he passionately embraced an interpretation of the gospels that demanded mercy rather than vengeance; peace rather than war. *'A little man trembling and most wretched, rowing through the infinite storm of this age'*, was how he described himself. Yet his extraordinary messages reverberated through Scotland. Later, with St Aidan's founding of Lindisfarne Monastery (see page 105), Iona's influence spread to northern England and beyond.

Nothing remains of the original wooden monastery, but it is known through the writings of St Adamnan, Columba's successor as Abbot of Iona, that the cult of Columba rapidly spread with his burial place attracting pilgrims in great numbers. A tradition grew of people of wealth and eminence being buried along Iona's Street of the Dead. On this route lie the remains of 60 Irish, Norse and Scottish kings including Macbeth, Macduff and Duncan who was, in Shakespeare's words, *'Carried to Colme-kill, the sacred storehouse of his predecessors, and guardian of their bones.'* John Smith is the most recent adherent to this custom.

During the 9th century a series of Viking raids devastated Iona, culminating in the slaughter of virtually all the monks at Martyrs Bay just south of the present ferry terminal. Columba's relics were divided and taken to Ireland and Scotland, and Iona was abandoned. However, within a century more peaceful Vikings, now converted to Christianity, returned and spread the word still further of Iona, Columba's sanctity and miracles performed through his intercession.

Under the patronage of Raghnall, son of Somerled, King of the Isle, the Benedictines re-established the monastic tradition, building Iona Abbey in the 12th and 13th centuries. An Augustinian nunnery was founded next to it. The mind boggles at what Columba might have made of such proximity, in light of his views about women and their bovine counterparts.

Monasticism ended and destruction came again after Scotland's break with the papacy in 1560 leading to the Scottish Reformation. Hundreds of stone crosses were thrown into the sea (only a few survive) and both monastery and nunnery were ransacked and subsequently fell into dereliction. In 1899 the Duke of Argyll, the then owner, donated the abbey ruins to the Church of Scotland, and its restoration began. In 1938 the Rev George MacLeod, the Presbyterian socialist, founded the Iona Community under whose auspices the rebuilding of the abbey and cloisters on their 700-year-old foundations was completed.

Today, there are some 80 permanent residents, most of them living in the stone cottages with black slate roofs which comprise Bail Mór. About 250,000 people a year visit, as day-trippers or for short stays.

Iona Abbey

PA76 6SN ☎ 01681 700404 ⊕ www.iona.org.uk. Free access.

The abbey church is in the care of Historic Scotland, and is the heart of pilgrimage and ecumenical worship on the island by the Iona Community and others. It is simple in style but huge for an island of this size, though somehow it manages to blend into, rather than impose on, the landscape.

The simplicity and modesty with which it was rebuilt and restored in the 20th century, is what contributes most powerfully to the abbey's sacred character today. Many of the original features have been incorporated, such as medieval side chapels and tomb effigies including that of John MacKinnon, the last Abbot of Iona. The cloisters were completely rebuilt in the 1950s and are a favourite place for pilgrims to pace in silent contemplation.

The approach to the abbey is along the pink-tinged cobbles of the Street of the Dead. Don't miss **St Oran's Chapel** in the burial-ground. This was probably the original abbey church built by the Benedictines when they arrived, and hence the oldest structure still standing on Iona. There are also three surviving Celtic crosses dating from the 8th and 9th centuries in front of the abbey. More than 300 others were thrown into the sea during the Reformation.

Little, if anything, remains from Columba's time on the island. There is a tiny chapel, '**St Columba's Shrine**', on the left of the main entrance to the abbey nave; this, according to some traditions was put there by the Benedictines because it marks the spot where the saint was buried. Certainly, it is a place of rich aura and somewhere to meditate on Columba and his legacy. However, other accounts have it that a mound a little way inland marks his cell and stone bed, and that this was his resting place.

Getting there

The passenger **ferry** takes 5 minutes to cross from Fionnphort on Mull, where cars must be left. This route and Oban to Mull are available on Caledonian MacBrayne (*0800 066500; www.calmac.co.uk*).

Where to stay and eat

Argyll Hotel PA76 6SJ ☎ 01681 700334 ⌨ www.argyllhoteliona.co.uk. A family-run hotel in the village looking across the sound to Mull.

Iona Abbey PA76 6SN ☎ 01681 700404 ⌨ www.iona.org.uk. Accommodation is mostly in bunk-bedded rooms for between 2 and 5 people. Guests share all aspects of life – meals, daily worship, activities and chores.

Martyrs Bay Restaurant and Bar Top of the Pier, PA76 6SP ☎ 01681 700382 ⌨ www.martyrsbay.co.uk. Self-service restaurant. The place to go for some wholesome grub and a pint of beer.

St Columba Hotel PA76 6SL ☎ 01681 700304 ⌨ www.stcolumba-hotel.co.uk. Exceptionally friendly and welcoming. Good dinners in the restaurant, including home-grown organic vegetables.

Tourist information

Iona Heritage Centre and Tourist Information Centre PA76 6SJ ☎ 01681 700576 ⌨ ww.isle-of-iona.com.

④ St Mungo and Glasgow Cathedral

Glasgow's striking, early-Gothic cathedral deserves to be better known. It is the only one of its kind on mainland Scotland to have survived the Reformation with its roof on. It is also subtly different from any of its English counterparts. Additionally, this church is the very essence of Scotland's largest city, in the sense that it marks the spot where Glasgow was founded by its patron saint. Today, George Street from the city centre and the High Street from the Clyde lead up to the cathedral area.

St Mungo – history and legend

St Mungo had bizarre beginnings, to say the least. His mother was the 6th century St Thenaw (also known as Thaney), daughter of King Loth who ruled over a swathe of southwest Scotland, and after whom the region of Lothian was named; one of her siblings, Sir Gawain, turns up in Arthurian legend as a Knight of the Round Table. Thaney's fate was to be seduced by a cad called Owain mab Urion, the son of another king, by whom she became pregnant. When he found out, Loth flew into a rage and had his daughter hurled off Traprain Law hill. She survived the fall, and was instead cast off alone in a boat which came ashore at Culross off the Fife Coast. Here she was rescued by Serf, a monk and saint ministering to the Picts, and gave birth to a son, Kentigern.

The little bastard was brought up at Culross monastery and cared for by St Serf who gave him the pet name Mungo (meaning 'dear friend') by which he was always, and still is, better known.

Most of this information we owe to Jocelin of Furness, a Cistercian monk and hagiographer who in 1185 wrote a *Life of St Mungo*. It is impossible to tell to what extent fact and fiction were fused over the five or six centuries since Mungo had lived; however, Jocelin claimed to have drawn on both ancient Gaelic documents and on oral traditions.

At the age of 25 Mungo began his own missionary work. On his way west from Culross he came across a holy man named Fergus on the point of death. Fergus requested that his body be placed on a cart to be pulled by untamed oxen which would, he said, be directed by God to his resting place. The destination turned out to be a burial site consecrated two centuries earlier by St Ninian (see page 189) near the River Clyde. Here, on the spot where Mungo buried Fergus, the cathedral that bears his name was to arise. Mungo later named the place 'Clas-gu', meaning 'dear family' in reference to the community he established there.

Mungo went on to rank among the most important figures in the 6th- and early 7th-century Church. He became bishop and evangelised in central and southern Scotland, northern England and Wales. Despite his elevated position, he dwelt in a small cell and lived a life of austerity and labour. There are accounts of his meeting both St David (see page 157) and St Columba (see page 181). In addition to his founding Glasgow with the assistance of God and oxen, four particular miracles are credited to Mungo.

Two were during his childhood at Culross. First, he restored to life St Serf's pet robin which had been killed by some jealous classmates who were trying to frame him for its death. Next, he was left in charge of the fire at the monastery but accidently let it go out; he took a branch from a tree and re-ignited it. The third legend is about a bell which Mungo brought back from Rome and used to mourn the deceased and call the faithful to prayer. (I agree, this story does not quite add up to a miracle, but there it is.) The final marvel involves Queen Languoreth who was falsely accused of infidelity by her husband. The king threw her wedding ring into the Clyde, claiming she had given it to her lover. Mungo intervened by ordering a servant to catch a fish in the river; they slit the fish open to find that it had, hooray for the queen, swallowed the ring.

To this day, Glaswegian schoolchildren learning about the four legends which are depicted on their city's coat of arms, are taught the following mnemonic:

Here is the bird that never flew
Here is the tree that never grew
Here is the bell that never rang
Here is the fish that never swam

Mungo died on 13 January 613, and was buried in the church he had founded, on the spot where the cathedral dedicated to him now stands. As his reputation for miracle-working spread, pilgrims arrived and his tomb grew into a popular shrine.

St Mungo's Cathedral

Cathedral Sq, Castle St, G4 0QZ ☎ 01415 528198 🖥 www.glasgowcathedral.org.uk. Free access (but donation expected).

From the outside St Mungo's has a gloomy mien, its sooty stonework making it look like a blackened cut-out. The interior, however, is majestic: I entered the lofty, early Gothic nave which immediately struck me as completely unlike any cathedral I know. Because it is built on the side of a hill, it has two separate parts: the 'upper church', and the so-called 'crypt' which, rather than being underground, is simply a lower section. My eye was drawn to the unusual feature of a series of steps along which pilgrims used to flow up from the nave, sideways through the transepts, then down both sides into this lower part.

I think it is fair to say that this has been a place of Christian worship since the 4th century, when St Mungo built his first church on a site blessed by St Ninian as a place for Christian burial. However, the cathedral was founded by King David I in 1136 to house St Mungo's shrine. The original building was destroyed in a fire and reconstructed in 1197, and not much remains from this era. The crypt, tower and choir were completed in the 13th century, with the nave being rebuilt over the following two centuries.

While so many of Scotland's great cathedrals and abbey churches were left to crumble after the Reformation, St Mungo's fared better. The town council was given responsibility for the church in 1583, since when it has been officially a Presbyterian Kirk (so its status as cathedral is merely honorific). Nevertheless, reforming zealots hell-bent on ridding it of all traces of idolatry stormed the cathedral smashing the statues and St Mungo's shrine. The last bishop, James Beaton, escaped to France with the episcopal treasures plus, some say, St Mungo's relics.

Others believe that Mungo's earthly remains still lie beneath the existing tomb, on the same spot to which pilgrims once flocked. This is in the crypt, into which I crept via the ancient pilgrim steps over the transept. Mungo's simple memorial is the centrepiece, lying guarded by a forest of columns, piers and arches. The gloom is brightened by a dash of colour in the form of a modern tapestry by a contemporary designer, Robert Stewart, depicting Mungo's four famous miracles.

St Mungo's Museum of Religious Life and Art

2 Castle St, G4 0RH ☎ 01412 761625 🖰 www.glasgowlife.org.uk.

Whatever the 6th-century saint's views on ecumenism or inter-faith dialogue may have been, I feel sure that this museum in the cathedral forecourt would please him. In a city which suffers its own sectarian tensions, the aim of the museum is to promote understanding and respect between people of different faiths. Displays explore the tenets of six of the world's major religions: Christianity, Buddhism, Hinduism, Islam, Judaism and Sikhism.

And because art has the capacity to bridge divides in belief systems, the museum also houses a collection of faith-inspired paintings and sculptures. There is a breathtaking statue of the Hindu god Shiva, called *Lord of the Dance*. In pride of place, however, is Salvador Dali's extraordinary, though rather unsettling, *Christ of St John of the Cross*. There is also a Japanese Zen garden outside.

Mungo would have been filled with joy. At least, I hope he would.

Getting there

Glasgow is 344 miles north of London and 52 miles west of Edinburgh. The city is at the hub of several **rail** routes, and is served by **air** from London, Manchester and various other cities.

Where to stay and eat

Babbity Bowster 16–18 Blackfriars St, G1 1PE ☎ 01415 525055. A magnificent merchant's townhouse just off the High Street and quite near the cathedral, now a hotel. There is a lively bar and hugely popular restaurant. Booking essential.
Cottiers 93–95 Hyndland St, G11 5PU ☎ 01413 575825 🖰 www.cottiers.com. It is not only because it is housed in a former church that this restaurant is

recommended after paying your respects to St Mungo. The food is great and the atmosphere even better.

Malmaison Hotel 278 W George St, G2 4LL ☎ 01415 721000 🖰 www. malmaison.com. Good, boutique-style modern hotel with an excellent restaurant.

The Cabin Restaurant 996–998 Dumbarton Rd, G14 9UJ ☎ 01415 691036 🖰 www.cabinglasgow.com. Superb Scottish food, followed by an eccentric after-dinner singalong led by the waiting staff.

Tourist information

Glasgow Tourist Information Centre 11 George Sq, G2 1DY ☎ 01412 044400 🖰 www.seeglasgow.com.

⑤ Whithorn

This out-of-the-way village near the tip of the Marchars peninsula in Dumfries and Galloway, straddles one main street. Out on the big bulge of southwest Scotland, I found Whithorn neither easy to reach, nor particularly prepossessing once I got there. However, to many hearts and minds Whithorn harbours the very soul of Scotland.

It is at Whithorn that the story of Christianity in Scotland begins. Near here, St Ninian landed from Ireland in AD397 at the start of his mission to preach the gospel to the southern Picts.

History and legend

Ninian remains a rather tricky figure to get to grips with. There are no contemporary written accounts of him, in fact nothing at all until good old Venerable Bede (see page 113) and his *Ecclesiastical History of the English People*. Despite the title, Bede occasionally touched on Scottish history and in this instance passed on what he termed the 'traditional' belief that Ninian was a Briton who had studied in Rome. Bede wrote of Ninian and Whithorn as:

an episcopal see, called after St Martin the bishop, and famous on account of the church where he rests in body, along with many other saints. The place belongs to the province of the Bernicians (Northumbrians) and is commonly called The White House. It received this name because he built the church there of stone, not a common practice among the Britons.

About 400 years after Bede, St Aelred (he of Rievaulx Abbey, see page 131) wrote with greater certainty that Ninian was the son a Christian King who was consecrated a Bishop in Rome and that he had known St Martin of Tours to whom he dedicated his church in Whithorn on learning of Martin's death in the same year he arrived in Scotland, AD397. Aelred also attributed numerous miracles to Ninian, performed both during Ninian's lifetime and through intercession after his death. One story tells of him relieving food shortages at a monastery by planting seeds which (in a pre-GM age, remember!) miraculously grew to fruition in a matter of hours.

Rewinding to the time of Ninian's arrival, most of Britain had been impervious to the new religion preached by Romano-Christians. What the latter had succeeded in doing, was converting some of the Celts out on the fringes of Britain and, via St Patrick, Ireland.

Ninian sailed from Ireland and landed on a beach near the Isle of Whithorn where he initially found shelter in a sea cave. Here he would retreat to meditate in solitude whenever he needed to over the coming years. Ninian then built a small stone church nearby which he painted white so it could easily be seen. This he called the Candida Casa – Latin for 'white house'. It was from this base, Whithorn, that he set out to proclaim the gospel to the heathens of southwest Scotland.

There are frustratingly few further details about Ninian's teaching and ministry to the southern Picts (as distinct from the Picts further north who had to wait another century and a half before St Columba arrived on Iona to preach the gospel to them). However, he gained the moniker 'Apostle to the Southern Picts' and his burial place at Whithorn became a shrine and perhaps the earliest place of Christian pilgrimage in Britain. From AD731 Whithorn came under the control of the Northumbrian bishops, and churches across northern England and further away in continental Europe, as well as in Scotland, were dedicated to St Ninian. In the 11th century a small cathedral was built by Fergus, Lord of Galloway, on the foundations of earlier churches.

The venerated memory of St Ninian, and Whithorn's tradition as a sacred place, inspired the Premonstratensians order of complemplative canons to reinvigorate the holy site and found a priory here in the 13th century, next to the 11th century cathedral. The Premonstratensians, an off-shoot of the Augustinian order, were particularly important in Scotland and founded several monasteries, most famously Dryburgh Abbey (see page 203) in the borders.

Kings and queens of Scotland made pilgrimages to St Ninian's shrine, staying at the priory which consequently grew opulent under their patronage. In the 14th century King Robert the Bruce went to Whithorn to pray for a cure for the 'unclean ailment' (possibly leprosy, possibly an STD) that was afflicting him. Two centuries later, King James IV made an eight-day walking pilgrimage to Whithorn, distributing alms as he went.

After the Reformation the cathedral was confiscated by the Scottish Crown and later granted to the Scottish Episcopalian Church. However, over the centuries it was abandoned and fell gradually to dereliction.

Whithorn Visitor Centre, priory and museum

45–47 George St, DG8 8NS ☎ 01988 500508 🖰 www.whithorn.com.

It is probably because there are so many archaeological scraps from different eras that my imagination proved stubborn about leading me to the age of medieval pilgrimage. Fortunately, the film and 'Through the Ages' exhibition at the visitor centre did a better job. These set the tone for a visit to the priory ruins of which the pinkish, roofless walls of Fergus's simple, Romanesque cathedral nave are the most conspicuous.

It was hard to make head or tail of the site of an archaeological dig carried out in the 1990s. Nothing was unearthed of St Ninian's Candida Casa despite Bede's reckoning that it had been built of stone, though the excavations revealed that several churches were built, altered and rebuilt on the plot over the centuries. A museum displays the finds along with carved headstones and crosses from the 10th and 11th centuries discovered in St Ninian's Cave, and others recovered from the cathedral ruins in the 19th century.

The Isle of Whithorn

My first impression of this little fishing village built round a natural harbour bobbing with fishing and leisure boats, was that it is blessed with a charm and attractiveness that eludes nearby Whithorn. Isle of Whithorn has not been as 'isle' since the 17th century, when a causeway was built joining the island to the mainland. First I climbed up a grassy bank just behind the harbour to the ruined 13th-century **St Ninian's Chapel** where pilgrims to Whithorn arriving by sea would pray, giving thanks for a safe voyage.

The Witness Cairn, a pile of smooth sea stones topped with a wonky-angled wooden cross near the chapel, commemorates St Ninian's landing and looks as if it might also be very ancient. However, I learnt that it was started only in 1997 – testament, then, to the enduring power of this sacred place. I added my stone before continuing round the bluff of Burrowhead to the Physgill estate, and walking for about 1½ miles along the cliff and down a wooded path to the stony beach.

I finally climbed a pathway of stones up to **St Ninian's Cave** itself, where the whole story started. The cave entrance looks wide, but surprisingly is only a few yards deep. Votive crosses, said to go back to the 8th century, are carved into the rocks outside and also within the cave. It is known that pilgrims over the ensuing centuries would also have visited the cave, as excavations beneath the breakdown of a piece of collapsed roof have revealed crosses and other Christian symbols.

It was not hard to imagine the saint finding solace in this sheltered place, with the rhythmic crashing of waves as a constant backdrop.

The cave remains a sacred spot in the 21st century, particularly for participants in youth pilgrimages organised by the charity Christian Aid, and the annual Catholic Diocese of Galloway pilgrimage on the last Sunday in

August. I saw that pilgrims had laid crosses, crudely fashioned from driftwood perhaps just weeks before my visit, in the very place where others have been doing the same for more than a millennium.

Getting there
Whithorn is 15 miles south of Wigtown, reached via the A75 to Newton Stewart, then the A746.

Where to stay and eat
Corsemalzie House Hotel Port William, Newton Stewart DG8 9RL
☎ 01988 860254 🖥 www.heavenlyhotels.co.uk. A tranquil and comfortable hotel with a highly rated restaurant about 10 miles west of Whithorn.
Steam Packet Inn Harbour Row, Newton Stewart DG8 8LL ☎ 01988 500334
🖥 www.steampacketinn.biz. A friendly pub on the quayside with a restaurant serving good food, especially fish, and rooms overlooking the harbour.
The Pilgrims Tea Room 45–47 George St, Newton Stewart DG8 8NS
☎ 01988 500508. A good place for a snack lunch if you are visiting the priory. Soups, sandwiches and cakes. Not licensed.

Tourist information
Whithorn Visitor Centre 45–47 George St, DG8 8NS ☎ 01988 500508
🖥 www.whithorn.com.

There is no tourist information centre in the Isle of Whithorn.

⑥ Kagyu Samye Ling Tibetan Centre
Eskdalemuir, Langholm DG13 0QL ☎ 01387 373232 🖥 www.samyeling.org.
Free access.

There seemed to be an air of forgottenness about the western side of the Scottish Borders, as I drove through heather-carpeted hills and empty green valleys dotted with ruined keeps and crumbling fortified farmhouses dating from the lawless 16th century. This was the age of cattle thieving and border raiding, when every landowner's survival depended on a private army.

More peaceful times have left the area untouched, unnoticed almost, with demure villages scattered in clusters of grey stone along the banks of shallow, rattling rivers. Typical of this country is the valley of the White Esk River, whose meanderings I followed along the little-used B709 north of Carlisle and Langhorn. Then, round an unremarkable bend just beyond Eskdalemuir, came the startling apparition of a turn-tile golden roof atop a riotously colourful oriental temple. From the second-floor balcony a glittering, eight-spoked dharma wheel radiated out across the heather.

Samye Ling Tibetan Temple was completed in 1998. Or, as I learnt from a plaque on the outside wall, it was, '*Consecrated by the XIIIth Kentin Tai SituPa on the 10th day of the sixth month, male earth dragon Year, 17th cycle.*' The interior is a mass of gilt statues, stunningly bright Tibetan art and huge velvet cushions where monks of the 'Kagyu' school of Tibetan Buddhism sit to chant holy mantras.

The main shrine room is dominated by a Buddha statue; there are prayer wheels, statues and thousands of tiny bowls replenished daily with offerings of water. Ceilings are painted with dragons and Sanskrit calligraphy.

The temple has been built in the grounds of a former hunting lodge, the rather grand and English-looking Johnstone House which in 1967 was bequeathed to a small community of Tibetan monks who had fled the Red Guards of the Chinese Cultural Revolution. They established the first Tibetan Buddhist monastery and centre for study, retreat and meditation in the West. The name they chose was Samye Ling, namesake of the very first monastery in Tibet.

I entered through the Samye Liberation Gate, the formal entrance carved with Tibetan mantras. The original house is still there at the end of a gravel drive lined with oak trees and flapping prayer banners. However, it is now incorporated into the much larger Kagyu Samye Ling Monastery with a new adjacent wing while, at the time of going to press, a third and fourth were under construction. When finished, these will complete a quadrangle in the traditional style of a Tibetan monastery.

In the grounds are a 60ft white gilt-topped stupa and an enormous golden Buddha. Monks flit about in wine-coloured robes, or tend the immaculate flower and shrub garden in jeans and big woollen jumpers. I wandered through the Tara Healing Garden planted with herbs in petal-shaped beds which, according to a lone monk, a Tibetan who was tending the plants, 'have the power to overcome both physical and mental ailments.' Then he added, unexpectedly, 'Scotland is not so unlike Tibet sometimes, here in the empty mountains'.

There are about 60 full-time residents at Samye Ling – monks, nuns and lay volunteers. Only ten of them are Tibetans, the rest Westerners. I was welcomed by Ani Lhamo, a lass originally from the Scottish Highlands who, after university, worked as a computer programmer in Glasgow before becoming a Buddhist nun (and changing her name). Ani, in her beautifully soft voice, told me that the only regret she had ever had, was for the initial disappointment her parents had felt about the course her life had taken. 'My becoming a nun was difficult to accept. But I believe they are OK about it now.'

And the best thing about being a nun? Ani's eyes sparkled as she almost whispered, 'Oh, my retreat. It is simply such a wonderful thing … there are not words to describe it.' Ani was referring to the four years she spent in silent, solitary meditation at the nearby Pureland Retreat Centre, in preparation for her ordination as a Buddhist nun. 'Yes, without a doubt the most amazing thing I have ever done', she repeated.

Ani introduced me to Lama Yeshe Losal Rinpoche, the current abbot who was born in 1943 in eastern Tibet and spent his early years at Dolma Lhakang Monastery. He escaped from the invading Chinese army in 1959 along with the Dalai Lama, and lived in India before coming to Scotland 1967 as one of the founders of Samye Ling. The Dalai Lama, by the way, paid a visit in 1993 while on a visit to Britain.

Lama Yeshe said, 'There is something about Tibetan Buddhism which has appeal for people in the West. There is so much stress here. So many lives lack any spiritual aspect. Some of the people who arrive here are lost.' I am not sure he meant the better-known faces who take refuge at Samye Ling from time to time. Actor/comedian Billy Connolly for example, or singer Annie Lennox. Lord David Steel, the former leader of the British Liberal Party who lives locally, is also a regular visitor.

About 35,000 people a year visit – an extraordinary number given the remoteness of the location. According to the Scottish Tourist Board, this makes Samye Ling the tenth most visited 'attraction' in Scotland. The number includes day visitors, and people who just stop by on a whim. Said Ani, 'All people are free to wander around, or visit the temple. We ask only that people are respectful.'

About 3,000 more visitors every year take part in residential courses. There is a constant stream of these on offer, the majority over weekends. As well as instruction in various forms of meditation – for beginners, intermediates and upwards – 'guests in quest' can study traditional Qigong medicine; 'The Tibetan Way of Painting'; 'Ground, Path and Fruition'; and numerous others things. The art of stupa painting, even. 'We welcome people from across the social spectrum. Many busy professionals find peace and harmony here. Families, too', said Ani.

Most course participants also join in the daily rhythm of the monastery, which starts with an hour of mantra recitation and meditation in the temple shrine room before work or study. The day ends with another meditation session.

I had arrived with a feeling of dislocation about this bit of Tibet in the heather. By the time I left, I could see what that monk was getting at – the one who reckoned that, 'Scotland is not so unlike Tibet sometimes.'

Getting there
Samye Ling is 30 miles north of Carlisle and 50 miles south of Glasgow.

Where to stay and eat
Samye Ling offers a variety of accommodation at the centre, with single and twin rooms and dormitories. For some residential courses, meals are included. Alcoholic drinks are not permitted on the premises. **The Tibetan Tea Room/Café** at Samye Ling is decorated in traditional Tibetan style and offers snacks and meals

Holy Isle

Lamlash Bay, Isle of Arran KA27 8GB ☎ 01770 601100 🖥 www.holyisland.org.
One night in 1990 Mrs Kay Morris, an Irish lady and devout Roman Catholic
who with her husband owned tiny Holy Isle in the Firth of Clyde off Arran, had a
dream. In it, a vision of the Virgin Mary asked her to pass the island to the Samye
Ling community. She travelled to Samye Ling and approached Lama Yeshe who,
it turned out, had himself had a vision many years previously, of an island where
people of all faiths, not just Buddhists, could retreat and find peace. He visited
Holy Isle and felt an immediate affinity with its rugged terrain and sacred past.
So much for synchronism; it appeared to be a done deal. However, there remained
the small matter of the cost, about which little guidance had apparently been
revealed in the visions. The market price turned out to be an impossible sum for
Samye Ling to raise. Lama Yeshe climbed to the summit of Mulloch Mor, the
island's highest point, to meditate upon the conundrum. The solution turned out
to be that Mrs Morris should lower the price to a level more affordable to the
Samye Ling community.

In truth, far-flung Holy Isle feels too remote to be a 'centre' of anything. It
has a long history as a holy place, going back to St Molaise who was born a
nobleman in Ireland in the 7th century AD, but turned his back on wealth and
privilege to settle on the island where he lived as a hermit. After his death the
island became known as Eilean MoLaise (Molaise's Island) and the cave on the
western shore where he dwelt became a place of pilgrimage. The spring from
which the saint drank was held to have healing properties.

Since acquiring the island the Samye Ling community have established a
small, residential Centre for World Peace and Health where meditation and
other courses are held. The centre operates on strict environmental lines with
solar heating and a reed-bed sewage system. A community of Buddhist nuns on
long retreat live, separate from the centre, at the southern end of Holy Isle. The
rest of the island is a nature reserve, home to wild Eriskay ponies, Soay sheep
and Saanen goats.

Day visitors arrive via a short ferry hop from Lamash on Arran. The
Centre is reached along a path
lined with stupas, while
multi-coloured prayer
banners flap in the
wind. As at Samye
Ling, guests are open-
heartedly welcomed,
and asked to treat the
island with the respect
due to a sacred place.

to residents or passers-by from 09.00 to 17.00 on weekdays and until 22.00 at weekends.

Balmoral Hotel High St, Moffat DG10 9DL ☎ 01683 220288
🌐 www.thebalmoralhotelinmoffat.co.uk. A traditional Scottish coaching inn serving meaty dishes and good beer. Feels very remote from all-things Tibetan.

Tourist information
Moffat Tourist Information Centre Churchgate, DG10 9EG ☎ 01683 220620
🌐 www.visitscotland.com.

⑦ St Andrews

Next time I am driving round a town in a state of frustration about its pointless one-way system, I shall offer an intercessionary prayer to St Andrew. 'You got me into this', I shall remind the saint and apostle of Christ, in reference to the town bearing his name having been, quite possibly, the birthplace of one-way traffic. In the medieval heyday of pilgrimage to the shrine of St Andrew, when perhaps a quarter of a million supplicants a year made their way here, an innovative system of transport management was in operation: pilgrims were instructed to flow up North Street in a single direction to the west face of the great cathedral; when they were done they would file back, one-way, along South Street.

More seriously, the layout of this character-charged small town in east Fife really does reflect its history as a place of pilgrimage. And, to be fair, it is open, airy and simple to navigate with the same two main avenues still streaming towards the (now ruined) cathedral. These days the traffic flows in both directions on each, but I did not find it hard to imagine flocks of pilgrims, exhausted and emotional as they ended their journeys. Many had walked from distant parts of Europe to venerate the relics of one of Jesus's apostles.

Between the two roads there is narrower Market Street where a medieval hospitality industry catered for the needs of hungry and parched pilgrims. No doubt all kinds of religious trinkets and other tat were also for sale. There were numerous inns and hospices (which in those days meant shelters for pilgrims), many of them run by religious orders. Market Street today seems to be a place where students – huge numbers of them, I found – hang out. And alongside the names of predictable high street retailers, shop after shop sells equipment and memorabilia to golfing pilgrims.

History and legend
St Andrew and his brother Simon Peter (the 'rock' on which Christ built his church) were working as fishermen on the Sea of Galilee when Jesus of Nazareth said he would make them 'fishers of men' and they promptly became

his apostles. A fact the gospel evangelists failed to foresee, was that Andrew would end up patron saint of Scotland with a little town of exceptional character on the Fife coast named after him.

After Christ's death, Andrew travelled to Greece where one of his converts to Christianity was the wife of the Roman Governor of Patras. Enraged and jealous, the governor ordered his crucifixion. Andrew submitted to this fate, requesting only that he be executed on a cross of diagonal planks to avoid any comparison of himself with Jesus.

Here we leave Andrew till the 4th century AD, with his remains kept in a Patras reliquary. Then the guardian of the relics, one Regulus (also known as Rule), later a saint himself, dreamt that they were in danger of being confiscated and taken to Constantinople. To avoid this, he must carry at least some of the relics to the outer limits of the Roman Empire for safekeeping. So off he sailed with a chest containing various body parts including a hand, three fingers, a kneecap, an arm bone and a tooth.

But Rule was shipwrecked off the Scottish coast. He struggled ashore and built the first shrine on the remote headland that was to become, in the name of his precious cargo, the ecclesiastical capital of Scotland and one of Europe's major pilgrimage destinations.

We know that in the 8th century the cult of St Andrew was going strong. This was the century in which the (Christian) Pictish King Angus beefed up his prospects on the eve of a battle against the Saxons in the south, by praying to St Andrew. In inspirational answer to his prayer, Angus saw a white diagonal cross outlined against the blue sky. You've guessed it, the Scottish Saltire flag was born. Moreover, from Angus's time onwards St Andrew was the patron saint of Scotland, with a particular role as protector of the Scots against the English.

The first records of pilgrims coming to St Andrews are from the 10th century. The east coast of Scotland was a remote place, but an apostle is an apostle, and the numbers coming here to venerate his relics grew exponentially in the medieval golden age of pilgrimage. Andrew's bones were retained in the large Church of St Rule (whose tower survives) until the arrival of a community of Augustinian canons who in 1160 began building the huge cathedral that would house a new, bejewelled shrine. It was finally consecrated is 1318 in the triumphal presence of King Robert the Bruce who four years previously had defeated the English at Bannockburn. Robert may have learnt the virtue of patience from a spider, but the victory he nevertheless credited to St Andrew.

The pilgrimage era all came to an end for St Andrews at the Reformation. Whereas the Scottish Reformation was by and large a gentler business than in England, with monks remaining to live out their days in their monasteries (as in the great border abbeys, see page 200 for instance), things were very different at St Andrews.

Nowhere else in Scotland experienced anything like the fury with which the St Andrews Cathedral was sacked in 1559. John Knox, the

Protestant revolutionary, leader of the Scottish Reformation and founder of Presbyterianism had been educated at St Andrew's University and, as a priest here, was powerfully influenced by the likes of European Protestants Luther and Calvin. Knox came to abhor the cult of St Andrew – particularly the veneration of body parts and all the trappings of pilgrimage. At Knox's instigation the cathedral was laid waste in righteous rage; the glittering shrine was destroyed with no trace surviving.

And so the end was one whose nature is all too familiar in Britain. However, an immensely important legacy of the ecclesiastical supremacy of this town survives in the form of the University of St Andrews, founded in 1410 by Bishop Henry Wardlaw. It is the most ancient seat of learning in Scotland and the third oldest in Britain after Oxford and Cambridge.

No parallel connection can be made between the saint and the motivation for the Pringle pullover-wearing devotees of the sand wedge and number six iron in pilgrimages to the 'home of golf'. Let us just say that the Royal and Ancient Golf Club of St Andrews, the oldest in the world and headquarters of the sport's governing body, honours a pastime with origins and legends almost as hard to pin down as those surrounding the 'fisher of men' from Galilee.

St Andrews Cathedral and St Rule's Tower

The Pends, KY16 9RF ☎ 01334 472563 🖰 www.saint-andrews.co.uk.

The ruins of **St Andrews Cathedral** are perched on a rocky cliff overlooking the grey North Sea. There was not as much remaining of the pale stone as I was expecting, but I was captivated by the atmosphere of the site as a salty zephyr wafted in and gulls wheeled and screeched above the broken bits of arch and column. Striding across the spongy turf covering what was once the nave floor, I could only marvel at the size of this place of worship built around a few scraps of bones believed to be those of St Andrew the apostle.

The distance from the west entrance to the east end is a staggering 475ft. For some reason the bizarre image came to me of a starting pistol firing and Usain Bolt dashing 100m within the nave before reaching the crossroads with the transepts. The ruins around me, I calculated, were of a stadium-sized cathedral of similar dimensions to its counterpart at Durham (see page 121) or York Minster (see page 136).

Those pilgrims must have been overawed by the scale as they processed towards the jewel-encrusted casket behind the high altar where lay those scraps of limb and digit. In the same way as for the relics of St James at Compostela, or for that matter those of Andrew's own brother, the first pope in Rome, it was the belief that these holy bones belonged to a saint personally chosen as a companion by Jesus of Nazareth. This is what imbued them with such potency.

Next to the cathedral are the ruins of **St Rule's Church**, where the relics were held before the cathedral was built. It struck me as extraordinary that alone among all these remnants of buildings, the church's 12th-century

Romanesque tower survives more or less intact. You can even climb to the top, which I did panting up the 151 steps of a steep spiral staircase. My rewards were commanding views over the cathedral ruins, the town, and fishing boats moored in the harbour immediately below. This reminded me that many pilgrims – especially those from Scandinavia, Germany and the Low Countries – arrived by sea. They would approach the cathedral from the opposite direction to the foot pilgrims, entering the precincts through the impressive Pends stone gateway, which survives to this day.

St Andrews Castle

The Scores, KY16 9AR ☎ 01334 477196 🖰 www.historic-scotland.gov.uk.

There is not much left of the castle, just a few crumbled vestiges of towers and ramparts on a rocky promontory overhanging the sea. Built mainly in the 12th century it was part of the Palace of the Bishops and the Augustinian canonate, as well as a stronghold in the wars with the English. This helps

explain why, come the Reformation, it went the same way as the cathedral. I stood among the roofless ruins reflecting that, in contrast with the cathedral, they felt rather bereft of aura.

Perhaps it was because this is a place that has been stained by religious strife and violence. It was easy enough to imagine bishops dressed in their finery sitting on silken cushions as they presided over the burning at the stake of the Protestant 'heretics' opposed to what they saw as corruption at the heart of the Roman Church. Near the entrance you can see the initials 'GW' in white cobbles on the road: this is in memory of George Wishart, the martyr and friend of John Knox whose burning was ordered and watched by the infamous Cardinal Beaton in 1546. In retaliation, a group of Protestants murdered the cardinal and hung his butchered body over the battlements.

Getting there

St Andrews is 55 miles north of Edinburgh, reached via the A91. The nearest **train** station is 5 miles away at Leuchars on the Edinburgh–Dundee line. From here, **buses** run by Stagecoach (*01592 642394; www.stagecoachbus.com*) connect with St Andrews.

Where to stay and eat

Old Course Hotel KY16 9SP ☎ 01334 474371 🖰 www.oldcoursehotel.co.uk.
Large, luxurious and world famous among the golfing fraternity. Top-notch food.

The Albany Hotel 56 North St, KY16 9AH ☎ 01334 477737
🖰 www.thealbanystandrews.co.uk. A Georgian townhouse right in the heart of
St Andrews. An easy walk from everywhere.
The Pitcher House 119 North St, KY16 9AD ☎ 01334 478479
🖰 www.thepitcherhouserestaurant.co.uk. A fun, lively, bistro-style restaurant.
Popular in term-time with students.
Vine Leaf 131 South St, KY16 9UN ☎ 01334 477497 🖰 www.vineleafstandrews.
co.uk. Wonderful contemporary-style food. Quite expensive.

Tourist information
St Andrew's Tourist Information Centre 70 Market St, KY16 9NU
☎ 01334 472021 🖰 www.standrews.co.uk.

⑧ The border abbeys

What is it about the remains of medieval monasteries and their surroundings
that they create indelible impressions and arouse such deep emotions? The
period between the establishment of the monastic orders and the Reformation
was, after all, relatively short. In Scotland it was only about 400 years.

The key figure was King David I who became King of the Scots in 1124. It
was under David's auspices, both before and after he succeeded to the throne,
that the thriving monastic orders of Europe came to southern Scotland and
built abbeys on a scale that must have overawed the population. As at other
great monastic foundations, from Glastonbury (see page 55) to Fountains (see
page 128), there seems to me to be an inescapable paradox in the fact that they
were founded on principles of simplicity, prayer and austerity, but burgeoned
into institutions of incalculable power and wealth.

Today, the great border abbeys are the roofless ruins of walls, columns,
arches and flagstones. Skeletal windows let sunlight through on to grass where
once there was a daily round of work, study and prayer.

Jedburgh
Abbey Bridge End, TD8 6JQ ☎ 01835 863925
🖰 www.historic-scotland.gov.uk.
Driving through the Cheviot Hills and over the Carter Bar from
Northumberland to Scotland, Jedburgh was my first stop. The ruins of
Jedburgh Abbey appeared as a dark silhouette, strangely shifting first to deep
amber, then to a lighter honeyed hue as I drew nearer. The abbey faces away
from the town but even in its ruined state still makes a mighty impact. King
David may have been on close and friendly terms with his brother-in-law
Henry I of England, but this first glimpse of Scotland so near the strategic
border with Northumbria was clearly intended to demonstrate the strength as
well as the sanctity of the country.

There had been a Celtic church on this bend in Jed Water (a tributary of the Tweed) since at least the 8th century, but it was Augustinians from Beauvais in France who came to the Scottish Borders in 1118 to found a new priory. The Augustinian traditions of monasticism were less cloistered than others, with monks closely involved in local communities. Under the patronage of King David the priory

was elevated to become Jedburgh Abbey and was granted tracts of land and fishing rights leading to great power and influence.

There is not much left of the monastic living quarters, though I did amble through the foundations trying to imagine black-habited comings and goings all those centuries ago. The abbey church, on the other hand, is the best preserved of any in the borders. The three-tiered nave is a startling sight, especially if viewed from the balcony reached by a rare surviving staircase at the west front. I gazed up at the Romanesque columns and to the Gothic pointed window arches, the contrast reminding me of the transition of styles which the abbey's era spanned.

The other thing to ponder was that, unlike the ruined abbeys south of the border, the destruction all around me was caused by so much more than a mere Reformation. Jedburgh Abbey was fatally exposed and hence repeatedly raided and torched in wars with the English. Nevertheless, some form of monasticism continued until Henry VIII's 'Rough Wooing' war in the 1540s when the English king captured and held the town.

In contrast with the wholesale violence of the Dissolution of the Monasteries in England, the monks were initially allowed to stay during the Scottish Reformation, with the abbey being used as a Protestant kirk. However, the last of the monks finally left in 1604 when the abbey was formally secularised. Over the ensuing centuries, stone was taken for building projects elsewhere, as the abbey slid slowly towards its ruined state.

A visitor centre at the bottom of the hill offers a slick and concise computerised audio-visual presentation on the abbey. You can also see an extraordinary archaeological find unearthed from the abbey ruins: the 'Jedburgh Comb' carved from walrus ivory and decorated with a dragon and a griffin. Where it came from and how it came to be here are among the mysteries of Jedburgh.

Getting there
Jedburgh is on the A68, 10 miles north of the border with England.

Where to stay and eat
The Royal Hotel 21–23 Canongate, TD8 6AN ☎ 01835 863152

🖥 www.royalhoteljedburgh.co.uk. Very friendly, mid-range hotel with reasonably priced food in the informal bar/restaurant.

Tourist information
Jedburgh Tourist Information Centre Murray's Green, TD8 6BE
📞 01835 863170 🖥 www.visitscottishborders.com.

Melrose
Cloisters Rd, TD6 9LG 📞 01316 688800 🖥 www.historic-scotland.gov.uk.

Approaching Melrose through hillsides blanketed with gorse, my thoughts turned to a young boy tending sheep on the Lammermuir Hills over to the east, in AD651. Suddenly he saw a vision of St Aidan's soul being carried up to heaven by angels. Inspired by the vision, he walked to the monastery at Melrose which Aidan had founded, and became a monk. The boy was Cuthbert, whose CV was to notch up a stint as a soldier, the bishopric of Lindisfarne and a lengthy period as a hermit on Inner Farne, before his death in 687. Sainthood followed before he posthumously founded Durham (see page 120) where his remains lie.

My first observation about Melrose, then, is that this enchanted little border town nestling by the Tweed at the foot of the Eildon Hills has a very ancient monastic tradition. It goes back hundreds of years before King David and his enticing of the religious orders to the Scottish Borders. In reality, however, little remains of Aidan's Celtic monastery. Old Melrose Abbey – or 'Mailros' as it was known – is about two miles from the present Melrose Abbey on a peninsula formed by a bend in the Tweed.

A mound with a few protruding stones is all that can be made out at St Cuthbert's Chapel and the monastery which was to suffer plague, and eventual destruction on the orders of Kenneth McAlpin, King of the Scots, in AD859. These vestiges are now on a private estate and unconnected to the Cistercian abbey.

On the other hand, it was undoubtedly because of its monastic history and sacred associations with St Cuthbert, that King David offered the site of Mailros to the Cistercians of Rievaulx (see page 131) in 1136. Once they had arrived, they found that a nearby site called Fordel suited their purposes rather better. Fordel became the new Mailros, a 'daughter house' of Rievaulx and eventually the independent Melrose Abbey.

It is hard to say what is more shocking about first impressions of the ruins: their sheer scale and graceful bearing, or the extraordinary pink colour of the sandstone – almost red sometimes, if the light is right. Although the monastery was founded in the 12th century, most of the surviving structure is Gothic, dating from about 300 years later. By the 15th century Melrose Abbey had become hugely wealthy. Rich pickings, then, for English raiders. In 1544 it was severely damaged and burnt, although a few bedraggled monks lived on until it was finally secularised in 1609.

The west front has entirely disappeared, but the window arches and chapels of the nave are remarkably intact. So too is the stone screen in the choir which once kept the monks and lay brothers apart. I admired the delicate carvings and grotesque gargoyles, and was particularly impressed by a bagpipe-playing stone pig. However, I noticed that many visitors – in particularly a group of tourists from South Korea, curiously – were making a beeline for the small museum where Robert the Bruce's heart lies encased in a lead casket.

A legend had long existed that Robert the Bruce, who died and was buried at Dunfernline Abbey in 1329, had had this vital organ removed from his chest so it could accompany Crusaders to the Holy Land as a sort of talisman. On its return it was buried at Melrose, although for centuries nobody knew quite where, a mystery that strengthened rather than diminished the legend. Then in 1997 – yes, as recently as that – a lead casket of a kind suitable for interring internal organs was found during some excavations. It was the heart of Robert the Bruce, no question!

Getting there
Melrose is 30 miles south of Edinburgh, reached via the A6091 between Newsted on the A68 and Galashiels on the A7.

Where to stay and eat
Burts Hotel Market Sq, TD6 9PN ☎ 01896 822285 🖥 www.burtshotel.co.uk. An 18th-century inn in a picturesque setting. Meals made from locally sourced ingredients.

Tourist information
Melrose Tourist Information Centre Abbey House, Abbey St, TD6 9LG ☎ 01896 822283 🖥 www.visitscottishborders.com.

Dryburgh
St Boswells, TD6 0RQ ☎ 01835 822381 🖥 www.historic-scotland.gov.uk.
Dryburgh is only about four miles from Melrose, but to me it felt and looked completely different. This might sound a bit odd, since both are the ruins of pink-tinged sandstone medieval monasteries on the banks of the Tweed. However, the scale here is smaller and the ruins less imposing, romantically set among woods of cedar, beech and rustling lime trees. It is the youngest of the border abbeys, and the only one not founded under the patronage of King David I.

Instead, Dryburgh was established in 1150 by Hugh de Moreville, a Norman knight who had become Lord of Lauderdale. Although he had nothing like the resources of David, de Moreville invited the Premonstratensians of Alnwick Abbey in Northumberland to found a daughter house on this secluded meander in the Tweed.

The Premonstratensians 'canons' (as they were known), were an off-shoot of the Augustinian order. They were founded by St Norbert of Xanten from Laon in northern France, who had become disenchanted with the worldly ways of some of his brethren. Comparison with the Benedictines and the more austere Cistercians is tempting, but it was less their opposition to lavish lifestyle that distinguished the Premonstratensians, and more a desire to retreat towards a more cloistered and contemplative way of being.

I roamed among the pink ruins, captivated by the enormous, peppery-smelling cedar trees almost as much as by the medieval vestiges. It was hard to form a picture of what the abbey church might have looked like, since there is virtually nothing left of the nave. In fact, the remains of the transepts appear more as the main body. These have been brought back to life, if that is the right phrase (in one sense it clearly is not!) by the chapels being re-used as burial sites for notable Scotsmen such as writer Walter Scott and World War I Field Marshall Douglas Haig.

There were probably never more than about 25 canons at a time, living by the motto that they should be 'beacons of prayer in a sinful world.' This did not stop invading English armies from attacking Dryburgh in 1322, 1385 and 1523. The abbey was patiently rebuilt after each assault; however, after Henry VIII's plundering forces laid it to waste in 1544, enough seems to have been enough and the last canons left.

Even today, it is not hard to understand why they settled here in the first place. I cannot image anywhere better suited to a life of serenity and contemplation.

Getting there
Dryburgh is 11 miles southeast of Melrose, reached via the A6091 and A68.

Where to stay and eat
Dryburgh Abbey Hotel St Boswells, TD6 0RQ ☎ 01835 822261
🖰 www.dryburgh.co.uk. A superb country house hotel on the Tweed, right next to the abbey. The Tweed restaurant has some of the finest cuisine in the borders, while Abbey Bistro is more affordable.

Tourist information
The nearest tourist information centre is at Melrose (see above, page 202).

Kelso
D5 7JF ☎ 01573 460365 🖰 www.historic-scotland.gov.uk. Free access.
Although less survives here than at any of the other great border abbeys, Kelso Abbey was, in its time, the richest and most powerful of the lot. True, the thick-set Normanesque west end of the abbey church is pretty much intact, but beyond that there is precious little left. The best thing is that you can rove

among the vestiges free of any officialdom, which I did trying to imagine the hubbub of activity around the vast Tironensian monastery established by King David in 1126.

I cannot say that my imagination was as readily responsive as at other border abbeys but this must have been an astonishing structure in its time. Exceptionally, there were four transepts rather than two and a tower at each end. A sort of push-me-pull-you of an abbey church, if you must.

With this rather odd image in mind, I found that the town centre with its lovely cobbled market square had more immediate allure. Far from being remote and secluded like, say, Dryburgh, Kelso occupied a strategic position close to the English border at the confluence of the Tweed and Cheviot rivers. This key location, of course, gives us a clue as to why its eventual destruction was so unsparing.

The Tironensians, named after their 'mother' abbey at Tiron near Chartres in France, were a branch order of the Benedictines who were initially granted land at nearby Selkirk in 1136 before moving to the prime site at Kelso. Although records are sketchy, an indicator of how important an entity Kelso Abbey became lies in the fact that King James II of Scotland was crowned here in 1437, as was his son James III in 1460.

Inevitably, however, Kelso was on the front line in the Wars of Independence with England. The abbey was attacked time and again. The worst of these attacks was during the 'Rough Wooing' campaign in 1545 waged by the Earl of Hertford, when 12 monks and 100 other men were massacred.

As at other Scottish monasteries, a few miserable monks remained after the Reformation, but they died off without being replaced. Masonry salvaged from the rubble of the abbey was taken, over the centuries, to build today's charming little town.

Getting there
Kelso is 39 miles south of Edinburgh, reached via the A68 and the A699.

Where to stay and eat
Ednam House Hotel Bridge St, TD5 7HT ☎ 01573 224168
🖰 www.ednamhouse.com. A beautifully located Georgian mansion with views over the Tweed. Locally landed salmon sometimes on the menu.

Tourist information
Kelso Tourist Information Centre Town House, The Sq, TD5 7HF
☎ 01573 228055 🖰 www.visitscottishborders.com.

APPENDIX
A guide to the sacred sites in this guide

Many of the places visited in this book have been sacred to different peoples in varying ways over the ages. The following is a broad grouping of those covered.

Chalk hill carvings

Holy isles

Pilgrimage routes

Prehistoric sites

Religious sites

Sacred towns and cities

Secular sites

Other sites

Sacred tours

Ancient Sacred Sites Tours http://ancientsacredsitestours.com/.
Specialise in sacred and spiritual tours to sites in the UK and beyond. Experience
meditations, healing and rituals. Visits to stone circles, passage tombs and Celtic
and Arthurian myths and more.
Andante Travels www.andantetravels.co.uk.
Archaeology tours, including private access to Stonehenge and the surrounding
area, the Avebury complex, Cornwall and Wales.
Celtic Spirit Journey and Retreat e info@celticspiritjourneys.com.
High-quality, small-group tours providing sacred journeys and spiritual quests.
Divine Light Tours http://www.divinelighttours.com/.
Based in Glastonbury and specialising in guided tours to the most sacred sites in
Britain and Ireland. Families, friends, businesses and spiritual groups all welcome.
Goddess Tours http://www.goddess-tours-international.com/holidays_in_
cornwall.htm. Sacred sites tour of Cornwall for women only.
Gothic Image Tours http://www.gothicimagetours.co.uk/arthurian.html.
Trips involve meeting and spending time with some of Britain's most respected
teachers, authors and ceremonialists who share knowledge into our pagan and
Christian heritage.
Harmony Healing http://www.harmonyhealing.co.uk/sacredtours.html#UK_
Tour. Single day sacred site tours to Avebury and Stonehenge are occasionally
offered, along with additional trips lasting one week to the Sacred Triangle
(Avebury, Amesbury and Glastonbury). Subject to a minimum of two participants.
Histouries http://www.histouries.co.uk/.
Based in Salisbury and providing private guided tours to attractions such as
Salisbury Cathedral, King Arthur's Avalon, Old Sarum Castle, Glastonbury Tor and
Abbey, the Avebury complex, crop circles and more.
Journeys with Soul www.journeyswithsoul.com. Tours of crop circles and
sacred sites Includes the Women's Journey to Avalon Tour.
Magical Mystery Tours http://www.magicalmysterytours.com/index.html.
Very unique journeys through breathtaking scenery with adventures to crop
circles and exploration of ancient sacred sites. Personally escorted tours, off the
beaten track limited to 4--6 guests (depending on the tour).
Megalithictours.com e neil@megalithictours.com.
Visits ancient, mystical and historical sites throughout Britain.
Premium Tours http://www.premiumtours.co.uk/tours/subsubcategory/all-
stonehenge-tours.id12.id12.html.
Offers a complete range of sightseeing tours to Stonehenge, including a private
guided tour of Stonehenge at sunset allowing you to enter the stone circle itself.
Rob Speight http://www.robspeight.com/RS/Tours_%26_Courses.html.
Runs a series of tours and courses throughout the year that are aimed at
everyone who has an open mind.

Sacred Connections 🔗 http://www.sacredconnections.co.uk/
Sacredconnectionstours/p1geninfo.htm. Guided tours around Highland
Perthshire, Scotland.

Salisbury guided tours 🔗 http://www.salisburyguidedtours.com/day-tours-
from-london.htm. Tours from London lasting from 1 to 3 days with a maximum
of 16 people.

Secret landscape tours 🔗 http://www.secretlandscapetours.com/index.php.
Various countrywide trips, ranging from 1 to 10 days.

Spiritual Holidays and Wellbeing Retreats 🔗 http://www.spiritualholidays.
com/pages/retreats/england.html and 🔗 http://www.wellbeingretreats.com/
dartmoor_retreats.html. Small-groups tours.

Stonehenge Tours 🔗 http://www.stonehengetours.com/.
Trips depart from London to Stonehenge and beyond.

Stone Seeker 🔗 http://www.stoneseeker.net/#Fieldtripslist.
Has a huge variety of different sacred tours across the country, including day-
long pilgrimages and visits to crop circles.

Wholistic World Vision 🔗 http://www.wholisticworldvision.org/tours/celtic.
html. Tours to Britain's sacred and spiritual sites of power from Stonehenge to
St Michael's Mount.

INDEX